MW01249167

Also by Gordon Williams

FINANCIAL SURVIVAL IN THE AGE OF NEW MONEY

NO RISK

Gordon Williams' Step-by-Step Program to Safeguard Your Financial Future

Gordon Williams

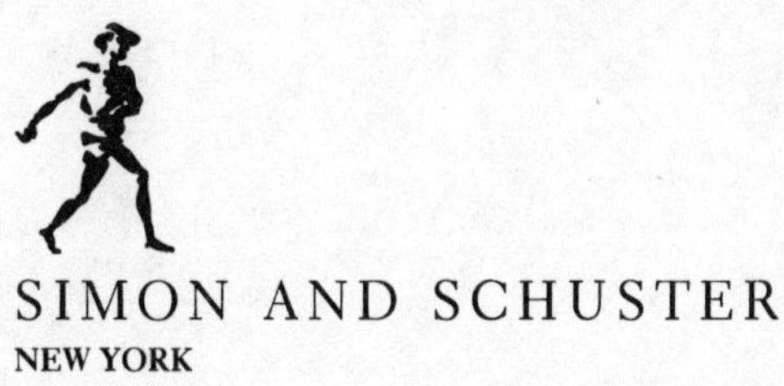

SIMON AND SCHUSTER
NEW YORK

Published by Simon and Schuster
A Division of Simon & Schuster, Inc.
Simon & Schuster Building
Rockefeller Center
1230 Avenue of the Americas
New York, New York 10020

SIMON AND SCHUSTER and colophon are registered trademarks of Simon & Schuster, Inc.
Designed by Irving Perkins Associates
Manufactured in the United States of America
10 9 8 7 6 5 4 3 2 1

Library of Congress Cataloging in Publication Data
Williams, Gordon
No risk.

Includes index.
1. Investments—Handbooks, manuals, etc.
2. Finance, Personal—Handbooks, manuals, etc.
I. Title.
HG4527.W467 1983 332.024 83-13531
ISBN 0-671-45171-5

To my mom

Contents

Acknowledgments

Even a book that flails away at the foibles of experts can't be written without some outside help—the advice and wisdom of friends and colleagues whom I turned to in my research and writing.

I can't thank enough those who read my book for errors of fact and interpretation: Seymour Zucker, Ephraim Lewis, Bob Mims, and Karen Pennar of *Business Week*; Karen Arenson of *The New York Times*; and Jill Bettner of *Forbes*.

David Kautter of the Washington office of Arthur Young and Company was a great help in answering technical questions on tax law.

David Jones, chief economist for Aubrey Lanston and Company—a major New York government securities firm—was a great help throughout the book as a consultant and then as a reader of my thoughts on the economy. Dave falls in a special category—an expert, but also a friend and neighbor. I rely on him—expert or not.

I am perpetually grateful to Patricia Lynn, who typed my manuscript and read it for spelling, style, and content. There was help beyond measure from my editor, Fred Hills.

What errors remain, I'll take the blame for.

I can't overlook the constant support I got from my superiors at ABC—Bob Benson and Peter Flannery from ABC News, and John Axten, Stuart Krane, Tina Press, Dick Rosenbaum, and Debbie Bernstein Golden from the ABC Information Network.

Lastly (but surely not leastly) there were all those hours of patience and forbearance on the part of my wife, Irene, and our kids, Debbie, Nancy, and Steve.

Introduction

You're only human.

You're not a trained economist, with degrees from here to Sunday, or a professional investor with a lifetime on Wall Street. You're just you—wise, alert, involved—trying to survive the most tumultuous years in American economic history. To help you get by, you have listened to those who claim to be expert about our economy.

Because you listened to the experts, the superinflation of the 1970s caught you by surprise. So did the recession of 1980 and so did the recession of 1981. The experts promised you that the economy would recover early in 1982. The recovery actually came at the start of 1983.

The experts told you to buy stocks and bonds as early as 1980. Neither market rallied until 1982, and when they did—the wildest rallies in our financial history—the experts never saw it coming. None of the experts prepared you for the dramatic break in inflation that came in 1982, even though it changed just about everything about our economy.

There were experts, in years past, who told you to forsake the American economy for gold and diamonds, and for German marks and Swiss francs. The prices of all of them plunged, and those who invested in them were pauperized. There were experts, a few years back, who told you to borrow fortunes to speculate in real estate—just as the highest interest rates in history, and two recessions in two years, turned real estate into a deathtrap. The real estate market rallied in 1982—but the experts didn't see that coming, either.

If you've put your faith in those who claim to be expert about our economy, you've learned a bitter, costly—but valuable—lesson: When it comes to our economy, most experts are mostly wrong most of the time.

That's too bad, because it's plainly a time to act in our economy. Inflation has been rolled back, and the stock and bond and real estate markets are working better now than they have in decades, with fascinating new markets appearing all the time, and with some key tax laws changed to your benefit. You can make money—maybe lots of money. All you need to know is what to buy in which market—and when.

It may not last. The biggest budget deficits in history could bring inflation back again, and whatever President Reagan is an expert in, it isn't economics. The Federal Reserve, which gets the credit for rolling back inflation, has made a hash of money policy more often than not over the years. It could easily do so again. The economic skies look bright today, but they could turn dark in a twinkling. Beyond knowing how to handle your money today, you must also be able to read the economic future, so you can spot trouble ahead early enough to save yourself.

So, it's a time for action. And yet, in deciding how and when and where to act, which experts can you listen to?

This brings us to another lesson: When it comes to forecasting the economic future, and to guiding your money through all the twists and turns our economy offers in profusion, there's only one expert worth listening to—and that expert is you.

It's time to wean yourself from those other experts and take command of your financial future, because no one can do a better job of it than you.

There is, within you, an instinct, a gut feel for how things work in our economy, which we'll call your economic sixth sense. When you've sharpened it and polished it and learned to make full use of it, you'll have all that you need to break loose from the experts and make it on your own.

There are as many reasons as there are stars why most experts are mostly wrong most of the time.

Some are merely slow of wit. Some insist on making economics more complicated than it need be—turning out convoluted mathematical models and abstruse theories, and forever losing sight of the economic forest for all the trees. Some toil in lofty ivory towers, remote from the real economy where you toil, and where the real decisions that affect the economy are made.

Some experts have political axes to grind, some make outrageous predictions to gain headlines, and some simply delight in being contrary.

Yet the real reason that most experts are mostly wrong most of the time, is that they are paid to serve other masters than you. Government economists want to sell you an economic policy, stock market economists want to sell you stocks, and bond market economists want to sell you bonds. Their expert forecasts aren't meant to enlighten you about the future, but to get you to buy whatever they're selling.

That leaves you as the expert you can always trust—the one person in the world with your economic best interests in mind.

These are the uncertain eighties, and this is a money book for the uncertain eighties—filled with the common-sense rules that will help you protect and increase your money, no matter which way the economy goes from here.

You already know more about the economy than you think, because you've lived in it, and worked in it, all your life, and because the decisions that most deeply influence our economy are made by you, and by millions of people very much like you. That's the basis of your economic sixth sense: the extent to which you're at the heart of the economy—your every action influencing the economy in some fundamental way.

If you spend money, our economy will go one way, and if you don't, it will go another way. You and your fellow consumers spend two of every three dollars spent in our economy. As you go, so goes the economy.

What you don't know about our economy, you can learn. All the information you need to observe the economy in action can be found in newspapers and magazines, on radio and television, and in volumes available at most public libraries.

Not only is the information available; the trials of our economy have turned it into headline news. You don't have to seek it out: It will seek you out.

Your economic sixth sense won't reach full flower overnight. It's a skill, which must be developed. But all of life is filled with skills that must be developed: driving a car, playing golf, operating a radial-arm saw. If you stopped to think about all the skills required to drive a car through rush-hour traffic, the sheer complexity of it would overwhelm you. But, step by step, through the years, you learned to drive skillfully. Step by step, through the years, you'll develop your ability to track our economy, until tracking our economy will be for you the most natural thing in the world.

That's what your economic sixth sense is all about: taking all that you know about our economy, combining it with a lot of common sense, and making it work for you.

Common sense helps a lot. You wouldn't buy a used car just on someone's say-so. You'd test-drive the car, poke around under the hood, and have a mechanic check it for hidden defects. Don't buy someone's expert economic forecast without giving it the once-over. Does it make sense? Does it sound reasonable? Must miracles happen for it to happen?

Did you really believe President Reagan could take all those big government spending programs—each the cherished darling of some special interest group—and dispose of them overnight? Did you really believe there was some special magic in Reaganomics that would enable the President to cut taxes, fatten defense spending, and still balance the budget? If you don't believe in the tooth fairy, why would you believe that?

Anyone who promises he can remake our economy overnight is selling snake oil in the economy-sized bottle. It's a $3 trillion economy—bigger than any other economy on the face of the earth—and it changes very slowly. It's like a gigantic supertanker that needs many miles of ocean just to slow down, and many more miles of ocean to change course. That's one key to tracking our economy: It takes time for anything very basic to change—and you can see changes coming in plenty of time to act upon them.

Another key to tracking the economy is that, if it happened one way before, it will happen that way again.

It's a cyclical economy. Booms will give way to busts which will give way to booms. The recession that began in 1981 was the thirty-fifth recession since they started keeping records in 1834. The recovery that began at the end of 1982, was the thirty-fifth recovery. The next recession—whenever it comes—will be the thirty-sixth. Since World War II, the average recovery has lasted three-and-a-half years and the average recession one year. Even the Great Depression was just another turn of the economic wheel. In fact, it was several turns: a slump that ran from 1929 to 1933, a recovery that ran until 1937, a slump that lasted until 1938, and a recovery that lasted until 1945.

Everything in the economy ties together—the anklebone connected to the shinbone, the shinbone connected to the kneebone, economically speaking. When consumers spend more, the stores they buy from order more. Factories then produce more, and to produce more, they hire more workers. Those workers then spend more, and the circle is complete. When consumers spend less, it goes the other way—fewer orders, less production, fewer jobs.

Think of the economy as a file of dominoes, standing on end, one next to the other. Topple the first domino and it will knock the next one down, which will knock the next one down, until all have fallen. Once you know the order in which things happen in our economy, you'll be able to spot the fall of the first dominoes—and you'll know in what sequence the others will fall, and how long it will take them to fall.

Money is at the heart of everything that happens in our economy. The more we have, the more we spend; the less we have, the less we spend. Nothing happens in our economy until someone spends money, so the supply of money in our economy is always critical. And since, of all the units of our government, only the Federal Reserve can create new money, its role is central to everything that happens in the economy.

Everything in the economy is relative to something else. There's the supply of money, and there are all the things we spend money on, from towering skyscrapers to toothbrushes. If there's too much money, relative to what's available for sale, we have that classic situation of too much money chasing too few goods. The price of what's available gets bid higher and higher, and we have inflation. It there's too little money, relative to what's for sale, some of what's available doesn't get sold. Unsold goods pile up, orders for new goods aren't placed, production dwindles, and so does employment, and we have a recession.

As the supply of money goes, so goes its cost—the cost of money being the interest rate. Money is a commodity, and, in time, too much money inflates the price of everything, including money. In time, too little money deflates the price of everything, including money.

As the supply and the cost of money go, so goes the economy—and so go the investment markets in which you risk your money.

You risk money, in hopes of making more, when the economy holds out the promise of noninflationary growth. That's when you expect your pile of invested money to grow—and you expect it to be real growth, not growth that comes only because prices are higher. When there's no growth in the economy, or when growth is due mostly to inflation, you safeguard your money because the risk of investing it becomes too great.

No investment market ever lives for the moment: All investments are made with tomorrow in mind. When the economy is booming, investors start looking ahead to the slump that must follow. When the economy is slumping, investors start looking ahead to the recovery that must follow. Not only is the economy cyclical, but when you invest your money, you're always chasing after the economic cycle.

Investment markets tend to turn in midcycle—the stock market rallying halfway through a recession and hitting a peak about two-thirds of the way through a recovery. You always watch the stock market because it will tell you where the economy is going.

It's pointless trying to forecast what's going to happen to our economy in the years ahead, and you'd go broke trying. Experts who try to forecast our economy years in advance are the wrongest of all, all of the time.

But you never have to forecast the economy years in advance in order to manage your money wisely and well. You only have to know what the next few months will bring, and there will always be clues aplenty to tell you where the economy will go in the next few months.

The one thing you always know is that the economy will remain cyclical. Armed with your growing knowledge of how the economy works, and with your economic sixth sense to guide you, you can make yourself the master of those economic cycles, rather than their victim. And that mastery is what taking command of your financial future is all about.

CHAPTER 1

How Our Economy Really Works

On the face of it, the American economy is vast beyond belief, and complex beyond comprehension. It's more than $3 trillion big—that being our gross national product, which is the sweeping measurement of all the products and services that our economy produces in the course of a year.

Even $3 trillion doesn't say it all, because beyond what we produce in America, we spend another quarter-trillion dollars each year buying products from other countries—automobiles from Japan, oil from Saudi Arabia, champagne from France.

Even $3 trillion *plus* the quarter-trillion dollars more spent on goods from abroad doesn't say it all, because beneath the visible economy is the "underground economy," in which transactions are mostly for cash and nothing is reported to the government. Its size is estimated at $400 billion, and while it embraces gambling, prostitution, and the drug trade, it also includes the hot dog you bought from a street vendor, the bud vase you bought at a garage sale, and the cash you paid to have your lawn mowed.

So the economy is vast and, without a doubt, it is complex. But it isn't incomprehensible and it certainly isn't irrational, and you really don't need those not-so-expert experts to guide you through it. You can follow the economy on your own, and you can forecast the economic future by yourself. The better you get at forecasting the economic future, the better you'll get at knowing which investment markets make sense at which time—and when to get out of all investments.

In short, you *can* take command of your own financial future—and you can do it well enough to ensure that you'll survive no matter what happens to our economy.

To begin with, there are six basic rules you should know about the economy:

1. Everything that happens in the economy is the result of a spending decision by some entity—the government, Exxon, you. Government spending is important because the government is the biggest spender of all, and because it writes our tax laws. Exxon's spending is important because it's the biggest company in one of our biggest industries. Your spending is important because you and your fellow consumers spend two of every three dollars spent in our economy.

2. Everything in the economy ties together. Spending decisions affect decisions on orders, which affect decisions on production, which affect decisions on employment. When you buy gasoline, the dealer will order more from Exxon, which will produce more, meaning jobs for those who produce gasoline. If you don't buy gasoline, the dealer won't order more, Exxon won't produce more, and those who produce gasoline will lose their jobs.

3. Whatever happens in the economy, money is at the heart of it. If there isn't enough new money to allow growth, the economy will slump. If there's more new money than the economy can readily absorb, the extra spending will produce shortages—too much money chasing too few goods—and there will be inflation. And the Federal Reserve is the master of our money.

4. No government economic policy will ever work as promised, because all government economic policies are political in nature, and politics will always win out over sound economics. Each new administration promises it will be different, but the promises quickly wear thin. That's why the stock market typically falls in the first year of a new Presidential term.

5. The economy will remain cyclical, with busts following booms, and booms following busts in predictable fashion. The

economy of the 1980s may feature less inflation and less growth than the economy of the 1970s, but then again, it may not. But it will remain cyclical, with periods of inflation and periods of recession.

6. No one can predict the long-term economy future, but it isn't necessary to do so. Armed with your growing knowledge of how the economy works, and with your economic sixth sense, you can predict what the economy will do a few months at a time, and that's all you need to do to take command of your own financial future.

Economic Paradise—And Paradise Lost

There is an economic ideal—a point of perfect economic balance: jobs for all who want to work, income sufficient to buy all we need, production sufficient to produce all that the economy needs, savings sufficient to finance all needed business investment, and prices stable enough to keep us at that point of perfect balance forever. The role of government would be to provide spending and tax policies to keep us at this ideal, and the role of the Federal Reserve would be to provide the requisite amount of new money to make it possible.

As with any ideal, we fail to achieve it for many reasons. The ideal always assumes a "frictionless" economy. But there's always friction in the economy—always bumps in the road that jostle us as we roll along.

Not all who can work will want to work, and there won't always be jobs for all who do want to work. It's no longer possible for our economy to provide jobs for all the Americans who make automobiles, steel, color TV sets, shoes, or any of the other products that other nations now make more efficiently and more cheaply than we do. The prolonged slump and high unemployment of the 1980s is, in part, a consequence of our economy's long-delayed response to this fact of international economic life.

A factory may produce all we need of a given product—jelly beans or woolen underwear—but it may do so at prices so high that none of us can afford to buy. Or it may produce a product so shoddy or so lacking in style that we exercise our right to buy a comparable product from a producer in Japan or Germany.

The demand for income sufficient to buy all we need may lead to wage increases so large that the payer of those wages will have to raise prices. Since higher prices will bring a demand for further increases in wages, we're soon caught up in what's called the wage-price spiral, which is what inflation is all about.

Acts of God (and acts of man) can disturb that perfect balance. A sudden freeze in Florida can send the price of orange juice to the skies—forcing us to spend more on orange juice and less on Wrigley's Spearmint chewing gum. The countries of OPEC have forced us to spend more on oil and less on other things, and adjusting our economy to more expensive energy is a further reason why our economy now runs so erratically.

So we don't have an ideal economy: we have a cyclical economy that is sometimes up and sometimes down—but which is always in motion. To study this motion, so you'll understand what really makes our economy tick, we'll approach the economy at a point in the cycle at which things have never looked better. The economy is growing at 5 percent a year, after adjustment for inflation. Not much of an adjustment is needed, because inflation is minuscule. Interest rates are low, the federal budget is in virtual balance, and the requisite amount of new money—not too much and not too little—is flowing into the economy to make it all possible.

True, things aren't as they once were in such basic industries as steel and autos, because both must share their markets with efficient and aggressive producers from abroad. Even that isn't so horrendous. Since our economy is in perpetual motion, there will always be older industries fading and new industries being born—as the auto industry succeeded the buggy industry. In America's younger days, we were the efficient aggressive producer from abroad, who challenged the industries of Europe for world markets. As steel and autos lose ground, newer industries take up the slack, and in our example unemployment is less than 5 percent, and our industry is running at more than 90 percent capacity. (As I write this, our unemployment rate is more than 10 percent and our industry is running at only two-thirds capacity.)

The Coming Storm

The only thing that mars the perfection of this image is that the seeds of impending economic trouble have already been planted—invisible to most of us—and you can start counting the days before inflation surges, and the days after that before we topple into recession. The economy is always eager to get to the next stage of the cycle.

The first signs of trouble seem, at first, like blessings. With unemployment down to 5 percent, more marginal workers find jobs. They don't have the skills that more experienced workers have. They produce, but less efficiently than those more experienced workers. Similarly, as we demand more production from our factories, we bring out older, less efficient equipment that was shut down because it is older and less efficient.

We're increasing employment and production, but we're also increasing costs, and as costs go up, so—slowly at first—do prices. As prices begin to go up, workers negotiating new contracts ask for more, and, because unemployment is so low and skilled, experienced workers are at such a premium, those demands for higher wages stick.

Prosperity has made us all want to live a little higher on the hog. Times are good, we're all earning more, and who's to object if we want a second car, a projection-screen TV set, and a steak every day. Now there are still greater demands falling on factories already producing at close to capacity. To satisfy those demands, still more inefficient workers are added, and the last, antiquated pieces of machinery are put into service. Now costs really begin to accelerate and the first signs of real inflation begin to appear. Price increases are bigger, and so are labor contract settlements.

Among those we ask for more is the government. We want better roads so we can drive our new cars, and more aid to colleges so all our children can be educated. We want the elderly to share in our prosperity, and we want the government to pay our doctor bills, and we want our shores made safe from foreign powers. Now the government begins to spend more. Shortly, it begins to run budget deficits, and it must borrow more.

But we're all borrowing more, to pay for those new cars and big-screen TV sets. And business is borrowing more to build the factories to produce the things we want. Because inflation today is worse than inflation yesterday, we assume it will be worse still tomorrow. Instead of saving and buying later, we're buying today to beat tomorrow's higher prices, and we're saving next-to-nothing.

The result of this greater demand on our dwindling pool of savings is that interest rates go up: inflation now inflating the cost of money. Until now, the Federal Reserve has had to add only a reasonable amount of new money to the economy each year. But now it's faced with a growing demand for money and with rising interest rates. It could let all of us compete for what money there is—allowing interest rates to go higher. Instead, it adds a little more money, letting more of us borrow as we want, without pushing interest rates to the skies.

The Fed has just done the equivalent of pouring gasoline on a fire. The extra money it has added to our economy—just to keep interest rates from further going up—adds to inflationary pressures. Those of us wise enough to know that inflation looms ahead whenever the Fed starts inflating the money supply, now know for certain that inflation tomorrow will be worse than inflation today. We respond by buying still more and borrowing still more and saving still less. And if interest rates did initially move lower as the Fed added more money, they're now moving still higher—inflation further inflating the cost of money.

Now the economic dominoes begin to fall—the first to go being construction.

We don't pay cash when we buy a home or build an office building; we do it with borrowed money. But now the cost of money is shooting up, and the idea of paying those high rates for the next thirty years sends more of us to the sidelines. Fewer homes are sold, fewer permits to build new homes are sought, and the pace of construction slows. First, construction workers are laid off; then the infection quickly spreads to all the industries that supply the construction industry: steel, lumber, glass, tools, paint, appliances, carpeting, furniture, and so on.

In each industry the process is the same. New orders decline, and inventories of unsold goods pile up. Manufacturers in these industries trim production, and workers are first worked shorter hours, then are laid off.

The Critical Stage

Companies in other industries decide that interest rates are too high, and they cancel projects, which leads to fewer orders, more inventories, less production, and fewer jobs. And now we're at a critical stage in the cycle. The seeds of recession have already been planted. Yet the rate of inflation continues to accelerate. (We were well into the recession of 1974–75 when President Ford launched his "whip inflation now" campaign.) It's usually at this point that the Federal Reserve launches an all-out drive against inflation—slowing growth in the money supply to a crawl—and ensuring that we will fall all the way into recession. It did it in 1980 and again in 1981 and, each time, we did have a recession.

Tighter money will first push interest rates still higher—a still-considerable amount of borrowing bumping against a dwindling supply of money. Now those high rates chase more and more of us out of the market and, now, what has happened to construction happens throughout the whole economy: orders down, inventories up, production down, and unemployment up.

The stock market does best when the economic outlook is the brightest—when the future holds the promise of a long period of uninterrupted economic growth. The market turned tail way back when interest rates began shooting up—holding its high ground for a while, but going no higher, and then falling back.

By now, in fact, nearly all the economic dominoes are falling, with only the rate of inflation continuing to accelerate.

By this point, you know full well that we're in a recession, because all the key economic signals tell you we are. You are shifting around your money accordingly, following the techniques that we'll be talking about in later chapters.

In fact, in only two places now is it not clear that the economy is in trouble: the White House and the Federal Reserve. Since incumbent Presidents regard recessions as being on a par with an outbreak of the plague, the man in the White House and his top advisers will assure us, speaking in chorus, that we absolutely won't have a recession. The Federal Reserve, unable or unwilling to admit that its policies have pushed us into a recession, will continue to regard inflation as the greater evil, and it will act accordingly.

But, of course, we are in a recession. The very last of the economic dominoes—the ones that stand upbeat until all others have toppled—are now falling, and it's hard times for nearly all of us. And yet, at this point, when everything looks the darkest, the seeds have already been planted for the coming recovery.

You are aware of all of this, and you are making your financial plans accordingly.

What Brings on the Recovery

There is immediate, nearly automatic, help for the economy from the government, since the onset of recession has triggered any number of government spending programs, from unemployment benefits to bigger welfare payments to more help for farmers.

One reason the Great Depression dragged on for so long was that such automatic help did not exist then. The economy had fallen, and since it got no help from the government, it just lay there until the spending of World War II finally brought the economy back to full-scale recovery.

That surely is not the case today and recessions make for gigantic budget deficits because the government is spending more, but because income and business profits are down, it's collecting less in taxes. It's a truism that each 1 percent rise in unemployment adds $25 billion to the budget deficit. President Reagan kept on talking about balancing the budget in 1981 and 1982, and the recession kept on piling up the deficits ever higher.

Still, all that extra government spending is balm for the ailing economy, and because private citizens aren't borrowing much, the government doesn't have a lot of trouble borrowing money to pay for the deficit.

Among those in government that refused to help our economy during the Depression was the Federal Reserve, which kept money tight throughout, under the belief—as late as 1937—that inflation and not depression was the more serious problem.

That is not the case today. Once a recession gets going in earnest, so that it is no longer possible for the Federal Reserve to ignore it, the Fed begins to feed new money to the economy at a handsome clip. The recession has finally stopped the advance in interest rates, because people just aren't borrowing money as they had been. The immediate effect of all this new money from the Fed is to pull interest rates lower—which starts us on the road back to economic good health.

The Fed increased our money supply at a rate of only 1½ percent in the first half of 1982, because it still worried about inflation, and because it refused to believe that the recession was so bad. Interest rates stayed high, and the recession persisted and all the experts who kept forecasting immediate recovery were as wrong as wrong could be.

The Fed increased our money supply at a 15 percent rate in the second half of 1982, because it was no longer so worried about inflation, and because it had come to realize just how bad the recession was. Interest rates fell, the financial markets rallied as never before, and the recession in short order came to an end. The experts who didn't see the recovery coming were as wrong as wrong could be.

As interest rates fall, a few borrowers reappear—starting with construction. Projects, from new homes to office buildings, that were put on ice when rates were high, are now revived. There are now the first flickers of life in construction: more homes sold, more new homes started, more permits granted to build new homes, more construction spending generally, and more construction workers hired. Those in the construction business now begin to place new orders—for everything from steel to lumber to toilet seats. This brings us the first pickup in production and employment in the industries that support construction.

The recession has brought inflation down. As demand dwindled and stocks of unsold goods began to pile up, companies had to cut prices to get rid of the stuff. Since everything from money to moose calls can be sold if the price is right, these lower prices do the trick and inventories begin to shrink. With both inflation and interest rates down, business investment plans are revived, and this steps up the demand for the whole array of capital goods, from machine tools to computers. As these new orders are placed, production and employment pick up on more industries. First the existing work force is worked longer hours and then, one by one, new workers are hired. Government spending is still hefty and the Federal Reserve, still obsessed with the recession, continues to pour in new money with a free hand. This will later lead to inflation and higher interest rates, but for the moment it represents more help for the economy.

The stock market continued to fall through the early stages of the recession, and as the recession got deeper, some of the plunges in the market were terrifying to behold. Yet as inflation and interest rates waned, the market began to stabilize. And then, on a day when times still looked hard to the rest of us, the stock market suddenly turned around—investors responding to falling inflation and falling interest rates, and starting to look forward to the economic recovery that was surely ahead.

The rally in the stock market is one sure sign that a recovery is ahead—and not very far ahead, either. Now, one by one, other signs of recovery begin to show up: still more activity in construction, spreading to shopping malls, office buildings, and factories. Watching the economy, you begin to see more new orders, workers working longer hours, and all the rest. And so the recovery goes. It will carry us back to full employment. Our factories will again run full-out, our incomes will be high, and there will again be prosperity for all of us. And since we've just emerged from a recession, it will take time for inflation to reappear. Interest rates will be low, the stock market will hum along, older ventures will find the money to grow and expand, and new ventures will find the capital to launch themselves in the world. For all of us, it's the best of times again. And yet, already the seeds of impending economic trouble have been planted—still smaller than the eye can see —the economy cyclical as it always is.

The Economy as It Really Is

That's the textbook version, of course. Of the thirty-five recessions and 35 recoveries we've had since 1834, no two recessions or recoveries have ever been exactly alike. The recession of 1980 lasted for less than six months and the slump of 1929–33 lasted for nearly four years. The recovery that began in the summer of 1980 ran for less than a year, while the recovery that began early in 1961 lasted until the end of 1969.

So some cycles are long and some are short. Some hit higher highs and some hit lower lows. Some touch just a few of us and some touch all of us. Never do the dominoes fall in exactly the same sequence.

Certainly this is a perverse time in our economy: the letdown after all the years of inflation, the long-delayed response to higher energy prices, the long-delayed response to the shift of so much of our production and so many of our jobs to other countries. After more than a century of the industrialization of America, we're seeing the "de-industrialization" of America. The basic smokestack industries are going and the age of advanced electronics and smart machines is coming. More and more we'll do the thinking and the planning and the selling here, while the making of things will be done in other lands.

So it's a time of great change for our economy and a time of great economic uncertainty. Yet the basic economic rules haven't changed. Our economy is cyclical. And because it's cyclical and mostly rational, it is predictable.

Each phase of the economic cycle will offer abundant clues

as to what's coming next. The clues won't be hard to spot, and they'll offer you months of warning, so that you can act appropriately. You don't need advanced degrees in economics, and you certainly don't need the wisdom of the experts. You can forecast the economy on your own, and the better you get at that, the more completely you'll take command of your financial future.

Guidelines for Action

Don't be intimidated by the size and complexity of our economy. It's understandable and predictable, and you don't need the forecasts of the not-so-expert experts to guide you through it.

Remember this:

—*The economy is always cyclical. Today's boom will be followed by tomorrow's bust, which will be followed by boom the day after tomorrow.*

—*Everything in the economy ties together. More sales produce more orders, which leads to more production and more jobs. Falling sales cut orders, which cuts production, which eliminates jobs.*

—*When a President (any president) says we aren't in a recession, we absolutely are.*

CHAPTER 2

Your Quick Guide to the Economic Guideposts

That's our economy in its broadest sense—vast, complicated, always in motion, and as it goes from boom to bust and back to boom again. Now it's up to you to break free of the experts and begin tracking the economy on your own.

Think of our economy as a highway and you as a driver, heading toward a distant destination. Your eyes tell you where you are. Etched in your memory are the places you've been. There are signs, every now and again, telling you where you're going, and how far it is to your destination.

Our economy offers in abundance recollections of where we've been, evidence of where we are, and signs pointing to where we're going: dozens of reports, scores of reports, on every facet of our economy—past, present, and future.

You could drown in statistics trying to keep up with them all. But you don't have to keep up with them all. Tracking a half-dozen reports will give you a pretty good sense of where the economy is heading, and watching a dozen will tell you enough about the economic future that you can take full command of your financial future.

You'll never have to look far to find the reports you want. All are made as public as their issuers can make them. Each is covered by radio and television and by such major newspapers as *The Wall Street Journal* and *The New York Times*. Each is analyzed in detail by such publications as *Business Week*, *Forbes*, and *Fortune*, and your library should have all on file. You can get still more detail from government publications that your library should also have on file: *The Federal Reserve Bulletin*, *The Survey of Current Business* (from Commerce Department), and *Economic Indicators* (from the President's Council of Economic Advisers).

A few warnings are in order:

1. Every report is just a spot-check, subject to revision. Government economists don't count every person out of work, or every package of Wrigley's Spearmint chewing gum sold in America. They count a few of whatever they're counting and then they make educated guesses. As more data come in, each report is revised and refined, and sometimes the revised reports will tell a different story from the original.

2. Every report has its flaws. Take just the report covering gross national product, or GNP, which is supposed to measure our total economy. It does count everything made in our economy and sold, as an addition to economic growth (which it is). It also counts everything made and left unsold on a shelf somewhere as an addition to economic growth. In a recession, a growing quantity of unsold goods is a sign of weakness, not strength. Stocks of unsold goods kept piling up in 1982—and according to GNP our economy kept growing, even through the worst of the recession.

3. Don't bank everything on a single report—or even on all the reports for a single month. Watch many reports, and watch them month after month, and then you'll know which way the economy is heading.

The Leading Indicators, Which Sometimes Do

Start watching the economy by watching the government's economic indexes, of which there are three: leading, coincident, and lagging. Each has its own place in the economic scheme of things. Together, the indexes are among the most useful economic reports around.

The three come out monthly, packaged as one. Each consists of a clutch of different reports, bound together for good reason.

There are a dozen leading economic indicators, and these dozen reports are chosen because each covers a slice of the economy that will turn up or down before the total economy does: one of the first economic dominoes to topple. Among the dozen leaders are the money supply, new orders for such things as consumer and capital goods, permits to build new homes, the number of hours worked each week by the average worker, the number of people each week first filing for unemployment benefits, and the stock market (as represented by the 500-stock index from Standard & Poor's Corporation).

The government compiles an index each month based on what these leading indicators are saying—called, as you'd suppose, the index of leading economic indicators. On average, since World War II, this index has turned higher on the eve of a recovery and turned lower about a year before the start of a recession. In theory, the leading indicators should always give you sufficient warning of the start of a recession, and alert you to the start of a recovery.

In fact, the indicators, while signaling every postwar recession, also signaled recessions in 1951, 1962, and 1966 which never happened. They underestimated the severity of the 1974–75 recession, almost completely missed the 1981 recession, and they kept signaling a recovery, starting in the summer of 1982, that didn't actually show up until early in 1983—months later than you'd expect it to. Still, the indicators correctly indicated recovery ahead in the summer of 1982, when the economy still looked hopelessly grim, and you must give them credit for that.

Regard any change in the direction of the leading indicators which lasts for at least three months as significant in terms of calling a turn in the economy—but don't regard it as an infallible guide to the future.

Those Other Economic Indicators

You can't ignore the coincident and the lagging indicators, because each gives you a different picture of the economy.

The leading indicators all have to do with things that will happen in the future. An order placed now will provide a job in the future. A building permit now will mean a house built in the future.

The coincident indicators tell you what the economy is doing right here and now: factory production, personal income, business sales, and the number of people working at non-farm jobs. The order placed (leading indicator) leads to production in some factory (coincident indicator) and to someone earning some income (coincident indicator).

Leading indicators tell you which way the economy is going, giving you enough warning to make all plans appropriate to your financial well-being. Coincident indicators tell you when the economy actually gets there. The leading indicators signaled recovery from mid-1982 on. Not until the coincident indicators signaled recovery early in 1983 could you be sure the economy had, indeed, turned into recovery.

Then there are the lagging indicators—those reports that trail the field. New orders (leading indicator) make for more factory production (coincident indicator). More factory production (coincident indicator) helps create new jobs and unemployment falls (lagging indicator). That's why unemployment doesn't begin to get bad until a recession is well underway. It is also why unemployment doesn't begin to get significantly better until the recovery is well underway.

So, you watch the indicators—leading, coincident, and lagging—for the story that each has to say about the economy. They appear at the end of each month for the previous month, and they get much publicity when they appear. And then, as you become an increasingly astute student of the economy, and as your economic sixth sense gets honed to a high degree, you learn to watch other things as well.

Relying on You

Pay close attention to your own best leading indicator—you. Nothing happens in our economy until someone spends money, and remember, you and your fellow consumers spend two of every three dollars spent in our economy. Finally, assume that your feelings about the economic future are shared by other consumers. If, deep down in your gut, where your economic sixth sense lives, you feel that times will get worse, assume that other consumers feel the same way, and will act accordingly. If you believe that times will get better, assume that other consumers feel the same way, and will act accordingly.

We're really talking about self-fulfilling prophecies. If we think that times will get better, we'll spend more and, lo, times get better.

Give yourself time to observe and analyze the economic world around you. Remember that you're at the heart of the economy: working, earning, spending, saving. You're constantly being exposed to clues about the economic future, and you must be alert to them:

1. What's happening at work? Is there more overtime or less? How quickly are job openings being filled? Has there been a change in the company's bonus policy? Is it suddenly taking longer to get requests filled for routine office supplies? Have any standard company events (Christmas party, company picnic, etc.) been canceled recently?
2. When you meet with friends, does the talk turn more frequently to the economy? Is the talk optimistic ("We're buying a new car.") or pessimistic ("Did you hear that Fred got laid off?")?
3. Do you find yourself doing less impulse buying because you think you ought to be saving more—or more because you feel you can spare the money?
4. Each time you go to a big regional shopping mall, checking the parking lot for vacant spaces, is it easier to find a space in a lot that used to be filled—or harder to find a space in a lot that used to be half-filled?
5. Are the stores you shop in running more or fewer sales?
6. Have any established businesses in your town shut down —or is there a sudden surge of new businesses opening up?
7. The next time you visit your doctor or dentist, ask if more or fewer patients are coming in for routine matters, as opposed to emergency treatment.
8. Are more than two people you know currently out of

work? Or have people you know who have been out of work, recently been hired?

The list can go on, but you get the idea. The economy doesn't turn on a dime: Things happen slowly, and you're always receiving signals that mean a change is coming—for better or for worse. Your economic sixth sense is nothing more than your ability to spot those signals as they appear: the subtle signs and warnings that change is coming.

Money—And Why It Matters

In watching the economy, remember that money really matters—and so does the Federal Reserve, with its unique power to create and destroy money.

You'd think that money is money, and that's the end of it. You should know that the Federal Reserve uses no fewer than four different measures of what counts as money in our economy, and that economists can offer at least that many more.

For purposes of watching the economy, you pay heed to two measures of money—each released often enough by the Federal Reserve to be useful, and each covered widely enough in the press, so you can keep track.

There is the most basic measure of money, called M1, which counts currency and coins, money in checking accounts, and money in those interest-bearing checking accounts called NOW accounts (for negotiable orders of withdrawal). The new super-NOW accounts, which pay a higher rate of interest, also fall into M1. The report on M1 is released each Friday afternoon by the Fed and enough fuss is made about the number that you'll have no trouble keeping track.

There is a broader measure of money called M2, which counts all the above plus money in savings accounts, including money in the new money market accounts at banks and thrift institutions, and money in money market mutual funds. (A thrift institution is the generic name for a savings bank, a savings and loan association, and a credit union.) M2 is released once a month by the Fed, and it's a little harder to track down.

You can quibble about which measure of money is the most important. Early in 1983, M1 amounted to about $500 billion and M2 to about $2 trillion, which is a considerable difference. The rates of growth between M1 and M2 have been considerably different over the years—sometimes one and sometimes the other growing faster. You can further quibble about how much money matters—whether it is the cost of money (interest rates) or the supply of money that is the most important. You can still further quibble about how much money matters—how much of a change in the economy you will get from a change in the money supply.

You can quibble about all of that, but you can't quibble over the fact that money—however you measure it—really does matter. A change in the supply of money will, after a certain amount of time, produce a change in the economy. So watch money, and everything connected with it: the stock and bond markets, mortgage rates, interest rates generally.

Further, watch the M1 measure because it's the easier one to follow—and understand what it is the Fed is supposed to be doing with the money supply.

Money as It Should Be

Ideally, the Federal Reserve should keep our money supply growing at a nice steady rate—the rate of growth in money being equal to the rate of growth you want in the economy. If you wanted the economy to grow by 5 percent after inflation, you'd want the Fed to keep our money supply—measured by M1—growing at a steady 5 percent a year, and the economy would take care of itself. Instead, the Fed keeps changing the rate of growth of the money supply to regulate the economy: faster money growth to pull us out of recession, slower growth to slow down inflation. Since it was the Fed that gave us the recession (too little money in the past) or the inflation (too much money in the past), the Fed's primary mission seems really to be to protect the economy from the Fed.

Be that as it may, the Fed keeps fiddling with the money supply, and with interest rates, and you have to watch it all very carefully.

Figure that a change in the money supply that lasts for a month will produce an effect on interest rates and that a change in the money supply that lasts for at least three months will produce a change in the economy. Take that 5 percent growth rate in that measure called M1 as your benchmark. A three-month period in which the supply of money grows by significantly less than 5 percent will slow the economy, and a three-month period in which the money supply grows by more than 5 percent will speed up the economy.

It will do either, no matter what the Federal Reserve insists it is trying to do to the economy. What the Fed says it is trying to do, and what it actually does, are often (usually, in fact) as far apart as day and night. Among the experts you want always to be most wary of are the officials of the Federal Reserve.

If you took what the Fed was saying at face value, Fed policy never varied an iota between 1979 and 1982. The aim was to wring inflation out of the economy—slowly, and gently.

Money as It Is

In fact, the Fed reduced growth in the money supply to near zero late in 1979 and early in 1980, and the economy plunged into recession. The Fed than gave us a burst of double-digit growth in the money supply midway through 1980 and the economy recovered. The Fed next cut money growth back to near zero early in 1981 and we again plunged into a recession. The recovery which was supposed to come midway through 1982 did not come because growth in the money supply still was close to zero. Around the middle of 1982, the Fed pushed the growth rate of the money supply from near zero to about 15 percent—which gave us the recovery that finally showed up at the tail end of 1982.

The experts missed the recessions of 1980 and 1981, even though a careful watch on the money supply would have shown both coming. The experts insisted the economy would recover in the summer of 1982, even though the absence of any growth in the money supply made such a recovery impossible. The experts were surprised when the economy finally recovered at the end of 1982, even though months of double-digit growth in the money supply absolutely ensured such a recovery.

Heeding the experts would have gotten you into nothing but trouble. Going off on your own, and keeping your own watch on the supply of money in our economy, would have allowed you to track the recovery very nicely.

As with any economic report, you never put much stock in what the money supply does in a single week. The numbers can be erratic—up one week, down the next. Watch for trends—for changes that last for more than a week or two. And, of course, keep watch on the other crucial indicators, too.

Wall Street as a Leading Indicator

That both the stock and the bond markets slumbered through the first seven months of 1982—ignoring all those expert forecasts of recovery just ahead—and then rallied brilliantly thereafter, is worthy of note.

Each market is a seismograph—perpetually monitoring the economy in general and the cost of money in particular.

The economy is important to investors because the better the economy does, the more companies should earn. The more companies earn, the more their stocks should be worth, and the better they should be able to pay off their bonds. The cost of money is important because there's not much point gambling on a common stock if you can earn 12 or 15 percent investing in a government-backed Treasury bill.

Since turning points in the economic cycle are marked by turning points in the cost of money—each market is a superb leading indicator. Later on, we'll talk about how you can make use of those turning points in interest rates in managing your money. Right now, we're using them to help you spot turns in the economy.

Nothing particularly good can happen to the economy, or to the stock and bond markets, when interest rates are high. High rates dampen the economic outlook, and they dampen interest in the investment markets. Lower rates brighten the economic outlook and prospects in the stock and bond markets.

The bond market—manned mostly by seasoned professionals—will tend to respond first, with the stock market in hot pursuit. The preferred stock market index is the Standard & Poor's 500-stock index (the one that's used in the index of leading economic indicators), and you'll find it reported each day in just about every newspaper across the land. Figure that if the stock market starts a broad, sustained advance, an economic recovery is no more than six months away. If the market hits a peak and just hangs there for a while, figure a recession is no more than a year away, and once the stock market begins to slide in earnest, figure that a recession is less than six months away.

That worked to a fare-thee-well in 1982. The rally in the stock market—the wildest rally in stock market history—began in August. The economic recovery began almost exactly five months later, which is as close to hitting the average as you can get.

Interest rates matter, not only in the stock market but in other key economic indicators—with construction being the best example, since all building is done with borrowed money.

As interest rates go up, there will be fewer new homes started and fewer permits granted to build new homes. Both these figures are reported monthly by the government. The volume of contracts for new construction will decline, and that total is reported monthly by the F. W. Dodge division of McGraw-Hill. There will further be a decline in the number of new homes sold (reported monthly by the government) and in the number of existing homes sold (reported monthly by the National Association of Realtors).

The reverse will be true as interest rates come down—increases in building permits, in housing starts, in construction contracts, and in sales. A decline in the number of building permits issued will give you as much as 15 months' warning of a coming recession, and a gain in the number of permits issued will give you around six months' warning of a recovery.

And the Other Indicators

There are still more indicators you should be aware of, because of the important things they have to say about the future. As with all the indicators I've included in this chapter, all are widely quoted on the air and in the financial press: often enough, they are sufficiently important to make headlines. You don't have to follow each one each time it's issued. Just have an overall feel for how these indicators are going.

You will note that some of the most widely publicized economic reports don't turn up on my list. That's because most of them aren't much good at calling the economic future. The reports on personal income and factory production are coincident indicators, meaning they track along with the economy, but they don't lead it. Unemployment is a lagging economic indicator which won't turn higher until a recovery is well underway—or lower until a recession has begun.

Released along with the monthly report on unemployment, is a report showing the average number of hours worked per week by the average worker. Although unemployment is a lagging economic indicator, the hours-worked figure is a leading indicator. Before companies lay off people, they start working their work forces shorter hours. Before companies hire people back, they start working their existing workers longer hours.

A shift toward shorter hours will give you about a year's warning of a recession, and a shift toward longer hours will give you about a three months' warning of a recovery.

All reports dealing with things ordered for future delivery (orders for durable goods, orders for capital goods, orders for factory goods generally) are important. When orders (leading indicator) decline, production (coincident indicator) will decline, and, in time, unemployment (lagging indicator) will decline. Of course, the reverse is true when the economy is turning around.

A change in the level of inventories relative to sales is important. When goods pile up unsold, new orders won't be placed, and then the economic dominoes begin to fall. When inventories are finally worked down—relative to sales—new orders will pick up and all else will follow.

The reports on new orders and on business inventories will each give you about 10 months' warning of a recession and about three months' warning of a recovery. In 1982 the big drop in business inventories of unsold goods began late in the summer and the recovery began about three months after that. The big surge in orders began about two months before the start of the recovery.

The list can go on and on—reports on the economy from the government, from private industry, from economic think tanks, and from experts of every stripe and persuasion. But you're weaning yourself from reliance on the experts, and learning to fall back on your own devices.

Keep watch on the economic reports—on the leading and the other indicators, on the money supply, and the stock market, and the cost of money. Apply all that you see against these eight rules of economic life, and you'll do just fine:

1. Changes in the money supply that last more than a month are always significant, even if the Federal Reserve insists that it has made no change in policy. Any change in the money supply that lasts for at least three months will change the direction of the economy.

2. Watch the reports on building permits, construction contracts, home sales, and housing starts to give you a very early warning of impending change in the economy.

3. Watch for changes in the level of business inventories, relative to sales, to confirm that warning of impending change.

4. All reports having to do with orders for things are important, since nothing happens in the economy until someone orders something.

5. Watch the stock and bond markets for signals that there has been a major change in interest rates. Changes in interest rates foreshadow changes in the economy.

6. Watch the leading economic indicators, but be very suspicious of an advance in the indicators that doesn't include a rally in the stock market. If the advance in the economic

indicators includes neither money nor the stock market, you have every reason to be very dubious.

7. Be impressed only when an indicator has gone in one direction for at least three months and wait until many dominoes have fallen before you let yourself be convinced that the economy is turning.

8. Don't be afraid to trust your own economic sixth sense. You're what makes the economy move, and you instinctively know and understand much more about the economy than you think you do. You really are your own best economic indicator.

Guidelines for Action

There are hundreds of reports you could follow in tracking the economy. Watch just a half-dozen of them, and you'll do fine.

Watching the leading economic indicators to tell you which way the economy is heading—and the coincident indicators to tell you when we've gotten there.

A change in the direction of the money supply will change the direction of the economy. If the money supply grows by more than 5 percent for three months, the economy will speed up. If it grows by less than 5 percent for three months, the economy will slow down.

Regard the stock market as a superior economic indicator; it called the upturn exactly in 1982. It will give you five months' warning of recovery ahead—and a year's warning of a recession.

CHAPTER 3

Taking Command of Your Personal Finances

You've seen it in the movies often enough: The covered wagons of the pioneers are ringed in a circle and from behind every wagon, guns blaze away at the marauding Indians.

You understand how our economy works, and your economic sixth sense is getting better and better at spotting impending changes in our economy. Now it's time to start taking command of your own financial future. You do that by doing the financial equivalent of ringing the covered wagons: making your money as assaultproof as possible against whatever economic marauders an uncertain future might bring—inflation, deflation, hyper-inflation, deep depression, or great, good times.

Things look pretty good right now—inflation down and the economy growing. But you can never be sure what tomorrow will bring, so you must build a personal financial strategy flexible enough to adapt to any and all changes in economic circumstance:

—You must put aside enough money as savings to live on for at least three months, as a hedge against whatever harsh things the economy throws your way.

—Once you've saved you must invest because the tax on investment income—capital gains—is tiny compared with the tax on wages, interest, and dividends, and because the more capital you pile up, the better insulated you'll be against the economic storms that swirl around you.

—In order to free up money for saving and investing, you must learn to budget your money—making every dollar go as far as possible.

And there's lots more to building a personal financial strategy appropriate to the eighties.

You must learn to use debt wisely and safely—and the rules about debt that applied in the 1970s don't apply in the 1980s. You want the most insurance for your money, and the basic insurance policy of the past—whole life—is fading and new forms of insurance are showing up in the market. You must make full use of all the benefits your employer provides—and there have been some changes there. And you must know what to do if you're in a situation in which you don't have a company benefits plan.

You could be fired someday in the future, and you may now have more going for you if that happens. Finally, just in case, you should know the new rules for going bankrupt. Thanks to recent legislation, you can now take refuge from your creditors while keeping your house, and a lot of other things, and a half-million Americans now go bankrupt each year. You hope it will never come to that. Should it, you'll know how best to weather the experience.

This is the dull and dirty work of managing your money. It doesn't offer the thrills and chills of a plunge into stocks, and it's not as much fun as shopping for some collectible. But it's as crucial to your financial well-being as fertilizing, watering, and mowing are to the success of your lawn. As you'll see in chapter 14, there are "smart" machines to help you—from advanced calculators that start at $25 to full-fledged home computers that start at under $100. Calculators and computers will both do the dirtiest of the dirty work of managing your money—in a tiny fraction of the time it would take you.

But even the smartest of machines can't do a thing until you've done the groundwork: collected, analyzed, and sorted through all the details of how you use your money.

Start building your money strategy by gathering together

every scrap of paper that shows how you've spent money over the past 12 months: canceled checks, credit card and charge account receipts, old bills, notes scribbled on the backs of envelopes—everything. Pick a rainy Sunday to give yourself plenty of time to do a thorough job.

It would be better if you could pull together everything for the latest 12 months and for the 12 months before that. This way you could make year-to-year comparisons: where you're holding the line on spending and where you're letting go. That's probably asking too much. You do want everything you can lay hands on for the past year, because that's what you build your budget on.

Group everything by spending category—broken down as many ways as you can. One way is to get a box of the cheapest letter-size envelopes you can find. Use a separate envelope for each category, and stuff all appropriate records in: mortgage or rental payments; food bills; utility bills, broken down by gas, electric, and telephone; car expenses; clothing, broken down by family member; medical bills, broken down by family member, with a separate envelope for drug bills, and another for cosmetics; house upkeep, broken down by type of expense; liquor bills; entertaining; eating out (it helps to charge everything and save the receipts).

Don't count department store charge accounts or credit card payments as a single category. Break out what the money was actually spent for—jotting each item down on a slip of paper and popping it into the appropriate envelope.

In later years you'll have the envelopes made up at the start of the year, and you'll put the receipts and bills right in each envelope as they come in. Or, if you buy a home computer, you can enter each spending item into the computer as it happens. Then, when you want it, it will all be stored in the computer's memory, waiting for you. For your first time, it's a big job of collecting everything, but it's worth the effort.

Next, total up the contents of each envelope. And then prepare a 3-by-5 card for each envelope: the spending category at the top of the card, and the amount you've spent during the past year, just below it. Now you have the basis for your budget, which will be a "zero-base budget."

Starting from Zero

As the term implies, you start from zero each year, as though you've never had a budget before, as opposed to just taking last year's spending and adding on. (If you're like most of us, you really haven't had a budget before—not a serious one, at least.)

You have that stack of 3-by-5 cards—one per envelope per spending category. First, pull out the cards that represent absolutely essential spending: mortgage or rental payment, utility bills, insurance premiums, installment debt repayment, the cost of commuting to work. These are bills that must be paid, come what may, and they represent your "minimum increment from zero."

Next, go through the rest of the cards, and rank them in order of priority—food, medical expenses, car upkeep, and clothing at the top, down to those impulse items that you spend money on but which you could live without.

Next, fill out additional cards, listing all the things you'd like to spend money on during the coming year which weren't in last year's budget: a fancier vacation, a new motor for the power boat, a new color TV set, whatever.

As you go through your 3-by-5 cards, you'll come across some one-time-only expenses (new transmission for the car, new burner for the furnace). Don't automatically discard them on the theory they won't occur again. You can count on a certain number of one-time-only expenses each year. If you go through a year without any, so much the better. Then you'll have some extra money left at the end of the year, to save or invest, or just have fun with.

Now start drafting your actual budget. Take last year's spending, and add an inflation factor of, say, 5 percent, which becomes your projected spending for the coming year. If it looks as though inflation is heating up, use a bigger inflation factor. If it looks as though inflation is cooling down, use a smaller inflation factor.

Prepare one final card, labeled "saving." Make it out for 10 percent of your take-home pay, and add it to your stack, just after those bedrock, minimum-increment-from-zero items.

That's your goal—to save 10 percent of your take-home pay. You may have to trim it a bit in light of your economic circumstance, but 10 percent is your target—and your income doesn't make a particle of difference. Aim for saving 10 percent of take-home pay whether you earn $25,000 a year or $50,000 or $500,000.

Finally, go through your stack of cards, and on each card, list any ways you can think of to cut spending. Is there work around the house you could do yourself? Could you do with fewer meals out? Could you wash the car yourself instead of taking it to the carwash? Could you buy cheaper cuts of meat? House-brand liquor? No-frills brands at the supermarket?

This is a dangerous time for all of us. The economy is stronger and we're less concerned about cutting back because times are hard. Inflation is down so our money goes further, and there's less pressure to scrimp and save, and more of a tendency to cut loose and spend.

You must fight that tendency tooth and nail.

If your money goes further, it's a time to gain ground—to build up your savings and your investment pool, after all the years in which saving was next to impossible. Again, you can't know what tomorrow will bring, and you must be prepared for anything. We squeezed inflation out of our economy in the late 1960s and again in the mid-seventies, and each time it came back.

Inflation could come back yet again, and you'll be ahead of the game, if you've done your saving now.

You may not want to take advantage of all cost-saving ideas. Your idea of bliss may be to have someone else do the lawn. Dinner out once a week may be necessary rest-and-recreation after a brutal siege at the office. Still, you want at least one cost-cutting technique per card, to be used if necessary. Since you're looking at your spending in a different way, you may find ways of saving money you hadn't thought of before.

Building on Your Budget

Now total up all the cards—last year's spending plus that inflation factor to give you this year's spending, plus those extras that weren't in last year's budget but which you'd like to spend money on this year. Then you strike the balance that really matters: proposed spending against anticipated income. If you know what this year's income is going to be, fine. If not, take last year's income from all sources and add a 5 percent inflation factor. If you expect to have income from other sources (interest, dividends, etc.), add them in. Remember, this is the bottom line we're talking about—after-tax income, what you actually have to spend.

If your anticipated income is $25,000 and all the spending items you've written down come to $30,000, you have a problem. Start discarding cards from the bottom of the deck, until you get your spending in line with income. Or, opt for some of those cheaper ways of doing things.

Tamper with savings only as a last resort. That's money you need to live on, if times get hard, and it's the money you'll invest to build capital. It's just below those bedrock items, and it should be the last item you trim to strike a balance in your budget. Even then, trim it gently.

That's your budget for the year, and once you've drawn it up, it becomes an important working tool. Check periodically to make sure you're holding the line: every month, ideally, but every quarter at a minimum.

If you come into more money, or if you find you're doing better holding the line on your budget than you expected, go through the leftover cards—those you discarded to bring your balance into line. If you do have extra money, and you aren't saving 10 percent of income, bring your savings closer to 10 percent before you start spending on anything else.

It's more likely that things will go the other way—spending outrunning your budget. Go through the stack of cards and discard some more, or adopt more of those cheaper ways of doing things, until you again bring spending into line with income.

There used to be guidelines about how to allocate your money—so much for food, so much for housing. It used to be that you tried to hold your housing costs to 25 percent of your income before taxes. You're doing well today if you can keep housing costs to under 35 percent of income. Forget about the guidelines. They're for the Average American Family, and you're you.

These days, that Average American Family (two kids, dad working, mom at home) embraces barely 10 percent of the population. You're more likely to be part of a two-income family or a single-parent family, or an unmarried couple living together. You may be in your twenties or your sixties. You may be a blue-collar worker or a high-level corporate executive.

Remember, you're taking command of your own financial future—weaning yourself from the experts and their guidelines and their rules of thumb.

It doesn't matter who you are or your age or how you live. The important thing is to draft a budget you can live with, and to stick to it—modifying it as circumstances dictate, but always remaining in control of your money. Each year, do it again—again starting from zero. Each year, you'll have some fresh insights on where to spend and where to trim. Each year, the budget will become just a little more tailored to you, the way you live and the way you spend.

Pennies Saved and Pennies Earned

We all learned to bargain-hunt when inflation was raging, because it was the only way to make our money go far enough. During the recession, business was stuck with mountains of unsold goods—a half-trillion dollars' worth in the autumn of 1982—that could be had at bargain prices.

Don't quit bargain-hunting just because times seem better. When you can buy for less, you're left with more to spend on other things, and more to save and invest. No matter what the economic season, a penny saved is even better than a penny earned because you don't have to pay any taxes on it.

That makes a penny saved worth as much as two pennies earned.

Don't always assume that posted prices are the final word—even in the most staid of stores. Make a reasonable offer—say 5 percent below the posted price—and you may be pleasantly surprised to find it accepted. When inflation is our lot, the store is paying sky-high interest rates to finance its inventory.

When times are hard, the store is most likely delighted to sell anything at all.

When you pay with a credit card, the retailer gets docked 4 or 5 or 6 percent by the credit card company. If you pay cash, the retailer gets it all, and he may be willing to shade the price just a bit.

Keep a "want" list in your purse or wallet of things you'll have to buy soon. When you go into a store, check to see if any of the items are on sale. Check the classified ads in your local paper to see if someone is selling what you need. Spend a couple of hours once a month checking out the garage sales in your town for the things you need. That want list imposes a discipline, so you don't come home from garage sales with a stuffed moose head when you really wanted a sled for the kids. The beauty part of garage sales is that you don't pay a sales tax and that immediately saves you a few pennies on each dollar.

Most towns have a Salvation Army store or a Goodwill outlet, and you can find bargains galore. I spent a fair amount of money on a handsome swivel chair for my study, only to have it fall apart after a few months of use. I went to the local Salvation Army thrift shop and bought a perfectly suitable chair for three dollars. In fact, I'm sitting on the chair as I write this.

Check into barter, in which you swap something you have for something someone else has. By one estimate I saw recently, Americans each year now barter goods worth $20 billion. Most newspaper classified sections have barter columns, and there are commercial barter services springing up, in which you pay a fee to get in on the action. At most companies, employee newsletters include a for-sale and a swap section, and there's rarely a fee for running an ad.

Every town has a few central locations where people post notices of things for sale. In my town it's a bulletin board in a big supermarket. Bargain hunting is fun, once you get in the swing of it. You stretch out your dollars, and that's good no matter what's happening in the economy. Along the lines of "you can't be too rich or too thin," you can't save too much money.

In *Financial Survival in the Age of New Money* I amused

some people with my tales about garbage bags, light bulbs, and size 13AA shoes.

The standard approach, when inflation was locked into double digits, was to buy today, because tomorrow's prices would surely be higher. In *Financial Survival,* I mentioned that I had saved $50 by buying a year's supply of light bulbs on sale, and $10 by buying a year's supply of plastic garbage bags, also on sale. I also noted that I had bought a pair of shoes on sale (my size being 13AA), the price reduced from $100 to $60, not because I needed new shoes immediately but because I assumed the shoes would probably cost $120 when I did need a new pair. (Waning inflation or not, the shoes, in fact, now cost about $130 a pair.)

Even when inflation was raging, I never did buy the idea of mortgaging the house to stock up on cases of canned corn or toilet paper, just to beat tomorrow's higher prices. It makes even less sense today, with inflation down. Your money is tied up in a non-earning asset, and whatever you save by buying before prices go higher, you lose by not being able to invest your money at a profit.

By buying in advance of rising prices a few years ago, you might have saved yourself from the ravages of 15 percent inflation. But you gave up the opportunity to invest your money at more than 15 percent. You can liquidate your position in a money market fund, or wherever, a lot easier than you can liquidate a house full of toilet paper. The same is true whether inflation is 15 percent or 5 percent.

I was simply bargain hunting when I bought my plastic garbage bags and my light bulbs and my size 13AA shoes. All were available at about half their normal price—and that's too good a saving to pass up, no matter what the rate of inflation.

Controlling Your Debt

It's hard to know how to manage debt in today's economy. In the days of high inflation, you made maximum use of debt, because you were paying back in depreciated dollars, and it was the lender who stood the loss. In times of disinflation (inflation is still there, but waning), that's less true. And in a period of deflation (prices actually falling), you're paying back in ever more costly dollars, and it's you who stands the loss.

Assume that even if our future holds the promise of less inflation, it doesn't hold the promise of no inflation. Assume that prices will go up by at least 5 percent a year—and maybe by more in some years. We could return to a double-digit inflation, but it won't happen overnight, and you'll have enough warning to change your borrowing strategy. As things stand now, continue to use debt—wisely, of course. You won't get the windfall you did when inflation was raging, but each payment you make on the loan will be in dollars worth just a little less—and maybe, at some point in the future, a lot less.

No matter what happens, stay a disciplined borrower. Buy only what you need and borrow only when you must. There's an obvious discipline when you buy a big-ticket item—a car or major appliance. You must take out a loan to pay for it, and the monthly payments go at the very top of your budget. You can get carried away on the day-to-day things if you don't exercise control over your credit cards. Whether you pay cash or charge, don't buy it if you don't need it. If it isn't on your want list, ask yourself why you're buying it. Credit card borrowing is expensive borrowing—18 to 20 percent as I write this. While other rates have come down, rates on credit card borrowing have not.

You can ride a credit card without running up interest charges, if you pay in full each month, and if you pay attention to the billing date for your account. That's the day each month when all your charges are totaled up, and your bill is prepared. Charge something near that billing date, and you get more than a month's free ride on your money.

I have a bank credit card, and the billing date is the twenty-first of the month. I have until the fifteenth day of the following month to get my payment back in the card company's hands before it starts charging interest. I could buy something on January 20, not get billed for it until the February bill, and not have to mail my check until the tenth of March—without paying any interest.

If you do let an unpaid balance run from one month to the

next, you do, of course, pay interest. Further, you'll start paying interest on each new charge as of the day it's posted to your account, not as of the billing date. Figure that the meter will start running within a day or two after you charge something.

The moral: You get that free ride if you settle in full each month, and you pay very dearly when you don't.

You're probably safe if debt repayment—not counting mortgage debt—comes to less than 15 percent of takehome pay. Beyond 15 percent, it's dicey, and when you hit 20 percent, you're in trouble. Again, that's one of those rules of thumb, and again, the idea is to use your growing knowledge of the economy to set your own rules. So shape this one to your personal situation as you shape everything having to do with money to your personal situation. Just remember that dept repayment is one of those minimum-increment-from-zero items, and the more you spend paying off debt, the less there is to spend elsewhere, save, and invest.

Where to Borrow

If you must borrow, shop your life insurance company first. If your policy dates to before 1971, the rate is probably just 5 percent. If it dates to between 1971 and 1978, the rate is probably 6 percent. Most policies written since 1979 carry an 8 percent rate. A few states now allow life companies to specify that loans against new policies will be at going market interest rates. Most don't—and you can repay the loan as you will.

You'll want to pay it back eventually, since borrowing on your life insurance cuts into the death benefit. Still, you pay back on your schedule, not that of the lender. All this assumes you have enough cash value built up that there's something to borrow. It also assumes you have whole life, and we'll talk in a bit about whether anyone should have whole life.

Next, check your credit union, bank, and thrift institution for their best rates. Credit unions usually offer the lowest rates, particularly on car loans, and it probably pays to join your company's credit union, if there is one, to have a place to turn to when you want to borrow.

You'll usually do better at a credit union or a bank—than by letting the retailer arrange the financing of a major purchase. But even that isn't an absolute rule. At various times in recent years, the automobile manufacturers, through their captive finance companies, offered car loans at rates far below the rates available anyplace else. The auto companies were desperate to sell cars, and rather than cut prices outright, they offered those bargain loan rates.

As with any big purchase (and what you're buying is money), shop around. The bank that holds your mortgage and/or your checking account will probably do a little better for you than an institution where you're a stranger. You and your credit standing are known quantities, and that's always important to a banker.

Savings and loan associations can now make consumer loans, so check with a couple of S&L's. They're new in the business, and they might offer the best terms just to build up a portfolio of loans. But steer clear of small loan companies—and mostly steer clear of personal loans generally. The rates are very high. And stay away from the finance companies that will lend you money in return for a second mortgage on your house. Again, you'd pay a very high rate for the money.

You're always better off doing all your financial business with a single institution. Just like any other retailer (and every lender you deal with is a retailer of money), a banker will tend to favor a regular customer over someone who just walks in off the street. When you must borrow, you're a familiar face.

I deal with a bank that holds my mortgage, my checking account, a car loan, and a student loan, plus various accounts that I have opened for my children. When I have banking business to carry out, even routine business, I drop over and say hello to the branch manager, just to keep in touch.

The law says a lender can't turn you down for a loan because of race or sex, and there probably is less rank discrimination than there used to be when it came to lending. If you're young, or a woman alone—newly divorced, for instance—you may very well have trouble borrowing simply because you haven't been on your own long enough to develop a credit rating.

For you, doing all your financial business with one institution is a must. Make sure the branch manager knows who you are. You may want to take out a modest loan—for a vacation or something else—just to establish yourself as someone who pays off a loan on schedule. Take out some credit cards and make sure you pay those off on schedule, so you build up a credit rating. Some banks have special departments for women—staffed by women. If there's such a department at a bank in your town, look into it.

Refinancing Your Mortgage

If you have a big expense coming up—college bills for the kids being the most likely—think about tapping the equity built up in your home, by refinancing your mortgage. If it's an older mortgage, the lender will welcome a chance to replace a low-yielding mortgage with a new, higher-yielding mortgage. If you've lived in the home for any length of time, inflation has pushed the market value of your home far above what you paid for it, so there's plenty of equity to tap.

The gain in the value of the house isn't doing you much good just sitting there. You'll pay a higher rate than on the old mortgage, but the interest payment is a tax deduction—meaning the government will pay up to half the cost. The more you've paid down on the old mortgage, the smaller the tax deduction, because the portion of your payment going to interest is declining.

This is one for you and your banker to work on together. What would another form of borrowing cost, against the cost of refinancing a mortgage? Don't forget all the costs connected with refinancing a mortgage: closing costs, loan origination fees, etc. What rate of interest would a college loan carry, and how quickly would you have to pay it back? A new mortgage would run for 25 or 30 years, while a college loan might have to be repaid in four years. How could the monthly payments stack up: old mortgage plus college loan versus new mortgage?

You'd get a large sum of money all at once by refinancing the old mortgage and you could invest that until the money has to be spent: income to offset the higher cost of the new mortgage. This makes the position: old mortgage plus college loan versus new mortgage less monthly income from the money you now have invested.

What Life Insurance Is All About

The next part of your personal financial strategy is making sure you have enough of the right kinds of insurance—on your home, car, health, and your life.

Insurance is supposed to insure, and nothing more. If you don't have enough, you can take horrendous losses. If you have too much, or the wrong kind, you're wasting money. If you're willing to pay the premium, you can buy life insurance enough to let your next of kin live like the Rockefellers.

It's more likely to be the husband who is the primary breadwinner—and the wife who is most likely to survive. At any age a woman can expect to earn only 65 percent of what a man doing comparable work will earn. If the surviving wife has young children, or if she's elderly, she may not be able to work at all. Expenses, such as mortgage payments, that were bearable when husband and wife were alive, will probably be beyond the ability of a woman alone—especially if there's still a family to be raised.

On that basis, you want enough life insurance to:

1. Pay your funeral expenses.
2. Pay off the mortgage.
3. Pay the college bills of your children.
4. Enable your family to live in reasonable comfort for three years.

If your income is $30,000 a year, that probably works out to between $150,000 and $200,000 worth of insurance you should have in your peak risk years (all your children still to be educated and the bulk of the mortgage still to be paid off). If your income is $50,000 a year, figure on a minimum of $300,000 worth of insurance.

Again, though, beware of formulas and rules of thumb, and the expert advice of others. Plan things out for yourself, because no one else knows your personal finances as well as you do. You need enough insurance to satisfy all four of those points. Whatever it takes is the right amount of insurance for you.

You'd modify those rules if your spouse is unable to work for one reason or another, or if you have a child who'll need special care in future years. Otherwise, you're safe enough sticking with this formula. You'll be doing right by your family, and the annual premium won't kill you.

You can buy whole life, which includes a savings feature, or term insurance, which provides only death benefits. Term starts out cheap, but the policy must be renewed periodically (hence "term"), and each time you renew, the premium goes up. Whole life is for life and the premium, while higher than term at the outset—never goes higher. In time, the premium on term will pass the premium on whole life. Still, over the life of a policy (your life, as it happens), you'll pay a lot more for whole life than for term, which is why insurance agents love whole life.

But the days of whole life are waning, and nothing made that clearer than when, early in 1982, the giant ITT Life Insurance Company quit selling it. ITT Life is a titan—a unit of ITT, the conglomerate, with some $4 billion of life insurance outstanding. Says President Robert W. MacDonald of ITT Life, "Whole life is no longer a viable consumer product. It just doesn't meet consumer needs."

The reason it doesn't is that while whole life uses part of your premium to build up savings for you, the interest paid on those savings has been tiny. "The average return on whole life policies," says MacDonald, "is in the neighborhood of 3 to 4 percent. Do you know of anyone today who would knowingly make an investment—and life insurance is, in the broadest sense, an investment as well as death protection—that returns only 3 to 4 percent?"

The insurance industry has learned a lesson by watching its customers put their money where the yields are—in areas other than insurance. To win customers back, insurance generally has come down in price. You can get more insurance for your money than you could a few years ago.

Also, the industry abounds with new products, of which "universal life" is the best known. In universal life, the savings portion of the policy is separated from the life insurance portion. You can pick the amount of life coverage you want, and you can change it at different stages of your life. Whatever part of your premium doesn't pay for life coverage, earns a return for you that's higher than the return on whole life. The 1982 tax law changed the tax situation of life companies to enable them to offer universal life.

MacDonald of ITT Life thinks the industry will create still more new products in the future—policies that offer more investment options, and pay a higher return than whole life. But he also thinks it will take a few more years to perfect these policies. In the meantime, he thinks, most people are better off buying term insurance and investing on their own.

"If you own whole life today," says MacDonald, "cash it in. Shop around first, and don't drop your current policy until you have a new one in place. But start now, because every day you wait costs you money."

Universal life does have some advantages over whole life, and the future may see still more types of policies that would pay more on your money. Examine everything that's available when you buy life insurance. It's possible that after you've examined all of them, you'll stick with term life and do your own saving.

Start out when you're young, and term will cost about one-third as much as whole life for comparable amounts of coverage. You need maximum protection when you're younger and the full cost of raising children is still ahead of you. By the time your children are out of college, the premium on term has gone up, but you need less coverage, and you can begin to scale back.

Since price cutting is rampant among insurance companies these days, it pays to shop around. Ideally, you should team up with an independent agent who can handle all your insurance needs and who, by dealing with several companies, can pick among them to get the best deal for you. But also check with agents for one or two of the life companies that use their own captive sales forces. If you live in a state with savings banks, check out the premium on Savings Bank Life Insurance (which is moderately priced term insurance) against what the life companies are charging.

Check for any discounts that might be available. Many companies offer lower rates to women, because of the life expectancy edge that women have. Some companies give a break to nonsmokers, and some offer lower rates to those who can prove they keep themselves physically fit.

Most likely, these days, you have life insurance as part of your company's employee benefits plan—with all or part of the cost paid by your employer. Make sure the company-provided coverage is enough to meet the four basic goals listed earlier. If it isn't, flesh it out with term insurance bought on your own. Make sure you understand what happens should you leave the company. As a rule, you can convert into an individual policy, without having to take a physical, if you act within a certain period—usually 30 days.

There can be a tax jolt when your company pays for your life insurance. Once the coverage goes beyond $50,000, the premiums paid by the company count as taxable income to you.

Spouse life insurance is a hot issue these days. Even if the primary breadwinner is the husband (which itself is no longer always the case), the wife's income plays an increasingly important role in many families today. If you're a two-income family, you must protect the family against the loss of that second income.

Say the secondary wage-earner is the wife, earning $15,000 a year and doing a lot of the keeping of the house. You'd want enough coverage to make up for that lost income for three years, plus the cost of a housekeeper for as long as you'd need one. Again, you're best off with a straight term insurance. If your spouse is covered by a company plan, so much the better.

So Long as You're Healthy

When it comes to health insurance, the way to go is with a group plan provided by your employer. The cost of health care has climbed faster than any other expense in our economy (health care inflation staying up in double digits when inflation in the rest of the economy has waned)—and the cost of private health insurance has climbed apace.

If you don't have a company plan and must buy coverage on your own, check your local Blue Cross–Blue Shield plan first. Talk to the agent who sold you life insurance to see what he can offer on health insurance. The best plans pick up 80 percent of your medical bills (after a $100 deductible), with almost no limit on how big your bills can run during your lifetime ($500,000 and more), and with a guarantee that your out-of-pocket medical bills won't top $1,000 or $2,000 a year. Hospital costs would be 100 percent covered, with no deductible, and so would surgeon's bills.

But such a plan will cost the typical family of four around $2,500 a year. Even a minimum plan, with far fewer features —will run at least $1,500. Yet you can't do without health insurance.

One alternative is a health maintenance organization. A good HMO should provide just about any medical treatment you might require—if you use the HMO's doctors and facilities—at a cost comparable to (and sometimes less than) a good private health insurance package. Many companies now offer membership in an HMO as an optional alternative to the company's health insurance plan. If you aren't covered by a company plan, check out the HMO's in your area. If you are covered by a company plan but are offered an HMO as an alternative, compare the costs and benefits of each.

Sometimes the HMO is a cliniclike affair, with all the staff in one location. Sometimes it's a group of doctors in an area who work for the HMO on a contract basis. Either way, visit the facility and look around. Talk to people who are members of the HMO. You'll be using the doctors who work for the HMO. Do you feel comfortable with them? Would you pick them as personal physicians? Is there provision for off-hours coverage? What sort of situations can't the HMO treat? If you have to be hospitalized, is the HMO tied to a hospital you'd want to go to? Is it a teaching hospital, with the staff and the facilities to treat serious conditions, or just a hospital in the neighborhood, with no particular claim to distinction?

An HMO makes the most sense if you have young children,

and lots of medical bills, or if you're elderly and need a fair amount of care (and you can reach the HMO without too much trouble). It makes less sense if you're middle-aged with relatively few medical problems.

When you change jobs, your company health plan will probably cover you for up to a month, but seldom can you convert to an individual policy without a physical exam. You can buy temporary coverage to tide you over from one job to the next—until the day you become eligible for coverage under the new plan, which isn't always right away. If there's a costly, chronic illness in the family, it can be a consideration when you're thinking about changing jobs. Most health insurance—group and individual—won't immediately pick up the cost of a preexisting condition. Some, in fact, won't pick up the bills for a year or two.

You always want the highest lifetime limit on medical expenses you can get: $250,000 per family member is the rock-bottom minimum and $1 million is a lot better. If the lifetime limit on your company plan is under $250,000, or even $500,000, shop around for a supplemental major medical policy called a piggyback. It can have a pretty high deductible—to hold down the cost of coverage—but it must have a high lifetime maximum. You can't be without adequate health insurance, and the more you can afford, the better.

Dental insurance is a nice adjunct to a company benefits package, and every day more companies offer it. It will take some of the sting out of expensive procedures, including root canal work, and sometimes orthodontia. It's also available to individuals, through private insurers but at a very high price.

What If You're Disabled

Most companies provide plans that will pay your salary through a short-term disability—typically up to 26 weeks. Fewer companies provide long-term disability coverage—the sort of thing that protects you against catastrophic situations that keep you out of work indefinitely. You need long-term disability protection, if you don't get it at work, particularly if you have young children. You have to figure out how much it would cost you to live at something above the barebones level, assuming a reasonable amount of income from your spouse. That much coverage won't be cheap, but it's necessary. Under what conditions will the policy pay off? How is total disability defined? If you work with your hands, will the loss of a hand count as total disability? As a broadcaster, I have a policy that covers me against damage to my voice.

Don't forget spouse disability insurance. It takes most families two incomes to get by, and protecting the family against the loss of your spouse's income, is as important as protecting the family against the loss of your income. If your spouse has coverage as part of a company benefits plan, fine. If not, you'll have to buy it. Long-term disability coverage is particularly important when there are still young children in the family. A serious disability could mean you'd have to hire a housekeeper to run the house and handle the children.

Whether it's for you or your spouse, shy away from those heavily promoted disability plans (sometimes even advertised on matchbook covers) that promise to pay so much a day for each day you're incapacitated. Most don't pay enough, or have so many limitations, that they're all but worthless.

Your Home and What's in It

You want enough property insurance to make your home and its possessions assaultproof—which means an adequate amount of homeowner's insurance, plus additional coverage to handle those things that fall through the cracks on a regular homeowner's policy.

Unless your house is insured for at least 80 percent of its replacement cost (not the market value, but the cost of actually rebuilding your home from the ground up), you'll get less than full reimbursement if there's damage to the dwelling.

Inflation over the years has pushed the replacement cost of your house to levels you never dreamed of. The cost of new construction went up by double digits for many years: Unless you've been very diligent, you're sitting on a financial timebomb—facing a major loss if your house is damaged.

If you haven't done it recently, find out how much it would

cost to replace your house. Some insurance companies have rather simple forms that will give you the replacement cost of your home. My company provided a form that took about 10 minutes to complete. I was stunned to find I was underinsured by about 40 percent of the replacement cost. The institution that holds your mortgage, or your real estate agent, can put you in touch with someone who'll do an appraisal of your home.

Most companies now offer an inflation feature on their homeowner's policies; this automatically raises your coverage by a certain amount each year. If the inflation feature isn't available in your state, then have your property appraised at least once every three years and adjust your coverage accordingly. Remember that while we may face lower inflation, only in a deep depression would we face zero inflation.

The contents of your house are normally covered to 50 percent of the total amount of your homeowner's coverage: $50,000 of insurance on the contents if your home is insured for $100,000. This guards against fire and theft on furnishings, clothing, and the like. But once you get into the area of valuables, limitations pop up all over the place.

The average policy will pay no more than $100 on any stolen cash, which is reasonable on the face of it. Otherwise, the woods would be filled with people claiming to have had a few dozen $100 bills around the house. But if you have a collection of rare coins, that's still money and it still comes under the $100 limitation. You're usually limited to a *total* of $500 on all furs and jewelry, and there are limitations on items kept at home that you'd normally use in your business. Often enough your regular homeowner's policy won't pay off on the "mysterious disappearance" of jewelry.

You need additional, specific coverage on these big-ticket (and very stealable) items. You'd usually buy a separate "floater" policy—which, more precisely, is known as inland marine insurance. (It's called a floater because the policy was developed to cover goods being shipped.)

Each item is listed separately. The company won't take your word for how much each item is worth. It will want bills of sale, or an appraisal done by a professional—just to make sure your diamond tiara really is worth $100,000. In case of loss the company has the option of paying you off at the appraised value, or of replacing the item.

All jewelry, arts and antiques, and assorted rarities should be reappraised each three years and adjusted for inflation. Should there be an explosion in the price of gold or of gems, you'll want the items reappraised more often. It's less important with furs, cameras, stereo equipment and the like, which depreciate in value fairly rapidly. If you lose a fur, the company will typically offer you the wholesale replacement cost (and it might send you to a furrier of its choosing, who'll replace the fur).

The 1982 tax law wiped out a few of what used to be money-saving approaches to homeowner's insurance (and auto insurance, too). The standard homeowner's policy carries a $100 deductible. You pay the first $100 of any loss, and the company pays the rest. You can cut your premium by as much as 20 percent by raising the deductible to $500. Until the 1982 law you could take any uninsured loss, beyond $100, as a casualty loss on your tax return. Thanks to that law the loss must go above 10 percent of your taxable income before you get any deduction. If you have a high deductible, lower it in light of the 1982 law. You can still gamble a bit and keep the deductible at $200 or $250, which will save a little on the premium, while putting a limit on what any loss will cost you out of pocket. Or, since the saving won't be that great, you might just say "the hell with it," hurl a few curses at Congress, and settle for a $100 deductible.

See if your insurance company offers reduced premiums if you install smoke detectors or a burglar alarm. I have smoke alarms in my house and that cuts my annual premium by about 3 percent.

In case of loss, you must prove to the insurance company that you lost what you claim to have lost. Everything on your floater policy is listed, but keep records on everything else in your house. You can simply go from room to room, listing everything in the house, and its value. If you have a cassette tape recorder, talk your way through the house. Another way is to photograph everything: distance shots to show all or part of a room, and close-ups to show individual objects. Show pieces of furniture and bric-a-brac in groups. Show suits and dresses hanging in closets. Or do it the 1980s way: borrow a videotape unit and go from room to room. You want to show the insurance company exactly the way things looked before a fire or theft, and you want to remind yourself of what you had.

Should disaster strike, you don't have to settle for what the insurance company offers. Get your own estimate of what the lost or damaged items were worth and how much it will cost to repair or replace them. You can hire a professional insurance adjuster who will handle things for a percentage of the final settlement. You'll find them listed in the Yellow Pages, or the National Association of Public Insurance Adjusters, in Baltimore, will put you in touch with an accredited member.

A Few Rules on Your Car

Finally, there's auto insurance. If you own a car, you have it, and you don't need much in the way of advice.

You must have adequate coverage against injuries you cause others—$500,000 at a minimum these days, given the settlements that juries are awarding. As with property insurance, rethink your collision deductible in light of the 1982 tax law, since your uninsured casualty loss most top 10 percent of taxable income before you can write off the loss on your taxes. You could cut the cost of collision coverage by up to 40 percent, if you lift the deductible from $100 to $500. Nowadays, you're better off with a $200 deductible on a new car (which will be about 15 percent less than $100 deductible). Go to the $500 deductible when the car is five years old (you're less likely to repair an older car). After eight years, drop the collision coverage altogether (you're more likely to sell the car for what you can get for it, than to spend much repairing it).

Many companies give a 10 percent deduction to graduates of driver education programs. Many give a break to students who maintain a high grade average, or to students who go to school far enough away from home that they won't be using the car very often. There may be further breaks if you don't drive the car very much each year, if you don't use the car for commuting, or if the car has anti-theft devices, or air bags. Some companies offer a break if you don't smoke or drink.

Benefiting from Your Benefits

For most of us, the basic protection against the bad things of the world is a company benefit plan. There will probably be a booklet listing all the available benefits, but don't feel shy about visiting whoever is in charge of the plan to make sure you're getting all you're entitled to. If you're not covered by a plan, you can use this to arrange for your benefits package.

There's no such thing as a perfect plan. Within any company, the benefits will vary according to your job, your salary, and how long you've been around. Executives get more than white-collar workers, who get more than blue-collar workers.

The Conference Board in New York has done a comprehensive study of benefits offered by 3,000 companies, big and small, in a variety of industries. It shows what the typical company offers these days, and what the "leading-edge" companies offer (companies that tend to do things first). The Conference Board study shapes up this way:

HEALTH INSURANCE. Most companies offer both a base plan and major medical coverage—the base plan covering specific routine medical services, with major medical picking up all the expenses for the treatment of a major illness.

Typically, the base plan will pay 80 percent of the cost of medical care, after a $100 deductible; full charges for a semi-private hospital room for up to four months; and "reasonable and customary" surgical fees. The lifetime limit on the major medical portion is at least $250,000.

The typical plan covers treatment of mental illness, and drug and alcohol addiction, whether or not it's done in a hospital. Usually, though, there are limits on treatment for mental illness on an out-patient basis.

It's common for a company to pay for your medical coverage, while you pay part of the cost of covering your dependents. Forty percent of the companies offered dental insurance, against 8 percent a decade ago. Nearly half offered a Health Maintenance Organization, as an alternative to health insurance, but only 3 percent of the employees opted for an HMO.

The leading-edge companies offered a single comprehensive medical plan, covering both basic coverage and major medical. Their plans put a limit on what you'd pay in any medical situation, and a very high limit ($1 million in many cases), or no limit, on the medical bills you can run up during your life. These leading-edge companies covered prescription drugs and offered, or were thinking about offering, an optical plan and a hearing-aid plan.

DISABILITY BENEFITS. Short-term disability pays part of your salary—sometimes your whole salary—for up to six months, depending on how long you've worked for the company. Long-term disability picks up after six months—typically paying 60 percent of your salary up to $2,500 a month, until retirement. After retirement, in many companies, there's a disability pension that takes over, integrated with your Social Security benefits. Most companies pay the whole cost of disability coverage.

The leading-edge companies pay full salary on short-term disability and as much as two-thirds of your salary, for life, on long-term disability.

PENSIONS. The typical company pays the whole cost of your pension, with the amount of the pension based on your earnings during the last years before retirement. (With Social Security, that should come to about 45 percent of your last active year's salary.) Retirement at age sixty would produce 80 percent of the normal payout. The typical company also contributes to a savings, profit-sharing, or stock purchase plan.

For inflation the leading-edge companies adjust the pension payout to retired people every couple of years. They offer a full pension in early retirement, and they pay more of the cost of an employee savings, profit-sharing, or stock purchase plan.

DEATH BENEFITS. The typical plan pays for group life insurance equal to twice your annual salary. For retirees, one-third of the preretirement insurance is continued at the company's expense.

The leading-edge companies extend coverage to your dependents, and they offer supplemental coverage, which you pay for, equal to two-and-a-half or three times your salary.

When a Cafeteria Is Not to Eat In

You may get it all in a single, comprehensive employee benefit plan. Or your company may offer what's called a "cafeteria" plan, in which you pick and choose from among all the benefits available to you. You get a little more in one area if you settle for less in another.

There are the "musts"—the areas in which you want maximum protection: health coverage, life insurance, and disability coverage. Profit-sharing and stock purchase plans are nice, but you can live without them. You can live with less vacation each year. But you must have the benefits that are essential to your financial survival.

You gain more flexibility if you and your spouse are both allowed to pick among employee benefits. You don't need two health insurance plans, so one of you can swap health insurance for something else (maybe company-supplied child care, or more time off so you can spend more time with the kids). If your company gives you a choice, draw up a list of all the benefits you can get, starting with those "must" benefits—health, life, and disability—and work your way as far down your list as you can. If you and your spouse both have a choice, eliminate overlaps.

But What If You're Not Covered

A harsh fact of financial life is that not all of us are covered by company benefit plans. The self-employed aren't, by definition. As noted, blue-collar workers are less likely to be covered than white-collar workers, who are less likely to be covered than the top brass.

If you're a woman, your job and your length of time on the job are less likely to provide you with anything more than barebones coverage, if you're covered at all. If you're an unmarried woman—especially if you have children—you've got your work cut out for you, because you're going to have to arrange coverage on your own.

I've tried to show in this chapter what protection you need —and how much of it—and which items take priority. You have to make your own decisions on how much of what sorts of coverage you can afford.

If you're a woman with children to raise, an HMO probably makes the most sense for you—and you might save money over buying health insurance. If you don't have a company benefit package, you're probably wise to shop very hard for an understanding insurance agent, and let the agent put together the best package you can afford of health, life, and disability coverage.

Someday the Axe May Fall

You hope that it will never come to that, but someday you could get laid off or fired, if times stay hard. You get government unemployment benefits, or course, but not every company has an established severance pay plan. Some will merely hand you a couple of weeks' salary and shove you out the door. Some offer severance pay according to a formula—typically one week's pay for each year of service.

You'll probably feel that you got fired unfairly, and your first thought will be, "I'm going to sue the bastards."

In fact, you'll have to play this one by ear, because it happens to be an area in which the law is changing rapidly. Mostly, the courts have—and still do—take the position that a company has the right to fire any employee, at any time, for any reason it wants.

But that is being watered down. You may very well have a case if you're over fifty, a woman, or a member of a minority group. If you are a member of a union, you're probably covered by a formal grievance procedure. You may have a strong case if you can argue that you were fired because you were trying to watch out for the safety of the public. There are laws to protect "whistle blowers" against retaliatory firing.

There was a big case in New York late in 1982, in which the state Court of Appeals ruled that an employee could sue his former employer because the employer's personnel handbook said that the only grounds for firing were "just and sufficient cause." That one could really rock the boat on firings and what to do if you are fired.

On occasion you'll have to turn to experts—in this case to a lawyer, if you are fired, to see if you have grounds for action. Most likely—unless you fall in one of the above categories—you don't. Then you try to see what—using appeals to common decency and fair play—you can get out of your company.

The longer you've been with your company, and the higher up the ladder you've climbed, the better your chances of negotiating a settlement. You want to walk out with as much cash as you can get, and you want life, health, and disability coverage extended as long as possible.

Go as high in the company as you can, but save your anger for outside the office. Your point is that you have legitimate rights that you're standing up for, based on your work for the company. Don't yell or pound on the table: Stress that all you want is what's fair. If you're over fifty, or a woman, or a member of a minority group, use the company's fear of a discrimination suit to buttress your position.

You want at least one week's severance pay for each year on the job. You want life, health, and disability insurance to run until you've found another spot. You want to be paid for any vacation you didn't take, and you want your prorated share of whatever bonus money the company pays. You may not get it all, but you'll do better if you make a stand rather than take the first offer that's made and slink out the door.

If You're Driven to the Wall

There's one last weapon in making your personal finances assaultproof. All has gone to hell in a hand basket, your creditors are beating on the doors and so you, regretfully, go bankrupt.

It's not a step to be taken lightly. But things can turn very bad for people very quickly these days, and if there's a danger of losing everything to your creditors, go bankrupt.

A new bankruptcy law that took effect in 1979 made it easier for individuals to hide from their creditors. Under chapter 13 of the new law, you simply ask for breathing room from your creditors. You pay a $50 fee and file in the nearest federal court, at which point your creditors must step back. Using the time you've gained, you work out a repayment schedule with your creditors: how much on the dollar you can pay and how long it will take you to pay (you have up to three years).

If that doesn't do it, there's chapter 7 of the law. You still pay $50 and you still file in federal court, but now you're tossing up most of your assets for your creditors to fight over. Once they've taken what there is to be taken, you're off the hook—able to start again, with whatever is left.

Even under chapter 7, your creditors can't take everything. You can keep $7,500 equity in your home ($15,000 if you and your spouse file jointly). You keep $1,200 of the value of your car; all household furnishings and clothing; $500 of personal jewelry; $750 of tools; and a few other things. Your creditors can't touch unmatured life insurance, Social Security money, welfare, unemployment, veteran's disability payments, alimony, child support and maintenance, or your pension or profit-sharing plan.

You don't need a lawyer to do any of it. You file your petition with a list of your assets, your debts, and your earnings. Legal stationery stores carry the forms. A lawyer can help you, but if you're so hard-pressed that you are considering bankruptcy, you probably don't have much left for legal fees.

You can file under chapter 13, and if the repayment terms drag you down, you can shift to chapter 7. You don't do it unless the wolf is banging on the door. A chapter 13 will stay on your credit records for six years, and a chapter 7 for 10 years. During that time, you won't be welcomed very warmly by any lender. But if the creditors are about to cart off the car and the furniture and the kids, then bail out and do it: your survival being what we're really concerned about.

Guidelines for Action

Budget your money and bargain hunt, whether the economy is soaring or sagging. You must put aside enough money to live on for three months, as a hedge against hard times. You must then invest your money, because our tax laws save their choicest rewards for those who invest.

You must have the right amounts of the right kinds of insurance—term life, not whole life. Don't forget spouse insurance—health and disability.

If you don't have enough of the right kind of health insurance, consider a Health Maintenance Organization as an alternative.

The courts are rewriting the rules on your rights if you lose your job. If you are laid off or fired, you may have the basis for legal action.

Should hard times drive you to the wall, don't be afraid to make use of the new, more liberal rules on going bankrupt.

CHAPTER 4

Managing Your Cash the Way Professionals Do

You must budget to save money, and you save money to invest it in hopes of making more money. And we'll get to the investment markets—in stocks and bonds and real estate—in just a bit. First, though, think about the woodchuck—that furry creature that lives in a hole in the ground. Each day the woodchuck ventures forth in search of food. He pokes his head above ground, looks around, and when the coast is clear, he darts into the open. The moment danger threatens, he dives back into his hole until all is safe again.

It makes great sense to invest your money these days because the climate for investing is right—as opposed to the late 1970s and early 1980s, when nearly all the investment markets weren't right at all.

Sometimes, though, taking command of your money obliges you to dive for safety because financial danger is threatening. Maybe inflation is resurfacing and interest rates are moving up and the stock and bond markets are starting to totter. Times are better now, but each time in the past we thought we had inflation on the run it came back again. Or maybe we face dark depression in which the fortunes of great companies are endangered. Either way, your hole-in-the-ground, when times get nasty, is the money you hold as cash—available to you, if not instantly, then reasonably quickly.

In the world of finance, cash is always money invested for a year or less. It includes money in checking and savings accounts and in those interest-bearing checking accounts called NOW accounts. It further includes money in money market mutual funds, bank and thrift institution money market accounts, Treasury bills, Treasury notes, the short-term issues of various agencies of the federal government, and anything else that has been invented by the time you read this.

The rules are changing by the hour in the world of cash, as the government throws away all the rules that used to apply to checking and savings accounts, and as the banking industry keeps inventing new places to save your money at a profit.

The way things line up now, in a nutshell, you:

—Hold your day-to-day living expenses as cash—preferably in a NOW account, in which you can earn some interest.

—Hold your three months' worth of savings in cash—balancing your desire for the highest possible return on your money with your need to keep your money safe and secure and readily available. That usually means a money market account at a bank or a thrift institution, or a money market mutual fund, or in short-term government securities.

—Hold everything in cash when danger threatens—abandoning stocks and bonds and pretty much everything else in order to keep your money safe until it's time to invest again.

Never hold more of your money in cash than you must, because the tax laws are stacked against you—as they are always stacked against those who save as opposed to those who invest.

What you earn from cash is interest income, and every penny of it is taxed at ordinary income rates (up to 50 percent). The first $100 of dividend income is excluded from taxation ($200 for a couple), but there's no comparable exclusion for interest. And a dollar held as cash is a dollar that won't earn you capital gains, for which the maximum tax bite is 20 percent.

But money held as cash is money that won't be lost in pursuit of a falling stock or bond. There have been plenty of years when you were best off staying in cash from New Year's morn to New Year's eve, because all else was too dangerous, and because the return on cash was better than anything else around. Through the 1970s and early 1980s, cash was the best investment for most people most of the time.

It's not like that right now: The investment markets beckon, and you're cheating yourself out of capital gains if you play it too conservatively. Cash was the only market in the bad old days and it's just a sometimes market now.

Manage your cash creatively, since cash invested one way can earn considerably more than cash invested another way. Keep on top of the market, because it is changing so rapidly as the rules that have governed banking for a half-century come tumbling down. Finally, since cash is always your refuge of last resort, there's a special premium on keeping it safe. Whatever new havens are invented for your cash by the time you read this, just remember that the highest return in the world doesn't mean a thing if your cash is not absolutely safe all the time.

The New World of Cash

The bad times of the 1970s made us all a lot more sophisticated about money, and there are more ways to manage your cash today than even the biggest corporations had barely two decades ago.

For years the typical family kept its money in a checking account, with the rainy-day money in a savings account that paid about 3 percent. We didn't know any better, that was pretty much all that was available, and—with inflation minimal, 3 percent wasn't such a bad return.

Until the early 1960s even big companies weren't doing it much differently. A company kept most of its money in a checking account, with its rainy-day money in short-term securities of the government called Treasury bills. And Treasury bills, circa 1960, paid less than 3 percent.

The postwar boom, and competition among financial institutions, changed that. Bankers traditionally waited until deposits came to them—it being regarded as vulgar for a banker to go out and solicit money. This wasn't true of the thrift institutions (savings and loan associations, savings banks, and credit unions). They could pay a little more for deposits than commercial banks, and they weren't a bit shy about grabbing every deposit they could get their hands on—mostly from consumers, but from business as well.

Much of America's banking talent in the early 1960s was concentrated at First National City Bank of New York (now known as Citibank), and in 1961 the bankers at Citibank decided it was time to join the competition for money. So they invented the negotiable certificate of deposit (or CD), which did for banking what the discovery of fire did for the caveman.

Citibank's real target was the Treasury bill, which is where most companies parked their idle cash. A Treasury bill, in common with all Treasury issues, is an IOU of our government—issued to finance the national debt. It's a bill if it matures in a year or less, a note if it matures in one to 10 years, and a bond if it matures in more than 10 years. Being an issue of the U.S. government, a Treasury issue (bill, note, or bond) is considered as good as gold. The trading market in Treasury issues is so vast (trillions of dollars' worth changing hands each year), that you can buy or sell in seconds, with a single telephone call. Treasury bills are issued for three and six months and a year, but you can always buy a bill with a few weeks, or even a few days, left until maturity, if you have cash to invest for a few weeks or a few days.

Citibank's certificate of deposit certified that so much money ($100,000 and more) had been deposited with the bank for a period of time (30 days and more), and that at the end of that time, Citibank would repay your money, plus an agreed-on amount of interest.

A Citibank CD paid slightly more than a Treasury bill. It didn't carry the good-as-gold name of the U.S. Treasury, but it carried the name of a gigantic bank. It was negotiable because it was a bearer certificate: Instead of being issued to someone by name, it belonged to whoever held it at the moment. That meant it could be readily bought and sold. In short order, a trading market in CD's developed, and you could buy a Citibank CD with just a few weeks or days until maturity.

Other banks recognized a stroke of genius when they saw one, and soon all big banks were offering CD's. Corporations bought CD's because they paid more than Treasury bills. The idea that a company, by shopping around, might earn more on its idle funds, lit a fire under corporate financial officers and suddenly cash became something to manage, at a profit.

Consumers Join the Rush

What turned consumers into aggressive managers of their own cash was the inflation that started building in the mid-sixties. Inflation swamped the return on savings deposits, whether at banks or thrifts, and it also swamped the stock market, which had become home for a lot of consumer money. Suddenly, there was a lot of consumer cash looking for something better.

There was first some nibbling away at the edges, starting with long-term consumer savings certificates, which paid more than regular savings accounts, if you didn't mind locking up your money for seven or eight years. The first money market mutual funds appeared in the early 1970s. The six-month savings certificate, for anyone with $10,000 to invest, appeared in 1978. The first 30-month savings certificate, for anyone with as little as $100, came in 1980. The interest-bearing checking account (the NOW account) appeared in New England in the mid-1970s, and became legal for all financial institutions everywhere in 1981. The three-month savings certificate—for anyone with $7,500 to invest, appeared in May of 1982.

Late 1982 brought the money market deposit account (a direct assault on money market mutual funds) and the super-NOW account (which pays more than a regular NOW account). The minimum deposit for both is $2,500, but that falls to $1,000 in 1985 and to zero in 1986. On Oct. 1, 1983, cash really got deregulated. All those complex rules on savings certificates were scrapped. Now you can negotiate a savings certificate, with any rate of interest, for any length of time beyond thirty-one days, with any minimum deposit the institution will accept.

Even that doesn't cover it all.

Merrill Lynch, America's biggest stockbroker, stunned

banks and rival brokers alike in 1977 when it launched its Cash Management Account, or CMA—a broker suddenly acting like a bank. If you're a Merrill Lynch customer with at least $20,000 of cash and securities in your account, you can write checks against the money in your account and you get a bank credit card. When your money isn't in use, it goes into one of the three Merrill Lynch money market funds. If you need lots of money in a hurry, Merrill Lynch's computer will first clean out the money in your account, then draw the cash out of your money fund, and finally borrow against the value of stocks held in your account.

There are close to 1 million CMA customers, with an average $65,000 in each account, and most other big brokerage houses have similar programs: Bache Command Account, the Active Assets Account at Dean Witter Reynolds, the Asset Management Account at E. F. Hutton, and so on.

Cashing In on Cash

When it comes to managing your cash, you want the best combination of liquidity, yield, and safety.

Liquidity is important because you must be able to move your cash quickly to where it can do the most good. Yield is important because you want to make as much money on your cash as you can. Safety is critical, because this is the money you live on, and it's your ace-in-the-hole money. And no investment is ever totally risk-free. The U.S. government, with $1¼ trillion in debt and not a prayer of paying it off, could conceivably default some day. Money market funds aren't covered by deposit insurance. Bank and thrift institution accounts are covered by insurance—but there's only $20 billion in insurance against $2 trillion in deposits. With cash, you want the risk kept as small as possible.

Ideally, every penny you have in cash should be earning something. Even your checking account money, if kept in a NOW account, will earn 5¼ percent interest. By shopping around, you should be able to find an institution that will let you open a NOW account with as little as $500. If you still have money in a 5¼ percent savings account (5½ percent if it's at a thrift institution), combine it with your checking account money and you'll surely have enough to meet whatever minimum balance requirements there are on NOW accounts.

As for the rest of your cash—your three months' living expenses, and whatever cash you're holding out of the investment markets—you have seven primary possibilities:

1. Short-term Treasury issues—bills and notes with a few weeks or months to go to maturity. All are fully guaranteed by the government.
2. Short-term issues of such federal agencies as the Federal National Mortgage Association, the Federal Home Loan Banks, and the Federal Farm Credit Banks. Agencies raise money to carry out some specific government function, and all have plenty of securities outstanding. Most agencies lack explicit government backing, but there's the implicit promise that the government won't let an agency default. Because there's no explicit guarantee, agency issues yield a bit more than Treasury issues.
3. The newly deregulated savings certificates.
4. Regular passbook savings accounts.
5. Money market mutual funds.
6. Bank and thrift institution money market accounts.
7. Super-NOW accounts at banks and thrifts.

The Cost of Entry

As far as the minimum investment goes, on a scale from dearest to cheapest, it takes:

—$10,000 to buy a Treasury bill or a short-term issue of the Federal Home Loan Banks.

—$5,000 to buy Treasury notes, newly issued for less than four years, or an issue of the Federal National Mortgage Association, or the Export-Import Bank.

—$2,500 to open either a money market deposit account or a super-NOW account. But recall that the $2,500 minimum is now set to drop to $1,000 at the start of 1985, and to vanish altogether at the start of 1986.

—$1,000 to buy Treasury notes, newly issued for four years or more; or the short-term issues of such federal agencies as the Federal Farm Credit Banks, Federal Land Banks, Maritime Administration, Tennessee Valley Authority, and the Student Loan Marketing Association; or a project note of the Department of Housing and Urban Development.

—$500 to buy into the least-expensive money market mutual funds, although $1,000 is more common, and $2,500 not unusual.

The $5,000 minimum on some Treasury notes is for new issues. Older issues trade in the secondary market in $1,000 units, and in managing your cash, you'll mostly be buying older issues in the secondary market, with just months or weeks to maturity. The $1,000, $5,000, and $10,000 minimums on the agency issues represent minimum denominations: They'll apply whether the issues are brand new, or whether they've been out in the market for some time.

You may pay $1,000 (or $5,000 or $10,000 or whatever) to buy a Treasury or agency security in the secondary market. But then again, you may not. You may pay more or less, and that gets into the whole matter of pricing—and discounting—bonds, which I cover in a lot more detail in chapter 6. For the moment, you get the short course.

A four-year Treasury note will cost $1,000 when it's first sold, and it will carry a rate of interest comparable to what other issues of its ilk are carrying. If other four-year Treasury notes are paying 10 percent, this note will pay 10 percent. But now say it's a year later, and new Treasury notes with three years until maturity are paying 15 percent. No one would buy that 10 percent Treasury note for $1,000 when they could buy a 15 percent Treasury note for $1,000.

That 10 percent return on your money is what you get when you paid $1,000 for the note. If you could buy it for $750, the return on your money would be, not 10 percent, but about 15 percent. And that's what happens. Prices of older securities are constantly going up or down in the market, to bring their yield (the return on your money, based on what you actually paid) into line with yields on comparable securities. If new Treasury issues carried rates of only 5 percent, someone might pay you close to $2,000 to get the 10 percent rate that your Treasury note carries.

As I write this, you can get 8½ percent on a brand-new six-month Treasury bill, and 8¾ on a six-month savings certificate.

On this day, there's an older Treasury note maturing in six months. It carries only a 7⅞ percent interest rate. But you can buy it for about $990, and at that price it would yield 8¾ percent on your money. You can do even better if you don't mind having your money tied up a little longer. There's another Treasury note maturing in seven months, and it carries a 14⅝ percent interest rate. You'd have to pay about $1,030 to buy it, but even at that price, it would yield about 9 percent on your money.

You can do even better with a federal agency issue. There's a Federal Farm Credit Banks issue maturing in eight months. It carries a 10¼ percent interest rate. You'd pay about $1,006 to buy it, and at that price, your yield would be about 9.2 percent—agency issues always returning a little bit more than Treasury issues.

All these issues reward you as well or better than you'd do on a savings certificate, or on a money market account or a money market mutual fund. Unlike a savings certificate, where your money is tied up for more than 31 days, you could sell the Treasury or agency issue in an instant, should you need the money.

You'd pay a commission to buy or sell a government issue—and you'll do better on that commission if you buy or sell more than $5,000 worth of anything at a time. But the interest on all Treasury issues (bills, notes, and bonds), and on the issues of such agencies as the Federal Farm Credit Banks, and the Federal Home Loan Banks is exempt from all state and local (but not federal) taxation. If you live in a high-tax state, that could make a difference.

Any broker can buy or sell Treasury or agency issues for you. You'll find price quotes for all outstanding issues, listed each day in *The Wall Street Journal*, *The New York Times*, and other major newspapers. Between all the Treasury bills, Treasury notes, and federal agency securities out there (about $250 billion in federal agency debt, beyond the $1¼ trillion in the national debt), there are plenty of issues maturing when you want them to: from a few days to a few years.

Your Other Choices

If all of that seems too much bother, you can choose from among money market deposit accounts, or a savings certificate from a bank or a thrift, or a money market mutual fund. Each offers its own combination of liquidity, yield, and risk.

You can buy into a money market mutual fund for as little as $500, and you can withdraw money by writing a check against your stake, with $500 usually the smallest check you can write. Money funds invest in the whole array of money market securities: Treasury and agency issues, CD's of U.S. and foreign banks, and the unsecured IOU's of corporations, called commercial paper. Money in a money market mutual fund isn't insured, and a fund is no stronger than the issues it invests in. There are funds that invest only in government securities, which should make them more secure. But they yield less than funds that invest in bank CD's and commercial paper.

Every fund has a prospectus that will show where it invests its money, and the funds all have 800 telephone numbers so you can check on the fund's yield for that day.

The bank and thrift money market accounts are insured up to $100,000, which may tip the balance in their favor. They pay rates comparable to a money market mutual fund—except that rates on money funds fluctuate day by day while the rate on a money market account, once set, stands for a month. But the minimum entry fee is $2,500 (against the $1,000 or less for the typical fund), and you can write no more than three checks against your money market account each month. And that $2,500 minimum is critical. Should your balance in a money market account fall below $2,500, your return suddenly falls to just 5¼ percent. Some institutions won't penalize you if your balance averages out to $2,500 or more over a month. Some will drop you to 5¼ percent for a whole month if your balance falls below $2,500 for just a single day.

Finally, there's the super-NOW account. It pays interest like a money market account, but you can write all the checks you want against it each month and for whatever amount you want. The minimum deposit is $2,500, as it is with a money market account. All that check-writing costs the bank more to keep your account, so it pays less than a money market account. Yet again, recall that the minimum falls to $1,000 in 1985, and to zero in 1986.

Since the money market accounts came into being late in 1982, the money market mutual funds have been offering additional financial services of their own, to hang onto your money. You have to decide if what a money fund offers is something that you need. If the money fund is part of a mutual fund family, you're usually able to shift money among funds—money fund, stock fund, bond fund—with just a phone call. That gives you an enormous flexibility that banks and thrifts can't match.

Setting the Rates

Money market fund rates change daily, and money market account rates stand up for only a month. With a savings certificate, you get a rate that stands up for three or six months —or however long it will be before your time deposit matures and you get your money back.

Actually, having a rate guaranteed for three or six months is fine if rates are falling. Other people are settling for less, but you're getting more until your savings certificate matures. If rates are going up, of course, others are getting more while you're still earning the rate set months earlier when rates were lower. The world can turn during the months your money is frozen, and you can't get at your money before the certificate matures, without paying a stiff penalty.

Banks and thrifts can pay what they want on money market accounts, and on super-NOW accounts, while money market funds pay a return based on what the securities they've invested in are paying. In practice, money market accounts and money market mutual funds usually return about the same. Again, the rate on a time deposit, or savings certificate, is whatever you can get the institution to pay.

There's a further consideration in weighing a money market mutual fund against something from a bank or thrift. If you're in the market for a loan—mortgage, college, home improvement, whatever—your banker will be very pleased that you've given him your money, as opposed to putting it in a money market fund. You've proven yourself a faithful customer, and that can tip the balance when your loan application is up for consideration.

If you're in the higher tax brackets, there's still another option to think about: money market mutual funds that invest in short-term tax-exempt issues, with the income from the fund exempt from federal (but not state and local) income taxes. You get a lower return on a tax-exempt money fund—maybe 60 percent of what a conventional money market fund is paying. But you keep it all because there's no federal tax bite. There are fewer tax-exempt money funds to choose from, and while all the top Wall Street names offer money market funds, not all offer tax exempt money funds. Still, once you get into the higher tax brackets, where the bite on interest income becomes truly burdensome, it can pay to get into a tax-exempt money fund.

Your Cash Strategy

In terms of liquidity, a money market mutual fund ranks first. You can write unlimited checks against your fund holdings, and you can shift your money from one kind of fund to another with a telephone call. Next would come a super-NOW account, and then a money market account at a bank or a thrift institution, followed by Treasury and federal agency issues, followed by savings certificates (the longer the maturity, the less liquid your deposit).

In terms of yield, it's usually federal agency issues first, with all others close behind. You'll pay a commission to buy a Treasury or an agency issue—but all Treasuries, and some agencies, are exempt from local taxes. There's no commission on any of the money market mutual funds, and obviously none on money market accounts, or on savings certificates. Some institutions might even give you a little present for buying a savings certificate.

In terms of safety, it's Treasury issues first, then agency issues just a quarter-step behind, followed by bank and thrift money market accounts and savings certificates, followed by money market mutual funds that limit themselves to government issues, followed by the rest of the money market funds. But even the insurance on insured deposits at financial institutions may be illusory, with only that $20 billion in insurance against $2 trillion in deposits. There isn't even enough insurance to cover the customers at a single giant commercial bank; yet that insurance is supposed to cover some 40,000 depository institutions.

You know when you buy in how much you'll get back on a savings certificate, and the rate on your money market account is guaranteed for a month at a time. You know what a Treasury or agency issue will yield when you buy in—but if prices in the market fall, you might take a loss if you have to sell your holdings in a hurry. Still, you're buying issues that are only a few months away from maturity, and the closer to maturity an issue gets, the closer the price in the market will cling to the price at which the issue will be paid off. At worst, you might have to hang on for a few months more—until maturity—and then you'd lose nothing.

You can go whole hog and opt for a Merrill Lynch Cash Management Account, or something comparable from another broker. But that's a different story altogether. If you have a brokerage house account with $20,000 in it, you probably don't need much advice about managing your money. Also remember that it's fundamentally a brokerage account. Lurking in the background at all times will be a stockbroker, using all his or her wiles to get you to invest in stocks or bonds or commodities.

You want to invest, of course, because that's where the capital gains are. But you want to invest only when you're ready—when your economic sixth sense tells you the time is right. Until then, recall the woodchuck and stay safely in cash.

Guidelines for Action

Cash is where your money goes for safety's sake.

Keep your three months' living expenses in cash, plus what you live on day to day. As soon as you see inflation hitting the investment markets (stock and bond prices going no higher, and sometimes going lower), prepare to shift all your money into cash.

Make sure all your cash earns some return—starting with your checking account money in a NOW account.

When you're ready for it, your cash will earn the most invested in a federal agency issue.

For the best combination of liquidity, yield, safety, and simplicity, use a money market account (if you can keep the balance above $2,500) or a money market mutual fund (if the balance might fall below $2,500).

If you're in the 35 percent tax bracket and beyond, look into tax-free money market funds.

CHAPTER 5

The New Rules About Investing in Real Estate

There are plenty of investment markets and more being born all the time, and we'll look into all of them as you learn to take command of your own financial future.

But first, look at the basic investment market, the bedrock market, the market you can never ignore: the trillion-dollar market in real estate, which has come back from the dead in considerable good health.

For starters, real estate offers tax breaks not found in such profusion in any other market. You invest to build your capital, and a dollar added to capital because you cut your tax bill is as good as a dollar made by picking a hot stock. And that's just for starters.

Remember this: Everyone has to live someplace. Similarly, everyone has to work someplace, and shop someplace. There is always a demand for real estate, and if things don't look right to you one moment, just wait, because sooner or later (and usually sooner) the real estate market always comes back.

Most investments in real estate make money most of the time, and you can't say that about any other market. When times are good, you can make gains as choice as you'll find in any other market. As bad as inflation was in the 1970s, the gains in real estate outran inflation year after year. When times are bad, you're better off in real estate than in any other market, because your money is in something tangible for which there's always a demand. As bad as the recession got, values in real estate stayed high, and it was among the very first markets to rebound as the recession began to lift.

In other markets, time is your enemy: If you stay in too long, you can lose everything you've gained. In real estate, values usually increase by a little each year and time is always on your side.

The experts were having a marvelous time in 1982, proclaiming the real estate market dead. While they were doing that, the Federal Reserve began feeding more money into the economy (as you knew, because you keep watch on the Fed), interest rates began to fall, and suddenly real estate was very much alive again. In fact, tracking the report on construction contracts from the F. W. Dodge division of McGraw-Hill, you saw real estate hit bottom in April of 1982 and start to recover —four months before the rally in the stock market.

Finally, the recovery in real estate was sure-fire evidence to you that the economy would soon be turning around—even as the experts were calling it the start of a new depression.

In watching the economy, it pays to have a real estate broker among your friends. When he or she tells you the real estate market is turning around, count that as another of your personal leading economic indicators. My source is a woman who sells apartments in New York. When the recession was in full flower, she told me the latest gag among New York real estate people:

Question: "What's the difference between a New York apartment and herpes?"

Answer: "Herpes is easier to get rid of."

When she told me that suddenly New York apartments were starting to sell again, I took that as an indicator that real estate was turning around (as it was), and that a turnaround in the economy was on the way (as it was).

Where to Look First

You must own real estate, for the stability and for the tax breaks. What you own depends on what your budget says you can afford—the monthly payment on what you own being one of those minimum increments from zero, which get paid off first. But that still gives you great buying power because of that wonderful concept called leverage—your ability to operate with borrowed money. In real estate, everything is done with borrowed money—typically $4 borrowed for each $1 you put up.

You start out with your own home (or cooperative or condominium apartment), and you go on from there.

There are small apartment houses, big apartment houses, small shopping centers, big shopping centers, regional shopping malls, small office buildings, big office buildings, towering office skyscrapers, raw land, farmland, vacation homes, resort condominiums, and still more. You can buy on your own or with partners that you've recruited. Or you can buy into a real estate partnership in which a few hundred partners each put up a few thousand dollars and the money is invested for maximum tax breaks, plus some income.

If none of these suit, there are real estate securities, the most notable of them being the passthrough certificates of the Government National Mortgage Association, which is better known to one and all as Ginnie Mae.

It would be pointless for me to tell you specific situations when you should invest (in real estate or in any other market). The market when you read this won't look like the market as I write it, because we're still coming back from disaster. Half the would-be home buyers still can't buy because interest rates are too high and terms are too tight. When you read this, the market will have either eased, because rates have fallen, or tightened up again, because rates have gone up.

Still, I can offer a few pointers:

—Unless the economy has changed dramatically, you're mostly likely to find bargains among homes or apartments selling for under $150,000. Recession hit the well-to-do less hard, and higher-priced properties tend to move well in good times and bad. You might do the very best, if you can find an older home that has been on the market for a year or so.

—For investment purposes, involving a reasonable stake, your best bet is most likely a smaller apartment building, 20 or 30 years old, catering to a market of young marrieds.

They're the ones obliged to rent because home ownership went out of sight. Because they're married, usually with young kids, they tend to be stable, rent-paying tenants.

—A second investment possibility is a small office building —preferably an older building fixed up. Later in the chapter, I'll explain about the special tax breaks available on such properties.

—For the foreseeable future, avoid raw land: The slump did sufficient damage to builders that they'll be slow to undertake new projects.

—For a far-out flyer, look into farmland. Between the economic recovery, and the Reagan administration's farm program, farm income is rising. The value of farmland—badly depressed in recent years—is finally starting to rise again.

We'll get into more specifics and more details later on in the chapter. For a start, we'll review the history.

The Changing World of Real Estate

Obviously things aren't what they used to be in real estate. No other market has gone through the turmoil real estate has, and it still isn't back to normal, even now.

Take buying a home. In years past, you picked the house you liked and got a mortgage at a rate about 3 percent more than lending institutions were paying on savings accounts. That usually meant a rate of 8 percent or less. Your mortgage was for 30 years, and the rate stayed the same through the life of the mortgage. Maybe your home increased in value, but you bought it because you wanted a place to live.

But inflation caught the market two ways: inflating prices and inflating mortgage rates. Other markets crumbled in the face of inflation, but home prices went up in line with inflation year after year, and even the family home became an investment instead of just a place to live. As inflation drove interest rates higher, the 8 percent mortgage became a 10 percent mortgage, and then a 12 percent mortgage, and then a 17 percent mortgage.

Nothing goes on forever, and in time the idea of "home as an investment" crashed against the reality that few of us could afford to buy a home. The average price of a new home went from $44,300 in 1976 to $78,200 in 1982. Add a 17 percent mortgage rate onto that, and the annual payment on a house jumped 182 percent during those six years, while income for the average family rose only 62 percent.

One casualty of inflation was the fixed-rate mortgage. A lender would make a 10 percent mortgage and then watch the cost of deposits jump to 15 percent. When expenses rise faster than income, you're in trouble, and by the start of the 1980s most mortgage-lending institutions—savings and loans and savings banks—were in very serious trouble. So in place of the fixed-rate mortgage, we got the variable rate mortgage, with the mortgage adjusted frequently according to rates in the financial markets.

With only one family in five able to buy a home, at inflated prices and inflated rates, the second mortgage became standard. You borrowed what you could to buy the house, and when that wasn't enough, you borrowed more through a second mortgage. Even the balloon mortgage came back—a throw-back to the bad old days, a half-century and more ago, when the balloon mortgage was standard and plenty of mortgages were foreclosed.

In a balloon mortgage, you pay a little each month until the final "balloon" payment, when you pay off the whole thing. If you miss the balloon payment, the balloon is said to have "popped" and the lender takes back the house. The balloon was standard back in the Depression, and countless Americans lost their homes as a result. After the Depression, the self-amortizing mortgage became standard—in which you paid off a uniform slice of the mortgage each month until, in 25 or 30 years, the whole mortgage was paid off. In the 1980s you took on a balloon that would run for maybe five years. You made the small monthly payments, praying all the while that mortgage rates would crack so you could replace the balloon with a conventional mortgage before that last, killer payment came due.

Usually, it was the seller of the house who provided the second mortgage (seldom with much joy). Maybe you got a first mortgage that required a bigger down payment than you could make. To sell the house, the seller would provide the second mortgage, which was usually a balloon done at below-market interest rates. The seller would then pray for a crack in mortgage rates just as hard as you were.

Nor was it a sometimes thing. The National Association of Realtors reckons that more than half the existing homes sold in the early 1980s involved seller financing. The world of finance abounds with euphemisms. The euphemism for "seller financing" is "creative financing."

There have been other wrinkles in home financing. There's the buy-down, in which a home builder pays cash to a lending institution which, in turn, provides home buyers with mortgages that are at reduced rates for the first few years. There's the shared appreciation mortgage (SAM), in which you get a mortgage at a bargain rate, but you share your profit with the lender when you sell the home. There's the graduated payment mortgage, in which you make a small payment each month in the early years of the mortgage and bigger and bigger monthly payments in later years.

Still newer—and potentially very interesting—is the growing equity mortgage (GEM), in which the monthly payment starts out small and increases, according to a set schedule, through the life of the mortgage. Unlike a variable rate mortgage, when fluctuating interest rates can make the monthly payment fluctuate, the holder of a GEM knows at the start that his monthly payment will increase by 3 or 4 percent each month. Each incremental gain in the payment goes to pay off principal, and a GEM is paid off in about half the time that a conventional mortgage would run. A 14 percent GEM might have a monthly payment of $650 at the start (nearly all of that paying the interest), climbing to $1,000 a month at the end (each step up from $650 representing an increase in the payment on principal). As you get older, your income should increase by enough to make those ever-growing payments bearable.

Take a 12 percent mortage rate as the cutoff. When rates are above 12 percent, the market will remain eccentric—with few people able to buy homes, and with the market littered with all those zany financing schemes. When the mortgage rate falls below 12 percent, and stays there for at least one year, things will pretty much return to normal.

Why You Buy

For all that, home ownership still is the best investment for most people most of the time. The lesson of the early eighties hasn't been to avoid the market but to approach it wisely. And that's true of every market.

Buy at the best terms you can arrange. If you get price appreciation on your home, so much the better. Even if you don't, you still get significant tax breaks—both the property tax and the interest on the mortgage loan being deductible. If you own the home for a year or more, any profit you make is taxed at the capital gains rate. If you sell, and buy a more expensive home, you don't pay any tax. And you have two years after you sell to buy that more expensive home before the tax bite hits. If you sell after age fifty-five, the first $125,000 in gains on your home are tax-free.

Unless the future holds nothing but black depression, you'll get some appreciation on your home—maybe not 10 or 15 percent a year, but not zero either. By every estimate, demand will outstrip the supply of homes for years to come. There are the millions of people who've wanted to buy the past few years and couldn't. The postwar baby boom generation is in its peak home buying years. There's a demand for at least 2 million homes a year, and we're building only 1 million homes. It's hard to imagine much prolonged price deflation under those circumstances.

Say the very worst happens and we fall into a depression in which the value of all investments tumbles. Because you're dealing with something tangible, and because everyone has to live someplace, home prices will fall less than most other investments, and they'll tend to recover more quickly. If depression hits, and you bought wisely, you're better off having your money in your own home than anyplace else. And the same holds true if the future should bring more superinflation.

If you already own a home, think about investing in sound improvements that will enhance its value. "Sound improvements" is the operative phrase here, since $50,000 worth of improvements won't turn a $100,000 house into a $150,000 house if you live in a neighborhood of $100,000 houses. You can spend $10,000 on a swimming pool, but it probably won't add $10,000 to the sale price of your house, because not everyone wants the expense and bother of a swimming pool in the yard.

An extra bedroom or bathroom will usually pay off. So will a modernized kitchen. So will a more efficient heating system, or central air conditioning. So will a sophisticated home security system. Talk to your real estate agent, and to the banker who holds your mortgage, for guidance on improvements that will increase the value of your home.

You can finance the improvements with a home improvement loan or with a second mortgage. Sit down with your banker and start making comparisons about the monthly cost of each, and think about what your budget can stand. The rate on a home improvement loan will be lower, but you might have to pay it back within three years while a second mortgage might run for 10 years. But if you sell during those 10 years, the second mortgage is just another mouth to be fed from your profit on the sale.

Shop around for the best deal you can get. Start with the institution that holds the mortgage, but also check at least one bank and one thrift institution for their best deal. Check your credit union. Check to see if the work you're doing qualifies for a government-insured loan, which can cut the rate.

Keep detailed records on all improvements to your home, since capital improvements (a new bedroom, but not a window air conditioner, or wall-to-wall carpeting) increase the cost of your house for tax purposes. And that higher cost reduces the gain—and the tax on the gain—that you'll owe when you sell.

We already talked, in chapter 3, about refinancing your mortgage if you need a lot of money—to pay college bills, for instance. You have the equity built up in your home, just sitting there. The lender is stuck with a mortgage paying less than the current rate. You might want to do a deal.

Say you bought your house for $30,000 in 1970, and got an

8 percent mortgage for $25,000. Now the house is worth $100,000, the mortgage is paid down to about $15,000, and with each monthly payment, the portion going to pay the interest is shrinking—and so is your tax deduction on the interest.

You might take out a college loan, or you might take out a new mortgage for $75,000 at the best rate you can get. It's a straight dollars-and-cents decision on which to do (monthly cost versus monthly cost).

The rate on a college loan is likely to be lower, but it would have to be repaid more quickly. Refinancing your mortgage would represent a longer-term commitment. With a variable-rate mortgage, the longer the commitment, the greater the chance that sometime during the life of the mortgage, rates will really run against you. If it's a fixed-rate mortgage, we could have a prolonged period of relatively low inflation and low rates, in which you'd be paying what, by comparison, might be a high rate for the money. But when you refinance, you do get that big wad of cash to be invested until needed. And the government will pay up to half the mortgage interest, depending on your tax bracket.

The equation, once again, is monthly payment on the old mortgage plus the college loan against monthly payment on the new mortgage less what your newfound cash (the freed equity in your home) is earning.

Nowadays, refinancing your mortgage must make sense on its own: it must give you money for less than you can get it elsewhere. You can't assume, as you once could, that rapid inflation will further increase the value of your home to $150,000—giving you more than enough profit to pay off the new $75,000 mortgage. You'll get some appreciation in the value of your home each year, but it isn't likely to be as it was in the inflationary 1970s.

A real possibility these days is that you have a high-rate mortgage from the bad old days and you've been thinking about refinancing with a mortgage at today's rates.

It may strike you as ridiculous that the mortgage lender would swap a 17 percent mortgage for a 12 percent or 13 percent mortgage. In fact, if you've been a good, loyal customer of the institution, you just might be able to work out a deal. Unless mortgage rates have fallen well below 12 percent —and stayed down—when you read this, it's likely the lender still has more money than takers and will do the deal. That makes it a question of whether you want to do the deal.

First, remember that the government is paying part of your mortgage interest, so the spread between a new mortgage and your mortgage is less than it looks. The various costs connected with taking on a new mortgage will further cut into your saving. If there's a chance you might sell the house and move soon (and most of us move once every 12 years), the saving won't mean much to you. Don't even think about it, unless you can get a fixed-rate mortgage with a rate at least three percentage points less than your current mortgage. Even then, compare all the costs—old mortgage versus new mortgage (counting in all the costs connected with taking on the new mortgage).

Shop Hard Before You Buy

Say that circumstance has put you in the market for another home. Maybe you're getting transferred, or maybe you just got a lavish promotion and your income justifies a move to someplace more imposing.

Buy at the best terms you can arrange—unless you think you won't be at the new place very long. With the market as illiquid as it has been, then think about renting. If you know you'll be there for less than eighteen months, you'll probably want to rent—giving up the tax breaks temporarily in favor of having something you can walk away from quickly when the time comes. You can wait two years before you buy again, without paying a tax on any gain from your last house. If you're going to be someplace for at least two years, then buy.

The old rule of thumb said you could afford a house priced at two-and-a-half times your annual salary. Like most of such rules of thumb, this one goes right into the ashcan. You buy what your budget says you can afford, since the mortgage payment goes right at the very top of your budget and you can't let the monthly payments eat you alive. Assume that the monthly payment will take at least 30 percent of your take-home pay. Once it goes beyond 35 percent, you're cheating yourself on other things—including saving—and you're probably getting in over your head. If it's much more than 35 percent, look elsewhere.

Test the market first by looking at both new and existing homes. Between the mad inflation of the 1970s and the record borrowing costs of the early 1980s, builders put up some awfully slapdash stuff. A lot of the newer stuff built the past five years you really don't want. On the other hand, the builder might be able to come up with some extra-good mortgage terms. An existing house is likely to have more extras in it, and it has been shaken down so that most of the bugs are out.

As I write this, you can probably do a little better on an existing home—and the longer it has been on the market, the better you should do. Just don't expect any great bargains. Home prices didn't fall all that much during the recession, and demand being what it is, prices firmed up as soon as the first signs of recovery came. Barring something close to depression, you aren't likely to see much in the way of bargain-priced homes in the 1980s.

Whatever the seller is asking, start by offering 20 percent less. That may do it, particularly if the house has been on the market for a while. Once you find the house you want, bargain just as hard on the mortgage. You may again find a conventional, fixed-rate mortgage, although the variable-rate mortgage is still more common. But that's not so bad, either. You'll get hit if interest rates go up, but you'll also be earning more on your money if they do. If interest rates fall, so will the rate on your mortgage. And if rates are going up, it means inflation is also going up, and you'll get some nice appreciation on your home.

Examine all the options the lender has: variable-rate mortgage, fixed-rate mortgage, growing equity mortgage, whatever. What will the monthly payments be for each type of mortgage—and which will do the least harm to your budget?

The shared-appreciation mortgage seemed like an interesting idea when it was introduced a few years ago. The lender would settle for a lower rate on the loan—about two-thirds of the going mortgage rate—in return for a piece of the profit when you sold. But most lenders want their money here and now, and the idea never really caught on. Nor did the Federal Home Loan Bank Board, which regulates savings and loan associations, ever warm up to SAM's. The growing equity mortgage is still new enough to be uncommon. Yet it's certainly worth looking at if you can find a lender that offers it.

Whatever deal you're offered, don't be afraid to haggle.

You'd like to keep the down payment to no more than 25 percent of the mortgage, and even less—if the lender will do it, and if the resulting monthly payments don't destroy your budget.

If the lender talks about a 14 percent mortgage, see if he'll do it for 13½ percent. Not until mortgage rates drop below 12 percent, and stay there, will it really turn into a seller's market. Until then, you gain bargaining power just by showing up ready to deal. Try to limit the number of "points" you're charged—a point being one percent of the loan, paid up front. Lenders used to charge a point or two to cover the cost of processing the loan. Nowadays, it's not uncommon to see a lender asking for five or six points—5 or 6 percent of the loan. Points are just more money out of your pocket. If the lender wants six points, offer four. Indicate that your willingness to do the deal depends on getting the right terms and that you are willing to walk away if you don't get them. There's nothing like the sight of a customer storming out the door to make a retailer see the light. The lender is just another retailer.

Beware the Balloon

If you're buying an existing house and the going mortgage rate is above 12 percent as you read this, the odds are at least 50–50 that the seller will take a second mortgage—that creative financing, as it's called. Most likely it will run for just a few years, and most likely it will involve a balloon. You're hoping that rates will come down sufficiently that you can refinance the whole mortgage, at lower rates, and with a big enough loan to pay off the balloon.

A balloon second mortgage need not be the end of the world, even if rates don't fall enough to let you refinance before the balloon falls due. Say that there's room in your budget to handle the monthly payments on a new house, but you can't quite swing the down payment that's required (not, at least, without stripping yourself of your last penny of capital). The monthly payment on the second mortgage, since it's a balloon, won't add much to your monthly payments. The big danger is that you won't have enough to make that final balloon payment, in which you pay off the balance of the second mortgage loan.

You really can do it only if you can make the monthly payments on the first mortgage—and set aside enough each month to pay off the balloon when it comes due. You become your own banker—setting aside money for that last balloon payment each month and investing it. You must bank enough each month so that your money plus the interest it earns will be enough to pay the balloon. Be conservative, and figure your money will earn 5¼ percent interest, while you're waiting for the balloon to come due. If it earns more, so much the better.

If your budget won't stand the strain of a payment on the first mortgage, a payment on the second mortgage, plus what you must put aside for the balloon payment on the second mortgage, the house isn't for you. Assume when you take on the commitment, that you're going to have to pay off the balloon—that mortgage rates and terms won't ease to such a point that you can get out from under the balloon by refinancing.

Home buyers (and sellers) were dealt a blow in 1982 when the assumable mortgage became a casualty of the times: hurt by a Supreme Court ruling and then done in by an act of Congress.

With an assumable mortgage, you take over someone's older, lower-rate mortgage when you buy the house. The going mortgage rate might be 14 percent, but if the seller had an 8 percent mortgage, made years ago, you could assume that mortgage and get the 8 percent rate for as long as the mortgage runs.

Lenders came to regard the assumable mortgage as only slightly preferable to yellow fever. Instead of replacing an 8 percent mortgage with a 15 percent mortgage, the lender is stuck with the 8 percent mortgage for many years more. Starting in the 1960s, lenders began writing "due-on-sale" clauses into mortgages. It means just that: When a house is sold, the full mortgage is due, and the buyer has to find a new mortgage at whatever the going rate is.

A number of states tried to block the due-on-sale clauses. In June 1982 the Supreme Court ruled that federal chartered savings and loan associations could write due-on-sale clauses into any new mortgage, and in October of 1982 Congress said that all mortgage lenders could write due-on-sale clauses.

Still, that's only on newer mortgages. If the house you cherish has an older mortgage, without a due-on-sale clause, you can still assume it. For all that, you may not want to.

The seller is well aware that, in terms of luring a buyer, an assumable mortgage is better than a kidney-shaped swimming pool. Nothing is for free, and the value of that assumable mortgage will be factored into the selling price of the house.

You want the old mortgage—but only if the price of the house hasn't been jacked up out of sight. If the premium attributable to the assumable mortgage can't be worked off through lower mortgage payments within seven years, it isn't such a bargain.

There is, finally, the government-insured mortgage, which used to be very popular, but which fell out of favor in the 1970s. In 1970 one mortgage in three carried a guarantee from the Federal Housing Administration or the Veterans Administration. By the early 1980s, it was one mortgage in 10.

One big disadvantage is the limited size of a government-guaranteed mortgage loan—typically under $70,000. Another is the time it takes to get a government-insured mortgage loan approved—government red tape being government red tape. But a government-insured mortgage runs for 30 years and carries a fixed rate. The biggest advantage, as I write this, is that the rate on government-insured mortgages is 12 percent, while the going rate on conventional mortgages is above 13 percent.

A fixed rate can be a mixed blessing. It's fine if you get the mortgage at one rate, and mortgage rates subsequently average out to a higher rate than what you're paying over the life of your mortgage. Think of a government-insured mortgage as still another avenue to be explored when you shop for a mortgage. Finally, consider one further advantage of a government-insured mortgage: It can be assumed, at the stated rate, by whomever you sell the home to. Under the right circumstances, that could be a considerable advantage.

Your next home may not be a house. The single-family house is horrendously inefficient in terms of capital, raw materials, and energy. In the future, more of us will live in apartments—cooperative or condominium—even in suburban areas. Mostly it's condos these days—the co-op apartment being pretty much limited to New York City and a few other markets. All the rules about buying and financing apply to both apartments and homes.

A Little Place in the Country

All the rules about first homes also apply to second homes—country places or whatever. As you study a neighborhood before you buy a house—looking into all the things that are likely to affect the future value of the house—look into the area before you buy a summer place or resort condo. Is the commute tolerable? Would it be an economical commute if the price of gasoline was to start climbing again? Are you relying on bargain air fares to get you there in a way you can afford? The price of gasoline could rise again, and the airlines may not keep offering bargain fares.

Presumably you'd use the place part of the time and rent it out the rest of the year. Is it in an area that visitors flock to? Is it, for instance, within reasonable driving range of a major metropolitan center? Is it so overbuilt that finding renters might prove a major problem?

All sorts of tax rules apply to a vacation home that you rent out. If you rent it out for fewer than 15 days a year, you can't deduct any of the expenses attributable to rental, but neither do you report the income you earned from the rental. If you rent it for more than 15 days, you are deemed to be in the rental business, and you are subject to the 14-day or 10 percent test. If you occupy the property for no more than 14 days during the year, or for no more than 10 percent of the days the home was actually rented, you can take all the deductions open to you as an owner of rental property: taxes, depreciation, and operating expenses—so long as the deductions don't exceed your income from the property.

There's the relatively new concept of time sharing. You—and a lot of other people—each buy a slice of a condominium apartment in some exotic spot. You each get to use it for part of the year, and since there's a mob of you buying the unit, the cost to each is relatively modest.

Unfortunately, it's one of those businesses that have attracted more than their share of sleazy characters. Some time shares have already failed, taking with them the money of those who bought in. Always have a lawyer check out any real estate deal, and that certainly holds true for time shares. In some cases you actually own a slice of the unit. In other cases, you get the right to use the facility for so many weeks each year. A "right-to-use" isn't necessarily inferior to outright ownership, but it should cost a lot less.

When it comes to pricing a time share, check out what resorts in the area charge for however long your time at the facility will be. The purchase price should be about 10 times what a resort would charge. If two weeks for four people at a nearby resort would cost $2,000, the time share should sell for about $20,000.

Beware of promises of how much the time share can appreciate in value. The right facility in the right area in the right economy might increase in value. But time shares haven't been around long enough to establish any rules about appreciation. It might appreciate and it might not. Don't buy to make a profit. If it happens, fine—but don't bank on it.

Now Think About Selling

For the moment, say that the shoe is on the other foot. Instead of buying a house (or an apartment or a resort condominium, or whatever), you're selling. Maybe, by the time you read this, the real estate market will have stabilized, with plenty of mortgage money around at 12 percent or less. The higher rates are above 12 percent, the greater the chance you'll have to provide part of the financing—creative financing, once again. If you can find a buyer who can make it on just a first mortgage, you're in clover. If not, get ready to play the second-mortgage game.

You'll get part of your money right away, from the first mortgage. Then you'll get dribs and drabs from the second mortgage. And then, if luck is on your side, you'll get the balloon payment. If luck is running against you, the buyer won't be able to make the balloon payment, and then you have a problem. As second-mortgage holder, you're down in the pecking order. You can sue, in hopes of getting your money, or you can rewrite the second mortgage and hope that things work out better the second time around. There's insurance to protect you against default. It's available through lending institutions, so check with the institution that holds the first mortgage. But it's fairly costly, and it will further reduce your profit on the home sale. To the extent that rates go down, you might be able to sell the second mortgage—but at a discount from its principal amount, and that, too, further cuts into your profit.

You're better off if the buyer can handle a nonballoon second mortgage, even if it has to run longer. You get your money back month by month, without having to worry about a balloon popping. Still, if the buyer could handle a conventional first and second mortgage, you wouldn't be stuck extending a second mortgage to begin with.

You may be better off renting your home instead of selling it. The rental would be for a few years, until the market opens up again. Since anyone who can't buy a house (meaning most people) is a potential renter, there's plenty of demand for rental property. Home prices stabilized in 1981 and 1982, but the rent on apartments went up about 10 percent a year. You don't get your capital out, but as owner of rental property you do get those tax breaks, and you should earn something each month beyond the fixed charges on the house.

If it's a company-sponsored move that has you selling your house, do all you can to get the company to take it off your hands. At one point, several years ago, General Motors found itself stuck with so many homes, bought from transferred employees, that it offered new cars to anyone who would buy them.

There's More to the Market

When you do think about real estate, you don't have to limit it to homes and apartments. There are plenty of other kinds available—from raw land to towering office buildings.

The conventional wisdom about raw land is that God only made so much of it, so it must increase in value. And so it might—but when? Areas that looked ripe for development a few years ago, looked less promising when rising gasoline prices put them beyond the point where commuting was economical. Builders, stuck with plenty of unsold homes now, aren't looking for new tracts to develop. Meanwhile, you keep paying taxes, and the interest on the loan you took out to buy the land.

Farmland was the hottest thing in the 1970s—everything from a modest spread that an individual might buy as an investment, to a sprawling cattle ranch that a gaggle of Middle East oil sheiks might have bought. Then the dollar so increased in value that investing in the U.S. became too expensive for foreigners. Interest rates reached a point where buying farmland didn't make sense unless you could turn a nice profit from farming—and it was at this point farm income fell to its lowest level since the Depression. By 1982, the value of even choice midwestern farmland was falling for the first time in three decades—offering bargains to those willing to bet on a turnaround in the value of farm property.

Any income-producing property, if you can swing it, is still one of the best things going. You operate mostly on someone else's money, you get as many tax breaks as are available in any investment, and your money is in something tangible that's likely to keep its value no matter what happens in the economy.

Real Estate Shelters Shelter Better

It's the tax deductions that make real estate so appealing. There are tax shelters galore—deals structured to shelter not only your income from the property but other income as well, from the grasping claws of the IRS. We'll go over tax shelters in more detail in chapter 11, when we cover taxes. Here we'll just touch on the high points as they pertain to real estate.

The rich put together deals that involve just a few partners, lots of money, and the help of highly paid lawyers and accountants, skilled in the back alleys and byways of the tax laws. You can buy into a tax shelter, put together by a brokerage house or a real estate developer, with shares sold to the public just as new issues of stocks and bonds are sold. Your ante might be just $5,000, and you'd be a limited partner in a deal put together to buy some piece, or pieces, of property. Whoever put the deal together would be the general partner.

What you buy in any tax shelter are tax deductions so big that they offset not only your income from whatever the shelter has invested in, but some of your other income as well. And no other form of shelter tosses off deductions the way real estate does.

First, there's the deduction for the interest on borrowed money—and all real estate deals are done with plenty of borrowed money: typically, $4 borrowed for every $1 you put up. And that gets into the "at risk" rule, which makes real estate such a favored investment.

In all other tax shelters your deductions can't exceed what you have at risk: the amount of money you actually put up plus whatever liability you have to the lender should the deal go bad. The key here is "recourse"—whether the lender can come after you for more money if the deal goes bad. If he can, it's a recourse loan. If he can't, it's a nonrecourse loan.

In every other kind of shelter, the IRS insists that if it's a nonrecourse loan, it isn't a bona fide loan, and you have no more at risk than the money you put up. Real estate debt is nonrecourse debt: If the deal fails, the lender takes the property rather than asking you for more money. Yet in real estate shelters, even nonrecourse debt is considered to be at risk, and your deductions can run up to the money you actually put up plus your share of the borrowed money.

Beyond the interest on the borrowed money, there's also depreciation—the money that, in theory, you're putting aside to rebuild when wear and tear have reduced your property to rubble.

All property has a useful life, and you once could determine that yourself, subject to IRS approval. A useful life of 30 to 40 years on an office building or an apartment house was pretty typical—meaning you took 1/30th or 1/40th of the cost of the building each year as a tax deduction. The 1981 tax law really changed that by giving all real estate a 15-year useful life. Instead of a mere 1/30th or 1/40th of the cost of the property as a tax deduction each year, you now take 1/15th of the cost. That, by itself, is a fine thing, 1/15th being a lot bigger than 1/40th. But Congress further said that on residential property, you can use "accelerated depreciation" in figuring the tax break on real estate. You write off more than 1/15th of the cost in the first years you own the property. In later years, you write off less than 1/15th a year, but by that time, you've sold the property and someone else is taking the depreciation.

Say that your share of a real estate shelter is $10,000, and that you have 99 partners who each put up $10,000. That's $1 million. The general partner who structured the shelter, takes that $1 million, borrows $4 million more, and with the $5 million, buys an apartment building. And the apartment building throws off a lot of tax deductions: the interest on the borrowed $4 million, depreciation, the taxes on the property, and the expenses of running the building. You share in all the deductions that $5 million has bought, even though you and your partners put up only $1 million in cash.

That will shelter what rental income there is from the building, and some of your other income as well. In time, when the depreciation is de-accelerating, the building will be sold, and you'll get back your $10,000 plus your share of the profits.

You have to be taxed at a high enough rate even to think about shelters, and since the Securities and Exchange Commission, and the various state regulators, take a dim view of selling shelters to people who can't afford them, you'll have to prove your financial "suitability" before you can buy. You can't use your last penny to buy in, because your capital—the $10,000 you put up—will be tied up until the building is sold.

It's a business made to order for sharpies. If you're rich enough to get into a big-buck private deal, you'll have skilled talent making certain that all is as it should be. In a public shelter, you're on your own—gambling your money, as you do in any investment, while further hoping that the IRS will think as highly of the deal as you do.

The IRS is the judge and jury on this one, and, by definition, the IRS doesn't think much of tax shelters. It can decide the shelter isn't legitimate and then you pay taxes—at ordinary income rates—on all the income you thought you'd sheltered, plus penalties that are getting stiffer all the time.

Also, the deal must make economic sense, as well as offering you shelter. There's no point in gaining some tax breaks if you lose your capital. If it's the wrong property, income may never measure up to expectations. Then you may have to sell at a loss. And if you must sell out early, the IRS can slap you with a tax bill—"recapture," it's called.

Buying on Your Own

No investment is every risk free, and that certainly goes for commercial real estate. It offers handsome rewards, but it also offers substantial risks. You don't do a thing until a lawyer or accountant has checked every detail.

Still, say that you and a few friends want to invest in income-producing property. Together, you can muster $50,000, and with that $50,000 in hand, you borrow another $250,000. With that, you might buy a small apartment building, a very small shopping center, or maybe a neighborhood medical center. With more money, you could acquire a bigger apartment building, a small office building, a bigger shopping center.

If it's an apartment building, think about what the neighborhood might be like 10 years from now. If it's a small shopping center, do the stores in it look durable? Do they appear the sort of businesses that might last 10 years, or are they "fad" businesses that might be gone before the snow falls? Is it in a neighborhood that people will want to shop in 10 years from now?

Beyond your lawyer or accountant, talk to your banker and your real estate agent. If it's an apartment building, talk to people in the neighborhood—especially local shopkeepers. If it's a shopping center, grab a few shoppers and talk to them.

Office buildings tend to be safer than apartment buildings, since office tenants are established in some business and are less likely to skip out in the night. Yet with home buying closed to so many people for so many years, the demand for rental apartments has soared. The right apartment building can be a choice investment now. An apartment building with married couples with children is safer than one filled with swinging singles. A well-built, older building can often cost less to keep up than a slapdash, newer structure.

There are even tax credits available for rehabilitating older structures. The credit is 25 percent, if you restore an authentic historic building (officially certified as such), and an old warehouse or factory can become a very appealing office building or apartment house or a shopping mall. There are lesser credits if the structure isn't historic: 10 percent if it's at least 20 years old, 15 percent if it's at least 30 years old, and 20 percent if it's at least 40 years old.

There's a growing trend toward office condominiums. You buy the structure, fix it up, and sell—rather than rent—the space. You get your money back right away. You get fewer tax breaks, but you get your capital back, plus a profit, very quickly.

All the rules about buying a home apply to any piece of real estate. You fight hard to get the price down, and you fight hard to get the best terms you can arrange on the mortgage. You're taking a gamble on the economic outlook, but it's a reasonable gamble. The tax breaks won't go away no matter what the economy does. You may not be able to sell exactly when you want to, and you never know for certain when a neighborhood is the right neighborhood. Still, real estate is bedrock—likely to appreciate in line with inflation if we get inflation, and likely to hold up well against the tide if we plunge into depression.

The Paper Side of Real Estate

Or, if you don't like any of the above, try real estate securities, starting with "passthrough" securities, available through "Ginnie Mae." Its function is to provide money to private mortgage lenders, which the lenders can then use to make new mortgage loans.

One way it does this is to put its guarantee on pools of government-backed home mortgages (insured by the Federal Housing Administration or guaranteed by the Veterans Administration). Slices of these pools are then sold to the public, and since Ginnie Mae guarantees that the mortgages will be paid off, they sell very well. They're called passthroughs because the monthly interest and principal payments on those mortgages are passed through the investors in the pool. The return on your money is super—as much as two percentage points above a Treasury bond of comparable maturity. The pool lasts until the last mortgage has been paid off—in about 12 years. But you get your capital back, bit by bit each month, as the principal on those mortgages is paid down. And a Ginnie Mae security is fully guaranteed by the U.S. government.

The steady return of capital each month can be a problem because you must stay on top of it, and keep reinvesting the money as it flows back to you. That you get capital back each month to reinvest gives you a little higher return on your money. A far more serious problem for most of us is that it costs $25,000 to buy a newly issued Ginnie Mae passthrough.

You don't have to buy a newly issued passthrough, though. You can buy an older one, which will cost a lot less than $25,000. As mortgages get paid down, the size of the mortgage pool shrinks, and it costs less to buy a share in that pool. If it's an older pool, offering a rate of interest less than going market rates, the price will have been cut to bring the yield into line with what newer passthroughs are yielding.

The secondary market in passthroughs isn't all that hot. You might have some trouble finding an older issue at the right price, and you might have trouble selling a passthrough if you want to bail out. But you can get smaller slices of Ginnie Mae passthroughs by buying into a unit trust—and you can do that for as little as $1,000.

A unit trust is created by a brokerage house to invest in something. Often it's municipal bonds, but in this case, it's Ginnie Mae passthroughs. Once bought, the passthroughs stay in the trust until they mature or are paid off. What you get for your money is a unit in that trust. You get the high rate of interest, and you get your money every month. You do, however, have to pay a commission that can run $35 or $40 per unit, which does cut your return. But you're buying in for as little as $1,000—or even less if you're buying a unit in an older trust.

Once Ginnie Mae invented the passthrough, other people followed, and private institutions also sell passthrough securities. Bank of America, the nation's largest, has already sold several billion dollars' worth of its passthrough securities. Any stockbroker can get you into passthroughs or into a unit trust that has invested in passthroughs.

The lower mortgage rates go, the better real estate generally should do, and the closer you look at the market. But that's true of all the investment markets. When rates are high, you stick to cash. When rates are toppling, you look at real estate —and at all the other markets as well. That's when you poke up out of your hole and scurry for capital gains.

Guidelines for Action

You can nail down capital gains in every investment market, but real estate is the bedrock market: tax breaks galore, the market that will hold up best when times are bad, the market that will come back first when the economy rallies.

Home (or apartment) ownership is almost always the best first investment for most people most of the time. When you buy, don't be afraid to haggle over the price—and the mortgage rate.

For an investment, look into a small apartment house, with mostly married couples as tenants.

Tax-sheltered partnerships are dangerous for most people most of the time, but accelerated depreciation and the way the "at risk" rule works in real estate could make a shelter in residential property worth looking at.

For a high return—and near-absolute safety—look at the current darling of the investment markets—Ginnie Mae.

CHAPTER 6

When to Try Your Money in Bonds

*"If this you know, you know it all . . .
When rates do rise, then prices fall."*

—ANONYMOUS

When you learn that bit of doggerel, you won't know all there is to know about the bond market, but you'll know a lot —why bonds rallied before stocks in 1982, why a stake in bonds can often make you more money than a stake in stocks, why the bond market is often easier to play than the stock market, and why—having said all that—most people mostly lost money in the bond market for most of two decades.

Play it right in the bond market and you can clean up. Play it wrong and you can get cleaned out. Yet even when you lose in the bond market, you can often do pretty well, because even a losing bond can pay you a sky-high rate of interest while you own it.

You're more apt to invest in stocks than bonds, for many reasons, which we'll get to shortly. But you have to understand interest rates to spot turns coming up in the stock market, and the bond market is *the* interest rate market. You keep a watch on bonds if for no other reason than rallies in the bond market precede—and signal—rallies in the stock market, which is what happened in 1982. More important for right now, perhaps, declines in the bond market precede—and signal—declines in the stock market, which has happened often enough in the past couple of decades.

We'll get to stocks in chapters 7 and 8. In chapter 9 we'll explore the new markets in stock options and financial futures: smart money tactics for stocks and bonds within your financial strategy. Once you learn your way, you can use those markets to stretch your investment dollars, and to limit your losses.

But first the bond market, and to put you into the picture, there are government bonds, corporate bonds, and municipal bonds. There are high-grade bonds, medium-grade bonds, and junk bonds. There are industrial bonds and utility bonds, revenue bonds and general obligation bonds. Some bonds are mortgage bonds and some are debentures. There are bonds so secure they can be bought with perfect confidence by widows and orphans, and bonds so risky they'd make a riverboat gambler turn pale.

There are $2 trillion worth of bonds and kindred securities, issued by everyone from the U.S. government to American Telephone & Telegraph to remote school districts.

With only a few exceptions (which we'll get to later), every bond carries a rate of interest that was fixed on the day it was issued, and that will remain fixed until the bond matures way off in the future. If on May 1, 1960, Consolidated Cotton Candy sold 30-year bonds that carried a 3 percent rate of interest, the rate of interest will stay 3 percent until the day in 1990 when the bonds mature and the bondholders are paid off.

There are bonds called convertible debentures, which can be converted at some future date into shares of common stock in the issuing company. But if the interest rate was set at 5 percent when the bonds were issued, it will stay at 5 percent until you make the conversion. There are floating-rate bonds, in which the interest rate fluctuates according to what rates in the market are doing. But there aren't many, and the bond market is called the fixed-income market, because that's what you get—a fixed return for the life of the bond.

And that's the rate side of it: a promise by the issuer (Consolidated Cotton Candy) to pay you a fixed return (3 percent) each and every year during the life of the bonds (30 years).

Everything Has Its Price

But there's a price side, too, and unless you know that, you can't know it all, and you can't know how to play the market for capital gains. Bonds are issued for the long term, but you can play the market for the short term.

We touched on this briefly in Chapter 4 when we talked about putting cash into short-term government issues. Now we'll get into more detail.

When bonds come to market, they're sold at what's called "par," which in the case of a corporate bond is usually $1,000. The $1,000 you paid to buy Consolidated Cotton Candy's bonds at par, brought you a guaranteed payment of $30 a year (3 percent of $1,000) for 30 years. In 1960, 3 percent wasn't a bad return. Now, more than two decades later, 3 percent is a pittance compared with what new bonds are paying. And the years haven't turned out so sweet for Consolidated Cotton Candy, either. Its profits are down, and there aren't many people who want its bonds. Certainly there isn't a soul in the whole world who'd buy a 3 percent Consolidated Cotton Candy bond unless he could buy it for a lot less than $1,000.

Of course, people can buy it for a lot less than $1,000. The instant a bond is sold to the public, it begins to trade—in some cases on the New York Stock Exchange, more often in what's called the "over-the-counter" market. The bond sold for $1,000 when 3 percent was still a good return. When market interest rates went higher, investors no longer would pay $1,000 for a 3 percent bond when for the same $1,000 they could buy a new bond yielding four and five times that. Anyone wanting to sell a Consolidated Cotton Candy 3 percent bond had to cut the price to find a buyer—which is exactly what the sellers of those bonds did.

The higher that current interest rates went—and the lower the fortunes of Consolidated Cotton Candy sank—the more the price had to be cut by anyone trying to sell one of its bonds. The bond returned 3 percent on your money if you paid the full $1,000. But if you could buy it for $500, it would return 6 percent, and if you could buy it for $250, the yield would be 12 percent. The obligation that Consolidated Cotton candy took on when it sold the bonds—to repay your $1,000 in 1990—didn't change; only the price changed.

The less you paid for those bonds, the greater the yield on your money. And no matter how little you paid for each bond, Consolidated Cotton Candy must (if it can) pay you $1,000 in 1990. You're certainly better off than the poor soul who paid $1,000 for the bond back in 1960 and who had to sell it to you for $250. Had he kept the bond, though, all he'd have to show was a measly 3 percent a year until he got his money back in 1990. These days, checking accounts pay more than 3 percent.

But now say that the world turns and the economy slips into deep recession. Interest rates fall, and instead of paying 12 percent and more, new corporate bonds pay only 6 percent. That 3 percent rate on the Consolidated Cotton Candy bonds no longer looks quite so ridiculous. Further, 1990 is drawing ever closer. Now the price of the bonds begins to climb—maybe not to $500, where the yield to a buyer would be 6 percent, but to $400, because Consolidated is far from a healthy company. You bought the bond for $250 and now you can sell it for $400. You held the bond for a year, earned 12 percent on your money, and now you've made a $150 profit. And since you held the bond for a year, you're taxed at the capital gains rate.

And that's the point of that doggerel. When interest rates go up, the price of older bonds will fall, until the yield (your return, based on the price you paid) matches the yields on new bonds. When interest rates fall, prices of older bonds will rise—until the yield again matches the yield on new bonds.

When to Buy

If you're holding bonds when rates go up, you're in trouble, because the price of your bonds will fall—maybe a little, but maybe a lot, depending on how much of a decline in price it takes to bring the yield on your bonds up to the yield on new bonds. And bond prices have fallen, more often than not, for the better part of two decades. You can hold on to your bonds until they're paid off—getting your money back, but earning a lot less than you'd earn if your money weren't tied up in low-yielding bonds. Yet if you sell, you sell at a loss, and maybe at a big loss.

If you're holding bonds when rates fall, several things can happen—all of them nice. As rates fall and prices go up, you can sell your bonds at a profit. Or, you can hold on to the bonds and earn a yield that's now higher than newer bonds are paying. And if you hold on long enough, the bond will be paid off at par—$1,000 back against whatever you paid for the bond, with that nice yield through the years.

The trick is to be holding no bonds at all when rates go up and prices down, and to be holding lots of bonds when rates start to fall and prices go up. "Calling the turn," it's called—buying in at that precise moment when interest rates start to fall, and it's the stuff of which legends, and fortunes, are made.

The trouble is that for the better part of 20 years, declines in rates were infrequent and of short duration. And if most experts are mostly wrong most of the time, when it comes to calling the turn on rates, nearly all experts have been nearly all wrong nearly all the time.

The experts said rates would fall in 1979. They fell—briefly—in 1980. Rates were supposed to fall at the start of 1981. They fell late in the year—again, briefly. The summer and fall of 1982 produced the wildest rally in bond market history—just when most experts were predicting higher rates ahead. And if calling the turn is the best thing to do in the bond market, being wrong on the direction of the market is the worst. You may get a nice return on your money—subject to taxation at ordinary income rates—but you don't get any gains. And if rates climb, when you were expecting them to fall, you either sit on those bonds until rates fall again, or you sell out at a loss.

Why Stocks Aren't Bonds

You might assume, having read all that, that the bond market is for masochists only—which could hardly be further from the truth. The rally in the bond market that began in the summer of 1982 made billions—hundreds of billions—of dollars for the fortunate holders of bonds. Almost certainly, more money was made in bonds in 1982 than in stocks. And one should be able to keep making profits in the bond market until the recovery is well established: not gargantuan profits on the scale of 1982, but profits just the same.

Finally, in many basic ways, it is easier to make money from bonds than from stocks. That's because—for reasons both structural and tactical—the bond market isn't the stock market.

When you buy stock, you're an owner of the company, entitled to share in its profits. When you buy a bond, you're just a nice person who has loaned the company some money. Your return on stock is based on what the company earns in future years. Your return on a bond is based on what the company agreed to pay you for the loan of your money—not a penny more.

If a company prospers, you can make a lot of money on a stock. When you own a bond, you only care that the company prospers enough to pay the interest on its bonds, and to pay off when the bonds mature.

You can pile up gains in both markets, but there's a significant difference in how quickly each market responds to changing circumstances. When rates fall, investors in the stock market will factor that into their calculations about the economic outlook, and, in time, the market will go higher. The same holds true when rates go up.

The response to rising or falling rates is much quicker in the bond market. You adjust the yield of a bond by changing the price, and that change is made at once. So rallies in the bond market will precede rallies in the stock market, and if you're nimble you can leap into the bond market the instant that rates turn, make a profit, and then move into stocks in time to catch the rally there. In 1982 the bond market started to rally nearly two months before the stock market did. And, of course, this makes the bond market a pretty reliable leading indicator for the stock market—on the way up and on the way down.

If you buy a stock and the price falls, you've lost your gamble and you sell at a loss. In bonds, you can hang on and earn a nice return until the day that bond prices do advance, allowing you to sell at a profit, or until the bonds mature and you get paid off at par. You can hold a stock as well. But if you bought the stock in hopes of a capital gain—as opposed to earning lots of income from it—it probably offered only a modest yield.

It's also easier to pick the right bond than the right stock. A stock will become enticing for a host of reasons: the company's current and anticipated earnings, the quality and uniqueness of its product, the quality of its management, etc. All you need pick in the bond market is a company able to pay the interest on schedule and to pay off the bonds when they mature. The rest doesn't matter a hill of beans to you. Every company that sells bonds has a credit rating, and the prices of bonds with like credit ratings will track pretty closely together. In stocks, you must pick the right time and the right stock. In bonds, you have to pick only the right time.

The right time—the perfect time—in bonds (as, as we'll see, in stocks) is right at the turn. Since that's beyond the skill of most of us, the closer the better. But you can count on the bond market advancing until the recovery is well along, because bond prices gain as long as interest rates fall, and interest rates typically fall well after a recovery has gotten started.

No market, as we'll see, ever moves in a straight line. Rates will fall (and prices rise) in the bond market, and then there will be an adjustment with rates rising (and prices falling). Then the market will rally again, slip some more, and rally again. But when rates hit bottom, that's it: You get out of bonds and into something else. The stock market will hold up at high ground even after interest rates have started moving up. You have time to get out gracefully. You have no time at all in bonds, since the price adjustment is immediate. When rates hit bottom, get out fast.

This obsession with falling interest rates does something to bond traders. The stock market investor wants lower interest rates as a means of turning the economy toward recovery—wherein lie fatter profits, fatter dividends, and higher stock prices. In the bond market, falling rates are an end to themselves, since it's falling rates that directly produce higher prices. And only in an economy that plunges into recession and never recovers do you get rates that keep going lower.

Stock traders are optimists by nature. Bond traders are born pessimists, always hoping for the worst. I once asked a veteran trader what it would take to produce a rip-roaring rally in bonds. He thought for a while and replied, "Total economic collapse."

Treasuries and Agencies Come First

The bond market breaks down into three main species—government, corporate, and municipal. We'll save municipal bonds for chapter 11 on tax-proofing your investments, which is where they properly belong, because all interest on municipal bonds is exempt from federal tax, and often from state tax as well. You may buy municipal bonds in hopes of a gain, but mostly you buy them for tax-sheltered income.

Each species of bond breaks down into several subspecies.

The government market, as noted in chapter 4, includes both issues of the U.S. Treasury, and of the various federal agencies, from the Federal Home Loan Bank Board to the Tennessee Valley Authority. The market further breaks down into bills (maturing in a year or less), notes (one to 10 years), and bonds (beyond 10 years). Only the Treasury sells bills, while both the Treasury and the agencies sell bonds and notes. The minimum purchase of bills is $10,000, while it's $1,000 and up on Treasury notes, and $1,000 on Treasury bonds. Each agency sets its own minimum, but it's most often $1,000 on notes and bonds.

You buy a Treasury or agency issue from a broker—paying a commission just as you do when you buy stock. With Treasury issues, you can also go to the source, placing your order directly with one of the 12 regional or 23 branch Federal

Reserve banks around the country. That saves you the commission. There's an auction every Monday of three- and six-month bills, with one-year bills sold monthly, and—the budget deficit being what it is—frequent sales of notes and bonds.

The Treasury borrows to finance the national debt, and all that it sells is backed by the might and majesty of the United States government. In theory the government could use its taxing power to pay off the national debt: raising all our taxes until it had collected $1¼ trillion. In practice, it prints up, and sells, new issues when older ones mature.

The various federal agencies borrow for just about any purpose under heaven: the Federal Home Loan Bank Board to finance housing; the Export-Import Bank to finance trade; the Bank for Cooperatives, the Federal Land Bank, and others to finance farming. Most agencies belong to the government. A few, like the Federal National Mortgage Association (Fannie Mae to its friends), merely have a close working relationship with the government. Each agency borrows when necessary to pay for whatever it's paying for, and agency debt is now $250 billion, on top of the $1¼ trillion national debt.

If Treasury issues are pure gold, the agencies have just a tinge of base metal. The issues of only a few of them are explicitly backed by the government (the Government National Mortgage Association—Ginnie Mae—being one). But again, there's an implicit promise the government won't let an agency default any more than it would default on a Treasury issue. Because it's implicit rather than explicit, agencies pay a little more than Treasuries are paying. And that makes them very tempting—virtually as good as Treasuries, yet paying a little more.

All Treasury issues are exempt from state and local tax (but not federal tax). If you live in a high-tax state, that can make a Treasury a better bet than a savings certificate, even if, on the face of it, the certificate is yielding more. It may not yield more after you pay state taxes. A few agencies—Ginnie Mae, the Federal Home Loan Banks, the Federal Farm Credit Banks—are similarly exempt from local taxes, but most aren't.

Any major newspaper will list the latest quotes on all Treasury issues and the more popular agency issues. There's a bid price at which a dealer will buy from you, and an asked price, at which the dealer will sell to you.

Each investment market has its little quirks. Stocks and corporate bonds are quoted in eighths of a dollar—32⅛ or 50⅞. Treasury and agency bonds and notes are quoted in 32nds of a dollar—95 24/32 or 102 5/32. That doesn't mean the dealer will sell you a government bond for $95 and change. All bonds—government, corporate, and municipal—are listed with the final zero dropped off. A quote of 95 means the bond costs $950. A quote of 101 means the bond costs $1,010. That saves space in listing, and it simplifies things when dealers are buying or selling.

A Closer Look at the Market

Take what was available on one typical day in 1982. There was a Treasury 7¼ percent bond maturing in August of 1992, available for 83 18/32 ($835.60). You wouldn't consider it if it still sold for the original price of $1,000, because 7¼ percent is still a pretty low yield compared with what else is available. You can, as I write this, get 8½ percent on a three-month Treasury bill, and 8¾ percent on a sixth-month savings certificate.

But you can buy the bond for $835.60, and your yield, if you buy this day, will be 9.92 percent on your money. (The same listing of prices for each bond that you'll find in newspapers will also show you the yield at that price.) And if you hold the bond until August of 1992, the government will pay you $1,000. You get nearly 10 percent each year on your money until 1992—free from state and local taxes—and you get a $164 capital gain in 1992.

Should interest rates drop sharply, so that 7¼ percent became a nice yield compared with other available securities, the price of your bond would climb from $835.60 to $1,000, or very close to it, and you wouldn't have to wait until 1992 to get your profit. In fact, interest rates have already dropped sharply as I write this. Four months earlier, you could have bought the same bond for $735.60. Had you done so, you'd already have a $100 gain. Or, based on the $735.60 price, you'd be earning an 11¾ percent return on your money.

Should interest rates rise sharply until new securities must yield 20 percent to lure investors, the price of your bond would plunge until, at the new, lower price, it would yield 20 percent, or close to it. You paid $835.60 for the bond, and while you'll get $1,000 in 1992, you might only get $300 for it if you had to sell in a time of soaring interest rates.

The shorter the time until a bond matures, the less you risk, because the closer you get to maturity, the closer the price moves to what the issuer must pay you at maturity. You might have to cut the price of an older, lower-yielding bond to $500 in order to sell it, if the buyer won't get the full $1,000 from the issuer for another 10 or 15 years. If maturity is only a year away, the same issue might go for $900.

The other side of that is that the further you are from maturity, the closer to current market interest rates an older issue will yield. By buying issues on the verge of maturity, you guard against loss from falling prices, but you also settle for a lower yield. In bonds, as in all investments, the greater the potential reward, the greater the potential risk.

When Business Sells Bonds

The corporate bond market is like the government bond market in one way: You're still lending money to someone who will pay you back in the future, and who'll pay you for the use of your money until then. But there's also a profound difference between the two markets.

A government issue will always be paid off because it's either explicitly or implicitly guaranteed by the government. True, the government replaces maturing bits of paper with new bits of paper, but the government always "pays" its debts. A corporate bond is no better than the corporation that issued it, and some corporations today are just a half-step from the poorhouse. A company can pay off your bond only if it earns enough.

In the government market you're gambling on the future course of interest rates. In the corporate market you're gambling on rates, but also on the ability of the company, whose bonds you buy, to pay you back. Because of that, companies pay more to borrow than does the Treasury.

There are two subspecies of corporate bonds—mortgage bonds and debentures. Mortgage bonds are secured by some piece of real property. Should the company default, you might become the part owner of a rolling mill or a locomotive. It would take time, but the asset could be sold, and you'd get some money back. Debentures are secured only by the company's promise to pay. Should a company default on a debenture, you take your place, somewhere toward the middle, in the line of creditors howling for their money. There are senior debentures, which move you toward the front of the line, and subordinated debentures, which move you toward the back of the line. There are also convertible debentures, which, as noted elsewhere, can be converted into so many shares of company stock sometime in the future. You take a lower rate of interest than market conditions would warrant—hoping you'll be able to convert into the stock at a price below what it's selling for in the market.

How to Read the Ratings

The ability of a company to pay off its debts is of paramount importance when you buy bonds. And while you could search the financial records of every American corporation, there are agencies that do this for you: examining the financial records of all the companies that sell bonds, and assigning a bond rating to each.

The agencies are Standard & Poor's Corporation a subsidiary of McGraw-Hill, and Moody's Investor Service, a subsidiary of Dun & Bradstreet. The issuing company pays the agencies to rate its bonds since buyers wouldn't touch an unrated bond. It's evidence of how sticky things have become in our economy, that the bond ratings of a record 167 companies were cut in 1981—more than double the total for 1977.

To the very crème de la crème go the highest of ratings: AAA at S&P and Aaa at Moody's. These are the pillars of corporate America—rich, profitable, conservative in their approach to all things, and likely to stay that way.

Next comes AA and A and then into the B's (starting with BBB at S&P and Baa at Moody's) down to B and then into the C's and finally down to D. Once you get to BBB and below, you're leaving the ground known as "investment grade" and you're getting beyond the point where widows and orphans should tread. By the time you hit C, you're dealing with a very sick company, and to get a D rating, a company must have defaulted on its bonds.

Once you get into the lower B's, you're moving into the realm of "junk bonds"—bonds that for one financial transgression or another, have fallen to the lower levels of the rating heap. But again, you get what you pay for. The higher the rating, the lower the interest rate it takes to sell bonds, and the less the price of those bonds will fall in a falling market (or advance in a rising market). Prices edge ever lower, and yields ever higher (and price swings are ever greater) the further down the rating ladder you go. By the time you reach junk-bond land, you're buying in cheap and hoping with every fiber of your being, that something astonishing will happen to make the company a winner again.

And lightning has struck—some hint of financial recovery ahead that has sent a junk bond soaring in price, and made a ton of money for some lucky investors on a modest investment. A typical play would be to bet on the bonds of a big-name company that has fallen on hard times—a Chrysler, or a Pan Am. As I write this, Chrysler is burdened with a CCC rating, and yet it clearly is doing better. Because of its low price, a junk bond will pay a handsome return (15 percent on a Chrysler bond, as I write this), assuming the company can afford to pay any interest at all.

A cut in a bond rating will produce an almost instantaneous drop in the price of a bond as it adapts to its new, lower standing in the world. You can scent a cut coming if company profits tumble—particularly if it has lots of bonds out. Now there's a question of whether it can earn enough to pay off its bonds. When a whole industry gets into trouble (automobiles, steel, airlines), figure that virtually all companies in that industry will suffer a rating cut.

In 1981, Standard & Poor's introduced its Creditwatch, to

alert investors to situations that could lead to a rating cut. It's usually well publicized when a bigger company goes on the Creditwatch list, and while a company can turn itself around, it's not a good sign. The price of its bonds will fall, and your chances of making a gain are reduced.

Even if you're just planning a quick in-and-out move in hopes of a quick profit, don't buy a bond without looking at its credit rating, and without making sure it's not on the Creditwatch list. Don't buy a bond of a company whose prospects are fading, or a company in an industry whose prospects are fading. You want a company whose prospects are improving, or a company in an industry whose prospects are improving. An improvement in a credit rating will produce an almost immediate rise in price as the bond adapts to its new higher standing in the world.

When you hit the turn in interest rates, or close to it, almost any bond will produce a profit. Later on, once the rally is established, you make your killings by latching onto bonds that are about to get upgraded. Now you're no longer talking about playing the whole market but about spotting opportunities. We'll get into that in much more detail in the chapters on stocks because that's the market where you are obliged to spot a limited number of winners out of a universe of stocks.

The quick, glib answer is that any company, or any industry that saw its fortunes hurt by a recession, is a candidate for a credit rating upgrading once the recession ends. Even the surviving companies in a sick industry can get a better credit rating once they can start boosting profits and socking away more capital.

Inside the Corporate Market

Even the bond ratings don't tell it all. Different kinds of companies sell bonds—the two biggest classes being industrial companies and utilities. Other things being equal, industrial bonds will yield a little more than utilities because industrial bonds are a little riskier than utility bonds. A utility will typically get frequent rate increases from its state regulators sufficient to produce a decent rate of return. If an industrial company gets into trouble, there's no one to turn to. Lately, plenty of industrial companies have gotten into trouble.

Bonds trade on the New York and other exchanges, and they trade over-the-counter, which is merely a lot of dealers linked together by telephone, Telex, and computer. One day in the summer of 1982 (just before the big rally got started), you could find New York Stock Exchange listings for no fewer than a dozen different AT&T bonds, each with its own characteristics.

There was an AT&T 3¼s84, selling for 89 and yielding 3.7 percent. It's an AT&T bond, carrying a 3¼ percent rate, maturing in 1984. In corporates, as well as in governments, that final zero is dropped off, so the 89 was really $890 per bond. Because you were paying $890 and not $1,000, the yield was 3.7 percent, not 3¼ percent. Granted, 3.7 percent wasn't much compared with what other bonds were paying, but you weren't buying it for the yield. In 1984, AT&T will pay you $1,000 for that bond—a profit of $110, taxable at capital gains rates.

There is also an AT&T 8.80s05. That's an issue, with an 8.8 percent interest rate, maturing in 2005. The price in the summer of 1982 was 73½, meaning $735, and at that price, the yield was 12 percent. Even six-month savings certificates weren't returning 12 percent. You get that 12 percent every year from now until 2005, even if rates plunge and new issues yield just 1 percent. In 2005, AT&T will pay you, or your heirs, $1,000 for that bond.

Testing the Waters

Say that on July 1, 1982, you took the plunge, and bought that AT&T 8.8 percent issue—gambling that interest rates were about to break and that you could pick up some handsome gains.

Mostly, you were flying in the face of expert opinion. The conventional wisdom was that the July 1 cut in tax rates would start an economic recovery in the summer of 1982, and that between the money needs of a recovering economy and the record money needs of the government to finance the record budget deficit, interest rates would go higher (and bond prices lower). But your economic sixth sense told you that interest rates were already too high to permit a recovery, that growth in the money supply was too slow, and that the Federal Reserve would soon have to act decisively to bring about a recovery. The leading indicators were up, but neither the stock market nor the money supply were contributing to that. On that basis, your sixth sense said "buy," and so you did.

You were, of course, exactly right. There was no economic recovery for six more months and in August the Fed did act to increase the money supply and drive down rates. You paid $620, on July 1, for each Telephone 8.8 percent bond. By August 15, the price of each bond had climbed to $675. By mid-September the price was up to $735, and by mid-October it was up to $880. You could have sold out in August, taken your profit, and gone on to catch the rally in the stock market. Or you could have held and watched the profits on your bonds build up.

It's seldom that clear-cut—the rally of 1982 being a most extraordinary thing. Yet it was a time when it was fairly easy for you to be right, while most of the experts were wrong.

The July 1, 1982, tax cut was coming up, and all the experts agreed that such a cut in tax rates must produce an economic recovery. We'd all get more money in our pockets—and people being people, and money always burning holes in our pockets, we'd spend it instantly. That extra spending, the experts agreed, would instantly turn the economy around.

That might have been true at other times. A glance at the real world—out where you live and work—would have shown many reasons why it wasn't likely to work that way in 1982:

1. Consumers might be getting more money, but with rates on mortgages and consumer loans at record highs, they weren't likely to spend it on the big-ticket purchases that move the economy.

2. Unemployment was rising, and when that happens, we tend to spend less and save more, because we fear we might be the next to be laid off.

3. The leading economic indicators were up, but the indicators linked to the cost and the supply of money—the money

supply and the stock market—weren't up, and that's always a bad sign.

4. Money growth was so slow as to make a recovery improbable. Further, Fed officials said again and again they would keep money growth slow to offset what they saw as the inflationary consequences of the record budget deficits. Fed officials might change policy—but not until it became clear there would be no summertime economic recovery.

A glance at reality would have shown the experts how wrong they were, but few seem to have glanced. You, operating in the real world, would have looked around and seen not a hint of impending recovery. You would have heard about friends being laid off. You would have seen extraordinary sales at the stores at which you shop, and you would have seen local businesses failing.

One by one, the forces that make for a rally fell into place, and then, first the bond market and then the stock market caught fire, as you suspected they would. There was no summertime economic recovery, and there were some well-publicized bank and business failures—plus the threat of default on loans by foreign countries. All of that showed that the Fed was keeping money too tight. President Reagan gave up a little on Reaganomics and persuaded Congress to raise taxes. Budget deficits would still be huge, but at least the President had rejoined the real world, and one could hope for lower deficits ahead. With that concession from the White House, the Fed could breathe a little easier about the deficits, and it could offer a quid pro quo—easier money. And with easier money, came lower rates, and with lower rates came that explosive rally in bonds and then in stocks.

Almost anything you bought then would have made you big bucks. Nor did you have to catch the market absolutely at the turn. The price of that AT&T 8.8 percent bond increased by $55 between July 1 and mid-August. Had you bought in mid-August, the price gained another $60 by mid-September. Had you waited to buy until mid-September, by mid-October the price had gained another $65. You could have missed the turn by a couple of months, and you still could have made a nice profit.

Even the mightiest can be brought down, and your flyer with AT&T would have hit an air pocket in March of 1983 when Ma Bell, and all of her operating companies, had their credit ratings cut by Moody's Investor Service. It was not unexpected: By court order, AT&T was in the process of being broken up on antitrust grounds. What would be left would be an entity one-third the size of the old AT&T, and a credit-rating cut at that point had to be expected. Possibly it wasn't, because the price of AT&T bonds dropped by about $10 each.

But it figures to be a short-lived thing, because AT&T successfully got out of the telephone operating business, which is a very expensive business to be in, and it is free to plunge into the computer-related businesses of tomorrow. It's a safe bet that Ma Bell will soon get her top-grade credit rating back again. Had you held those bonds when the rating was cut, you might have lost a little—after the choice gains you had already piled up. Unless you were mildly retarded, you wouldn't have bought the AT&T bonds without knowing about the antitrust suit, the break-up of AT&T, and the possibility of a lowered credit rating. All were well-publicized events.

Moving On Down

Maybe you tried a more daring play and paid a visit to junk-bond land. On July 1, 1982, you bought the 8⅝ percent bond of International Harvester, maturing in 1995. Harvester has had its problems, and on July 1 that bond was selling for 32½ ($325 a bond). At that price, the yield wasn't 8⅝ percent but 27 percent. It took a lot of faith to believe that Harvester would still be around in 1995 to pay off the bond. It has only a B rating, and its losses have been staggering. Yet the company has been working hard to turn itself around—selling off parts of the business to raise money, bringing in new management. Maybe it will make it, and so you gamble.

Again, you win. The rally pulled everything along with it, and two months later the bond was selling for 90 ($390). That's an immediate profit of $65 per bond. If you didn't want to sell, you had that 27 percent yield, based on what you paid—assuming the company can afford to keep paying the interest on its debt.

The more daring the play, the faster you take your profit and get out. A company in junk-bond land could collapse at any moment. There's an old Wall Street adage: "Bulls get fed and bears get fed, but hogs only get eaten."

Strategies for Bonds

All this drama is pretty heady stuff for a market that seldom saw much price movement at all. Widows and orphans and bankers used to buy bonds—not daring plungers. It isn't that way any longer, of course. As long as rates stay volatile, prices will stay volatile and the bond market will remain a market for the higher rollers.

Bonds certainly have their place in the scheme of things. There are plenty to choose from and they trade in organized markets, with quotes always available and with no problem about finding sellers when you want to buy or buyers when you want to sell. If you guess right, you can make some very choice capital gains. And if you guess wrong, you can still wind up earning a very nice return on your money while you wait for rates to fall and prices to rise.

You can buy bonds on your own, or you can buy into mutual funds that invest in bonds. Someone else, for a fee, picks the bonds, with enough buying power to pick an array of bonds, which limits the risk of one bad bond causing you a major financial loss. It will also save you commissions, which can be fierce when you just buy one or two bonds.

Some funds charge a commission of 8½ percent when you buy in, but there are enough "no-load" funds that charge no commission that there's no good reason for giving anyone that much money off the top. You can buy in modestly—fund shares usually selling for $10 and $15 each. Every major newspaper will tell you each day what shares in each fund cost. Most libraries have a copy of *Weisenberger Investment Companies Service*—a fat volume that lists all mutual funds, tells you what each fund specializes in, and details the fund's past performance.

As with money market mutual funds, you want to buy into a family of funds—a number of funds of different types run by one management company. You can then shift from a money fund to a bond fund or a stock fund, and back again, with just a single telephone call.

If you want to invest directly in bonds, government or corporate, here are the rules:

1. For income, buy newly issued bonds—as long as you understand that income will be taxed at ordinary income rates. For capital gains, when prices are low and you think they'll rally, buy older issues selling at a discount.

2. If it's a corporate bond, buy quality—but not too much quality. You can go as low as an A-rated bond without taking undue risk. The yield will be higher than on a top-rated bond, and price gains will be bigger when rates fall and prices rise.

3. Buy older bonds selling at between 50 percent and 75 percent of their face value. If it's above 75 percent, it's a bond with real problems.

4. Buy an issue that's between five and 10 years from maturity. The closer you get to maturity, the closer to par the price will go, in anticipation that the company will pay off the bonds at par. Beyond 10 years, it's too long to wait in case you decide to—or are forced to—hold the bond to maturity.

5. A good, cautious first step is to buy Treasury or federal agency issues maturing in less than 10 years. Price fluctuations will be less than in the corporate market—somewhat limiting your gain, but also limiting your loss if the market runs away from you.

6. Favor utility bonds over industrial bonds, for the greater safety factor. It will take years for industrial companies to repair the damage of the past two decades, while the helping hand of state regulators give the utilities that extra margin of safety.

7. A rating is fine as far as it goes, but do your own homework. Read annual reports and other financial information on the company you're investing in. Assume the rating agencies have caught the obvious things like excessive amounts of debt

and serious shortages of working capital. But let your instincts be your guide. Is the report too flashy? Are there too many superlatives? Does the company's story ring true? If something gets your economic sixth sense ajar, in all you read and all you hear, about the company, don't buy its bonds (or its stock either, for that matter).

You should know about "call" protection when you buy a bond—though this mostly applies when you buy a newly issued bond for the return. No company wants to pay yesterday's high rates forever if today's rates are lower. Most bonds, therefore, can be "called" by the issuer after a certain number of years—redeemed ahead of schedule so the company can float a new issue at a lower rate. Most bonds when issued are safe from call for at least five years, and 10 years is pretty common. If you're buying for income, seek 10 years call protection. If you're buying an older bond selling at a discount, there isn't much danger that it will be called, since the bond is selling at a discount because the rate is far below rates on new issues.

You hedge in bonds by buying several different bonds, rather than several bonds of a single issuer, so you don't have all your eggs in one basket. Still, that's kid stuff nowadays. You really hedge your position in bonds (and you speculate on changes in interest rates without buying bonds) by using the new markets in interest-rate futures, and interest-rate options on interest-rate futures. We get to those techniques in chapter 9.

And All the Rest

You normally wouldn't think of money in a bank as falling within the realm of fixed-income investing. Still, the array of things that financial institutions can offer keeps growing, and the line between money in a bank and money in a fixed-income investment is fast disappearing.

As part of its campaign for phasing out all interest rate ceilings, the government in 1983 lifted the rate ceiling on all time deposits beyond 31 days. You can open an account with any amount of money, at whatever rate of interest you can negotiate—for as long as the institution will keep paying you that rate. Obviously you can't play for capital gains, and your income is taxed at ordinary tax rates. But your money is insured, and it's still another option open to you.

Lastly, there's the basic rule that applies to bonds—and to every other investment: When you get a reasonable profit, take it and run. The longer you hang around, the greater the danger that the market will run away from you. If it's a choice between hanging in for the year, and risking what profit you have, take your profit and pay the taxes. A gain is better than a loss any day, even if the gain is taxed at ordinary income rates.

However you do in the bond market depends on how successful your economic sixth sense is at spotting turns in turns. Don't expect to catch the turn exactly: even the professionals seldom do that. Close is good enough—but the closer the better.

Guidelines for Action

Even if you don't want to invest in bonds, watch the bond market because it turns before the stock market turns—making it a leading indicator of the stock market (which, in turn, is a leading indicator of the economy).

If you do try bonds, buy quality, but not too much quality (A-rated, not AAA-rated).

Favor utility bonds over industrial bonds for that extra particle of safety.

It's easier to pick a winning bond than a winning stock—but don't buy any bond until you've read up on the company that issued it.

Buy an older issue, between five and 10 years from maturity—unless you're convinced interest rates have gone as low as they're going to go. If you think that, you shouldn't be looking at bonds, anyway.

CHAPTER 7

Why the Stock Market Behaves the Way It Does

When you think about investing your money, you have to ask yourself this question: Can 32 million Americans be wrong?

That's how many people own stock, according to the New York Stock Exchange. Standing shoulder to shoulder, they'd stretch back and forth across the country six times. That doesn't count another 130 million people who are indirect investors in the stock market because they have money in a pension fund, or an insurance company that owns stock. The aggregate financial wealth of all Americans is $7 trillion, and 15 percent of that is in stock.

The answer, of course, is that 32 million Americans can frequently be wrong. Unlike the stock market of the 1950s and 1960s, when prices mostly went higher most of the time, the market of the seventies and eighties has been treacherous. The image of those 32 million investors shoulder to shoulder isn't quite right. Most investors have spent most of the past 15 years on their knees, wondering what hit them.

Things seem to be different now, of course, with inflation on the run and the economy recovering from recession. The rally that began in August of 1982 was without precedent in its magnitude. Assuming we are in for a long time of noninflationary economic growth, we could be in for a long-running bull stock market. Economic growth is essential to the stock market's well-being, while inflation invariably knocks the market flat.

You can hardly take command of your own financial future without giving the stock market a try. Even now, most people don't realize all the nice things that an advancing stock market can do for them. Of those 32 million Americans who own stock, at least 10 million have just a few shares as part of a company stock purchase plan. Fewer than one American in 10 really invests in the stock market.

It needn't be the bull market of all time for you to move into stocks. As always, even in a bull market, stock prices will fluctuate. You can venture in and be pretty confident your economic sixth sense will tell you in plenty of time if it's time to clear out of the market.

You won't want for advice on how to play the stock market —and we'll talk about market strategies in chapter 8. There are those new tactics you can use to stretch your money and limit your risk—involving options and futures. We'll get to those in chapter 9. Right now, we'll stick to basics—how the stock market works and how the economy and the market interact.

Say you've built a better mousetrap. If you had money enough to build and market it, the world would surely beat a path to your door. But your banker has seen a lot of better mousetraps in his day. He might loan you money, but at a high rate of interest, and you'd have to repay the loan someday, whether your mousetrap made it or not. So using your persuasive skills to the utmost, you find friends and neighbors willing to become partners in the venture. You get their money to build mousetraps. They'll share in the profits if there are any. The more profits you make, the more there is to share. If you make nothing, there will be nothing to share, and your friends and neighbors will have nothing for their money but heartache. Should you make a bundle, your partners will soon find other people willing to buy their shares of the business for more than they put up.

What Makes a Winning Stock

That's what the stock market is all about. Every company that ever sold its stock to the public, did what you did—raised money by selling shares in the company to other people. In the bond market you're just a lender. When you buy a share of common stock, you become a part-owner of some business—entitled to share in its profits if there are any. The more the company earns, the more it usually will give you in the form of dividends. If there are no earnings, you get nothing back on your money. If earnings increase—and seem likely to keep increasing—someone will probably pay you more for your piece of the business. Should earnings dwindle, someone might still buy your share, but they wouldn't pay much.

The ultimate challenge in the stock market—the one that separates the men from the boys (or the women from the girls, since 47 percent of all stock owners are women)—is to find companies able to increase earnings year after year but selling at prices low enough so you can buy cheap and sell at an obscene profit.

When the economy is booming, most companies will increase their earnings year after year, and picking stocks that will increase in price is no great challenge. When inflation rages, it becomes harder, since fewer companies can increase their earnings faster than inflation. And when the economy slumps, it becomes harder still, since few companies will increase earnings at all. And inflation deals still another blow to the stock market—pushing interest rates so high that you can earn more on a risk-free Treasury bill or an insured bank deposit, than you can by risking your money in the market.

Nor can you look out the window and say, "This is how the economy is doing, so this is how the stock market must do." Today never matters in the stock market—only tomorrow. You buy the shares of Amalgamated Cough Drop at $20 a share because you expect to sell them for more than $20 a share in the future. You expect Amalgamated Cough Drop to increase its earnings—and to give promise of being able to continue increasing its earnings—so someone else someday will pay more than $20 for your share of those earnings.

You're always a hostage to fortune when you buy stock. When you buy a Treasury bill or a savings certificate or a bond, you know the day you buy how much you'll earn on your money if you hang on until the security matures. When you buy stock, you haven't a clue as to how much you'll earn. You could earn lots if the company prospers, and you could lose it all if the company doesn't. And since Amalgamated's future is tied to the economic future, you are similarly a hostage to economic fortune when you buy stocks. If the economic skies of the future prove sunny, Amalgamated should do very well. If the economy slumps, Amalgamated's earnings go out the window. If inflation rages, people will be too busy buying Treasury bills to buy Amalgamated shares from you.

Investing for Income

If you're approaching retirement, think about buying stocks for income—buying the stocks of companies that share their earnings lavishly with shareholders. Maybe the stock will increase in price, but that's secondary. You just want a yield high enough—based on the dividend—to represent a very high return on your money. If you were still in your peak earning years, the tax burden on those dividends would be killing. But when you retire, your tax rate will drop, and you'll keep most of what you earn.

You aren't terribly concerned if the price of the shares falls because you've bought them to hold. You're more concerned that the company will be able to pay that dividend year after year. Every broker has a list of income stocks—heavily laced with utilities and a few giant industrial companies. All carry top credit ratings and are likely to keep paying that dividend for years.

Utility stocks are favored for the same reason utility bonds are—because state regulators try to guarantee utilities a level of profits high enough to ensure their survival. And the 1981 tax law gave a nice break to investors in utilities—mostly electric utilities. You can take up to $750 of dividends from a utility each year ($1,500 for a couple) and reinvest them tax free in the stock of that utility. As long as it's reinvested, you don't pay taxes on the dividend income until you sell the shares. To encourage reinvestment, some utilities will sell you their shares at up to a 5 percent discount from the market price, with no commission charge.

If you're in the market just for income, you might also look at preferred stock, as opposed to common stock. With common stock, the dividend is based on what the company has earned and what it feels it can afford to pass on to shareholders. If earnings are sparse, there will be no dividend. With preferred stock, the company promises to pay you a set dividend every year, no matter what happens to earnings. The stock is preferred because you get your money off the top—your dividend will be paid before the common shareholders see a penny. If hard times hit the company, it must pay what it owes you before it can pay anything to the common shareholders. Price swings are typically smaller with preferred stock. That limits your chances for a gain—but also minimizes your chance of losing.

Going After Gains

If you aren't in the market for income, then you're in for gains, and that gets you into the hurly-burly of the marketplace.

At the very core of the stock market, and of every decision to buy or sell, is the interplay of price and earnings of each stock that's traded. The basic measurement of any stock is its price/earnings ratio—expressed as p/e—which is how much investors will pay for each dollar per share that the company earns. That's total earnings divided by the number of outstanding shares. Price is the current market price of the stock while earnings are for the most recent 12 months.

Say that Amalgamated Cough Drop earned $2 a share in the past year—$2 million divided by the 1 million outstanding shares. On this day, its shares are selling for $10 in the marketplace. Its p/e is 5, meaning that investors will pay a paltry $5 for each $1 of Amalgamated's earnings. Face it, Amalgamated isn't a very exciting company. Its earnings grow modestly, and it's unlikely we'll ever increase our buying of cough drops by any great amount. There's just no glamour there.

But look at that dazzling newcomer to the scene—Blueberry Computer. A few years ago, it didn't exist. Nor did its principal product—a higher-powered computer for use in the home and office. Now Blueberry Computer is very much in business, and people are buying home computers right and left. Two years ago, it earned a dime a share. Last year, it was $2, and for the future, the sky's the limit. On the assumption that Blueberry's earnings will keep growing at that heady rate, investors have accorded Blueberry's shares a p/e of 50—the stock selling at $100 a share, and earning $2 a share.

The classic prescription for making money in the stock market—or anyplace else, for that matter—is to buy cheap and sell dear. The way you measure cheap versus dear in stocks is by looking at the p/e. You want a stock with a low p/e that will, in the shortest possible time, become a stock with a high p/e. Of the thousands of people who make their money telling other people what stocks to buy, some embrace the "e" side of the equation. They are fundamentalists, who base their selections on how much a company has earned, and how much it's likely to earn. Others embrace the "p" side of the equation. They are the technicians who draw complex charts tracing the price of a stock in the past—the idea being that the past price movements predict the future price movements.

Four Things You Must Know

All the theories notwithstanding, there are certain things about the stock market you must know:

1. The stock market is inherently rational. Individual investors may be irrational, but the mass of investors together is pretty rational most of the time.

2. The market is particularly rational in its response to developments in the economy—which is why it's a leading economic indicator. If the economic future isn't right, then the "e" won't grow, and if the "e" doesn't grow, neither will the

"p." And if the "p" doesn't grow, you can't make any money in the stock market.

3. The market does best during periods of noninflationary growth. We're most likely to get periods of noninflationary growth as we emerge from recession, which is why market rallies begin in the depths of recession. When inflation heats up, markets hit a peak and then decline. That's because inflation brings high interest rates, and the combination of high interest rates and inflation bring countermeasures from the Federal Reserve which will produce recession.

4. The clearest line to track in forecasting the stock market is interest rates: the lower rates go, the higher stock prices will go, and vice-versa. As noted in chapter 6, let the bond market be your guide, and you should do just fine.

Why the Stock Market

You can never ignore the stock market, because no other market on the face of the earth can match its advantages. There are thousands of stocks to choose from, of every size and in every industry.

Of all the businesses in America, some 15,000 have shares available for you to purchase. The biggest and richest—some 1,500 in all—trade on the New York Stock Exchange, which accounts for 80 percent of all the stock trading on all markets. In 1981 the Big Board, as it's called—and for good reason—traded $400 billion worth of stocks, and the total value of all shares on the Big Board was $1¼ trillion. Next comes the American Stock Exchange, located just a few blocks west of the New York exchange. The Amex, as it is called, traded $26 billion worth of stock in 1981. Its companies tend to be smaller and less profitable than Big Board stocks, and many companies have moved from the Amex to the Big Board when they got big enough.

Next come the regional exchanges—the Midwest in Chicago; the Pacific, with trading floors in both Los Angeles and San Francisco; the Boston; and the Philadelphia. They trade some big-league stocks that also trade on the Big Board, and they trade some local issues—stocks of companies located in their region.

Finally, there's the over-the-counter market—the biggest in terms of number of issues. Most O-T-C stocks are small, Johnny-come-lately ventures, but with some exceptions. The stocks of many big banks still trade over-the-counter. In the past, trading literally was over a counter—buyer and seller face to face. Now, it's by telephone, Telex, and computer, as is O-T-C trading in bonds.

Wherever a stock is traded, you can get price quotes any hour of the day. You can buy or sell in a matter of minutes. All public companies must provide annual reports to shareholders, and they must file voluminous reports with the Securities and Exchange Commission, which are available for your study. You can assume that when it comes to the 500 or so most widely held stocks, a brokerage house somewhere has done a report, analyzing the company and its prospects. Most libraries have volumes from Standard & Poor's Corporation, listing all manner of financial facts and figures about every public company.

The various exchanges police their own affairs, and the SEC watches over the exchanges. Any new issue of stock must be registered with the SEC. The over-the-counter market has its own police force—the National Association of Securities Dealers. There are crooks in the market, because there's so much money around. But most of the unruly practices of the past are gone. You can invest in stocks and feel you're getting a fair shake.

Granted, as a small investor, you're a mouse going up against elephants. The giant institutions—the banks, mutual funds, and insurance companies—do 75 percent of the trading. You buy a few shares at a time and they buy by the carload. If you're in the way—holding a stock when a big institution is selling (or when institutions in general are selling)—you can get trampled through no fault of your own.

There's also the matter of inside information. The SEC says that neither a company nor its officers or big stockholders can reveal material information about the company to one investor without revealing it to all. In theory, you and the trust departments at the giant New York banks must be told the same facts about a company at the same time. You'd have to be pretty naive to believe that an institution, able to buy or sell 100,000 shares of some company's stock in an instant, won't be told things long before you learn of them.

Still, because they must trade in large quantities, institutions are limited in the stocks they can buy. Most of the wonder stocks of recent years don't have enough shares around for institutions to get involved. Nor—all that inside information notwithstanding—have the institutions been big winners in most years. Mostly they do no better than the key market averages (which isn't so surprising, since they tend mostly to buy the stocks that make up the key market averages).

Why You Look at Mutual Funds

You can opt for the stock market, and avoid all the fuss and bother by letting someone else do it: by buying shares in a mutual fund, of which there are hundreds. There are stock funds, bond funds, growth funds, income funds. There are funds that specialize in foreign stocks and funds that invest in things related to gold. Some funds buy everything in sight, and some limit their buying to a specific area—energy stocks or small growth stocks.

There are those families of funds—a single company that manages a variety of funds: stocks, bonds, money market, municipal bonds, etc. In almost all cases you can buy one fund and shift to another by making a phone call.

In every fund, no matter what type, you and your fellow investors put up the money and, in return for a fee, the fund managers invest where they think it will do the most good. You're buying into a pool of stocks selected by professionals, and you're buying into a greater array of stocks than you could possibly afford. It's an ever-changing array—funds constantly buying and selling stocks according to what they think will do the best at the moment. As a rule, the funds have tended to do just a little better than the key market averages. (Since there are hundreds of funds, but thousands of stocks, the odds are better that you'll pick a winning mutual fund than a winning stock.)

Some funds sell their shares through brokerage houses, and you'll pay a sales commission—usually 8½ percent—when you buy. Other funds, called "no-load" funds, are sold directly by the management company, and you pay no commission. Since every penny of commission reduces your investable pile, there's no good reason for buying a fund that requires a commission. There's no evidence that no-load funds do worse than funds that sock you with a commission charge.

When you want to sell, the management company buys the shares back from you at the net asset value—the wealth of the fund divided by the number of shares. Major newspapers list, each day, the major funds and the asset value on that day. You're earning dividend income (taxable, of course). If the value of your fund shares increases (and the 1982 rally produced some truly dazzling gains), you can sell at a profit (at the capital gains rate, if you've held on for a year or more).

Every fund has a prospectus that will show its objectives and its past performance. The same *Weisenberger Investment Companies Service* that we talked about in connection with bond funds, lists all funds, and their track records. The past is not always a sure guide to the future, but a fund that has consistently done well obviously is a better candidate than one that has trailed the pack. You want growth—so you want funds that stress growth. You want to buy one of a family of funds, so you can shift quickly from cash to stocks or bonds and back to cash.

With all that diversity of holdings, a fund isn't likely to own enough of any one issue to make a huge killing—not as well as you'd do if you picked a couple of winning stocks. But neither are you likely to suffer the loss you'd take if you just owned a couple of stocks and one of them went bad.

Picking a Stockbroker

If you want to plunge directly into the stock market, you first need a stockbroker who'll guide you. There has been a blood bath in recent years, and two of every three brokerage houses of 20 years ago are no longer around today. Those that survive often belong to someone else. Bache belongs to Prudential Insurance Company, Shearson Hayden Stone belongs to American Express, and Dean Witter Reynolds is part of Sears Roebuck. But Merrill Lynch still stands independent—America's biggest stockbroker—and there still are enough firms around, so that you won't come away empty-handed.

There are the financial department stores—Merrill Lynch and the others—which offer just about everything financial—stocks, bonds, commodities, real estate, tax shelter, and on and on and on. There are specialty houses that offer just a few products. There are firms like Morgan Stanley and Dillon Read that cater to the bluebloods. There are regional firms, operating in just one part of the country. There are discount brokers who'll buy and sell stock for you at a lower charge than the full-service house but which won't offer you any help in selecting stocks.

You're starting out small, and since brokers live from the commission dollars that come from trading stocks for clients, you'll have to shop around to find a broker interested in you. You want a broker who'll spend a reasonable amount of time with you—helping you pick stocks and holding your hand through the rough spots. You, in turn, hope that someday you will do well enough in the market to become a valued customer. Be honest about how much you have to invest, what sort of return you want, and the risks you're willing to take. The broker must be someone you can trust and with whom you feel comfortable, because you're going to be having some pretty intimate conversations about your money.

Ask among your friends. Ask your banker. Visit a few brokerage houses and see what your reaction is. You're probably better with a smaller, local house, but also visit the nearest branch of Merrill Lynch or Bache, or one of the other financial department stores.

Most firms have a "broker of the day"—often a new broker, who's assigned to handle off-the-street traffic. Instead, ask to talk to the manager and let him steer you to someone who might be interested in your account. If the manager doesn't seem much interested in you, walk away and try another firm. Use a discount broker if you think you'll be trading frequently and want to save commission dollars. Probably you won't be trading so much that the commissions will be a huge thing and you'll want the help and hand-holding that a full-service house can offer: stock reports, economic reports, plus the ability to handle not only stocks but every sort of investment you might have in mind, from bonds to commodity futures to a real estate tax shelter.

You're free to change brokers at will, and if you're not happy with your broker, do just that. But be realistic about what to expect from a broker. You can't monopolize his time. You can expect your broker to offer you a reasonable amount of research material about stocks as it comes out, and you can expect him to make periodic recommendations about changes in your portfolio. Beware, however, of the broker who makes too many recommendations. A broker hungry for business, can "churn" an account—lots of trading to produce more commissions.

Finally, a broker—no matter how good—is merely an ally. He (or she) can help you in the market, but there's no substitute for your doing the real work of watching the market and watching the economy. Your broker can advise and offer recommendations on specific stocks. But it's your economic sixth sense that will tell you when to buy and when to sell, and what to buy and what to sell.

And that gets us back to basics—buying cheap and selling dear. Remember that cheap and dear are relative. A stock can be cheap because it's a sleeping beauty that no one has discovered. Or it can be cheap because it's such a dog that no one else wants to buy it. Stocks can be cheap because most investors haven't yet realized what a great time it is to buy stocks. But they can be cheap also because investors realize all too well that to buy now is to dump their money in the sea.

Bringing You up to Date

A little history is in order here, to bring the market up to where it is now.

As the 1980s began, the experts saw it as a great decade for stocks because the average stock was selling at its lowest p/e since just after World War II. Years of inflation-cum-recession had made investors so gun-shy that Wall Street seemed to be littered with nothing but bargains. Assuming the economy got back to something approaching normal, prices of those stocks would go up, and things would be as they were in the early 1950s.

That's pretty heady stuff to think about, because the 1950s saw the start of the grandest bull market in American history —two decades in which the price of most stocks went steadily higher.

No one had bought much stock during the Depression and no one bought much stock during the war. In 1950 the average p/e for 500 stocks that make up the Standard & Poor's 500-stock index was seven. The market value of all listed stocks was less than $100 billion. Then came an economic boom that ran for 30 years and for the first 20 of those 30 years, the rate of inflation was minuscule. There's nothing better for the stock market than a noninflationary boom.

American business earned just $19 billion after taxes in 1945. By 1965 that had climbed to $73 billion—an increase of nearly 300 percent. During those same years, inflations averaged less than 2 percent a year.

That was the "e" side of the equation—earnings shooting up. And the "p" side wasn't doing so bad, either. The index that measures all the stocks listed on the New York Stock Exchange climbed from 8 in 1945 to 50 in 1965—an increase of better than 500 percent. Had you gone into the market in 1945 and done no better than the overall market had done, you'd still have $5 for each $1 you started with. And that was simply capital appreciation. You were also earning $3 in dividends for every $1 in dividends paid in 1945. And since inflation was modest, and most of us were still in low tax brackets, you surrendered very little of that profit. Against that seven p/e of 1950, the p/e of the average S&P stock had climbed to 17 by 1965.

That was the high-water mark. Things began to go to pieces after 1965 as inflation began to overwhelm us.

At first, inflation was seen as no big problem for stocks, because stocks were supposed to be the perfect inflation hedge. Inflation would hurt the bond market because a 3 percent bond would always pay the original holder 3 percent. But companies could increase their earnings and their dividends, and stock prices would keep going higher, at least as fast as the inflation rate. If the stock market was always the best place to be, the conventional wisdom went, during times of inflation it was the only place to be.

The years since 1965 have made hash of that conventional wisdom. The stock market might have been a perfect hedge against a little bit of inflation, but it wasn't much of a hedge against a lot of inflation—and after 1965, we got a lot of inflation.

Not only did inflation send interest rates to a point where Treasury bills became more rewarding than stocks, but each new wave of higher rates produced new competition for stocks —from new products in the commodity markets to six-month savings certificates, to gold and diamonds. And, of course, each new outburst of inflation was followed by tight money from the Federal Reserve, which cast the economy into recession.

There was tight money and a mini-recession in 1966, and the New York Stock Exchange index fell by 23 percent. The Fed eased up and the NYSE index advanced by 56 percent between late 1966 and late 1968.

There was a recession in 1969 and the NYSE index fell by 38 percent. The Fed eased again, and between 1970 and 1973 the NYSE index rose by 74 percent. Then came the killer recession of 1974–75, and the NYSE index fell by 50 percent. We think of 1929 as the blackest year for Wall Street, but what happened in the the mid-seventies was many times worse. Between 1929 and 1932 the total value of all stocks listed on the Big Board fell by $70 billion. Before the market hit bottom late in 1974, the total value of all Big Board stocks fell by $400 billion. The total value of all shares listed on all exchanges fell from $1.2 trillion in 1972 to $675 billion two years later—a loss of $525 billion. That doesn't count the bond market, the commodity market, or the real estate market—all hard-hit. Figure the total damage to all the markets at better than $1 trillion, making it the worst financial catastrophe ever.

After that, most people simply gave up on stocks. Not until the early 1980s did the market value of all listed stocks return to where it had been in 1972. Because of inflation, though, a 1980s dollar was worth about half what a 1972 dollar had been worth. You lost 1972 dollars and got back dollars worth half as much.

The market had its moments, but not many. Mostly we kept our money in savings certificates and money funds, and we dabbled in commodities, precious metals, precious gems, arts and antiques. For many people, home ownership became their only investment.

With few people buying, stocks did become cheap, and by early 1982 the average stock in the S&P 500 index was again selling at a p/e of well under 10. By any reckoning, there were bargains aplenty in the stock market, if only investors could be persuaded to buy.

In 1982, inflation finally cracked under the weight of two recessions in two years. In the summer of 1982, interest rates finally came tumbling down, and first the bond market and then the stock market caught fire, in the hottest rally in history.

Should inflation come roaring back, or if the recovery fails and we tumble into a deep, dark depression, you can write off the stock market. To the extent we have a long period of noninflationary growth, the rally could endure, and become a classic bull market—just made to order for you.

Guidelines for Action

There's an economic season for stocks—and a reason why the stock market is a good leading economic indicator.

Remember the p/e equation—"p" being the stock's price, and "e" being the company's earnings.

Buy at the bottom of a recession, because that's when it's most likely that "e" will go up and "p" along with it.

Sell at the top of a recovery, before "e" goes down and carries "p" with it.

Shop hard to find a sympathetic stockbroker—one who understands what your investment goals are, and how much you have to invest.

If you're new to stocks—or if you don't have time to be a serious investor—stick to mutual funds (and to a family of mutual funds at that, so you can shift to another fund when economic circumstances dictate).

CHAPTER 8

A Stock Market Strategy for All Economic Seasons

Venture near the stock market, and you'll be offered theories, maxims, and old wives' tales by the score. You'll be told the market ebbs and flows in line with women's hemlines, and in line with the changes in the water level of the Great Lakes. There are contrarians, who buy when everyone else is selling, and perpetual bears who've been predicting a market crash ever since the Depression. The position of the planets is said to influence stocks—as is the standing of the New York Yankees in the American League.

All of it is hogwash. As you've learned to shun all that expert advice about the economy, shun all the expert advice about the stock market, and let your economic sixth sense be your guide.

Remember these absolutely basic rules about the stock market, because they're the rules that really count:

1. The stock market is a leading economic indicator, and it will behave as such. It will start to rally when the economy hits bottom, and it will start to slide when the economy is at a peak.

2. Watch the bond market. It will rally as soon as interest rates begin falling, and when there's a sustained rally in the bond market, a rally in the stock market is seldom far behind.

Bond prices fall as interest rates climb. When bond prices fall for any extended period of time, a slump in the stock market is seldom far behind.

3. Today never matters in the stock market—only tomorrow. The market will do well only when investors can assume that tomorrow will bring noninflationary economic growth. It is most reasonable to assume this when the economy is still in the recovery stage. The more uncertainty there is about what tomorrow will bring, the more you think of staying out, or moving out, of stocks.

4. Inflation will always damage the stock market—but never more so than now. As strong as the stock market may look, our memories of the inflation of the 1970s and early 1980s are so acute, that the market will crumble at the first hint that inflation is coming back. It took us a generation, after the 1930s, to stop seeing our economy as Depression-prone. It will take a generation now to stop seeing our economy as inflation-prone.

To put the relationship between actual inflation and the stock market on a historic basis, Standard & Poor's Corporation checked its 500-stock index over a 46-year span. In the 10 of these years when inflation was the worst, the S&P 500 (400 industrial companies, 40 utilities, 40 financial companies, and 20 transportation companies) declined by an average 3½ percent. In the 10 of those years when inflation was the mildest (or when there was no inflation) the index gained an average 14.2 percent.

That's what actual inflation can do to the market. What you have to worry about now is perceived inflation—concern that inflation is on the way back. Of all the things that the market is vulnerable to, it is most vulnerable to that.

Take 5 percent inflation in the wholesale price index as a benchmark. As long as wholesale prices are moving up at an annual rate of 5 percent or less, the stock market can advance. If the rate of wholesale inflation runs above 5 percent for three consecutive months, expect the market to stall. If the rate of inflation accelerates beyond 5 percent for three consecutive months (6 percent one month, 7 percent the next, 8 percent the next) expect the market to retreat. A pattern like that would so ignite inflationary expectations that most investors would abandon stocks for cash in a trice. It would certainly set off alarm bells at the Federal Reserve.

Watch the money supply. Too much money, as you recall, can light those inflationary fires, and that fear alone can hit the stock market. A secondary fear among investors is that if the Federal Reserve gets sloppy or silly or whatever and allows the money supply to grow too rapidly, it will compensate for that by pushing interest rates up, and interest rates can do in the stock market.

Linking Stocks and the Economy

Recall how the stock market fits into the economic cycle—hitting bottom, on average, about six months before the start of a recovery, and peaking, on average, about a year before we fall into recession. Each turn of the cycle is a little different. In 1953–54 the market hit bottom 2½ months into a recession that lasted 10 months. In 1960–61 it hit bottom seven months into a recession that lasted 10 months.

The 1981–82 recession lasted 18 months and it seemed as though it would never end. But the bond market began to rally early in the summer of 1982, the stock market rally began in mid-August, and the economic recovery came at the end of the year. It was a long, nasty recession, but the stock market was a leading indicator, as always—rallying five months before the start of the recovery, which is pretty close to average for the postwar years.

That's not so surprising since neither the market nor the economy does well when inflation and interest rates are high, and both do well when inflation and interest rates are coming down. In 1982, by watching the turn in the bond market, you could see the turn in the stock market coming. By watching the turn in the stock market, you could see the turn in the economy coming.

Ideally, you want to buy into the stock market at the bottom, ride the market up to the peak, and move your money elsewhere before the inevitable slide consumes it.

You don't have to buy exactly at the bottom and sell exactly at the top: Close is good enough. There's a study by analyst Mallory Lennox of E. F. Hutton & Company showing that if an investor had bought all the issues in the S&P 500-stock index six months before a market bottom and held on for a year, he would have been rewarded with a 7 percent gain over that period. If the same investor bought in three months before the bottom and held on for a year, the gain would have been 12 percent. Buying in precisely at the market bottom and holding on for a year would have produced a 27 percent gain. Buying in three months after the bottom, and holding on for a year, the gain would be 24 percent. The study was done before the 1982 rally when gains along the way were even bigger.

If it's an authentic rally, the market will score a dramatic gain, then lose up to one-third of the gain, then advance to a new high. It will keep advancing, but with occasional setbacks along the way. Unless your economic sixth sense tells you the economy is about to turn hostile, each setback in the market should be followed by a fresh advance. You can score gains by buying in at almost any point during this advancing stage.

When the market peaks, it won't collapse overnight. There will be plenty of warnings—rising interest rates, rising inflation. The market will peak, and then sort of hang there for a while—not going higher, but not slipping much lower, either. That's the time to begin bailing out, because soon the market will begin to slide. All you need do, to buy in time and to sell in time, is to keep your economic sixth sense firmly fixed on the three months immediately ahead.

If it's an authentic bull market, it will be around for a while. Standard & Poor's counts nine bull stock markets between the start of 1949 and the end of 1980. The average bull market lasted 30 months, and the S&P 500-stock index gained 66 percent during that period. The shortest bull market (1960–61) lasted 14 months, and the S&P gained 34 percent. The longest bull market (1962–66) lasted 43 months, and the S&P gained 70 percent. If the rally is for real, you'll have time to make your moves, because barring a faster-than-expected return of inflation, the rally that began in August 1982 should still be running well into 1985, and maybe beyond that. And when the rally finally begins to poop out, you'll have plenty of warning.

Always listen to what the experts have to say about the outlook for the economy, interest rates, and the stock market. Then be prepared to do the opposite. The contrarians—those who are the most bullish when everyone else is bearish, and vice versa—have a point. Market bottoms and market tops both tend to come when least expected.

When recession strikes, stockbrokers, with lots of stocks to sell and few customers, will start talking about recovery months too early. Whoever is in the White House will have assured us there would be no recession—and will then spot a recovery on the horizon months before it's visible to anyone else. We were four months into recession in 1981 before President Reagan allowed as how we might be in a "light" recession. Hardly had he said that, when his aides began forecasting imminent recovery.

The closer we get to the bottom of a recession, the louder will be the cries of the gloomers-and-doomers that this is it: the recession without a bottom, the stock market that will fall forever. The market will take some sickening plunges just before it begins to turn around—which is what happened in the summer of 1982. The closer we are to a market peak, the more you'll hear rosy forecasts about the outlook for the economy and the market.

What to Watch For

Recall the sequence in which the leading indicators lead—going up when the economy is about to pop out of recession, and going down when it's about to fall into a recession. Sustained changes in the rate of growth in the money supply, and sustained changes in all the indicators relating to construction, give you your first clues. When the construction indicators—building permits, home sales, housing starts, and construction contracts—start to turn higher, a stock market recovery isn't far off, and a recovery in the bond market has probably already begun. When the construction indicators turn down, the bond market will probably turn down with them, and the stock market will be within a few months of a peak.

Take a 5 percent growth rate in the money supply as your benchmark, because the economy, interest rates, the inflation rate, and the market will all tend to do best when the Federal Reserve can keep the money supply in that area for an extended time.

An extended period of slower money growth will threaten an economic slump. Further, in the short run, at least, it will threaten higher interest rates as demand for money bumps against a dwindling supply. An extended period of faster money growth will initially pull interest rates lower (a greater supply to handle the demand), but it will threaten inflation and higher rates ahead, and it will almost certainly cause the Federal Reserve to tighten money.

Watch all interest rates, but pay particular attention to two of them:

1. The federal funds rate. Banks with extra money on hand will lend it for short periods to banks that are short of money. This trading of money is done in the federal funds market, and the rate at which this money trades is the federal funds rate. If the funds rate begins to move higher, it implies a growing shortage of money among banks, and that implies tightening moves by the Federal Reserve, even if they aren't visible to the naked eye. A falling federal funds rate implies a growing supply of money among banks, and that implies easing moves by the Federal Reserve. The Fed controls the federal funds rate with great precision, and it is always read on Wall Street as a clue to what the Fed is up to.

2. The broker loan rate. This is the rate banks charge when they loan money to stockbrokers. A change in the broker loan rate will often precede a change in other bank rates, and it's important for that reason. Beyond that, the higher the broker loan rate, the more it will cost brokers to borrow, and the more they'll charge customers who buy stocks on margin. The more it costs to borrow to speculate in stocks, the less attractive it becomes. The reverse is true when the broker loan rate falls.

The Federal Reserve stands ready at all times to loan short-term money on an emergency basis to banks that run short. The rate banks pay to borrow this money is the discount rate. Whenever the Fed changes the discount rate, it's always a clue to Fed intentions. When the discount rate goes up, it's a warning from the Fed to the economy to slow down. When it comes down, it's a signal that the Fed is willing to tolerate more vigor in the economy.

When the Fed changes its discount rate more than once, regard it as a clear signal. If it goes up at least twice, move away from stocks. If it goes down at least twice, prepare to move into the market. The more times the discount rate is raised or lowered, the more emphatic a signal the Fed is sending to the financial markets.

Never forget that you're a leading economic indicator—constantly picking up and sifting through the clues about the economic future. You're not trying to forecast the economy long-term, which is a mug's game, anyway. You're just trying to figure out what the next three months will bring. That's how you build your view of the future—a few months' worth at a time. When you're sure we're in a recovery, assume it will last for a minimum of two years, and act accordingly. If you're sure we're in a recession, assume it will last for about a year, and act accordingly. If the economy doesn't run true to form, there will be sufficient warning of that in all the economic signs you watch, and you'll be able to change your investment plans accordingly.

Once again, the immediate danger to the economy (and to the investment markets) is a resurgence of inflation which would panic investors and oblige the Federal Reserve to counter with tight money. Creating enough new money to finance those record federal budget deficits, without creating so much new money that inflation threatens, may be impossible. Even as I write this, growth in the money supply has been rapid enough for long enough to make one wonder about the dangers of rekindled inflation.

The concern, in fact, is twofold: renewed inflation, which would force the Federal Reserve to tighten money, which would cast us back into a still worse economic slump than the recession of 1981–82.

It may happen, but it may not. If it happens, it won't happen overnight and it won't happen without warning.

In watching the economy, at all times be dubious. The economy abounds in false signals that, in the long run, signify nothing—which is why you don't leap into the market the instant that interest rates break, and why you never respond to a single economic indicator, or what all the indicators do in a single month. Again, it is always the weight of evidence you're looking for: not one domino falling, but one domino after another falling.

The Market as Indicator

Watch the stock market itself, because it's always sending out clues about what it intends to do next.

The market averages have their own story to tell. Once we're in a recession, a succession of very steep declines in the Dow-Jones 30 industrials, the S&P 500, and the New York Stock Exchange index, frequently means the market is approaching a bottom. After a recovery has been running for quite a while, a series of sharp advances in these indexes can signal trouble. It could mean that smart money is moving in for one final fling before the top blows off. If you buy then, you're the greater fool that shrewd investors are counting on to take them out of the market.

Watch the odd-lotters—those who buy stocks in less than 100-share lots. Do the opposite of what the odd-lotters are doing, even if you're an odd-lotter yourself: Buy when they're selling and sell when they're buying.

It's a Wall Street truism that the behavior of the small investor is always a contrary indicator of the market's future direction—the small investor being regarded as always wrong. And that often is the case. Unsophisticated investors will watch cautiously as the market advances, and finally drawn in by all the contagious excitement, they'll buy—just as the market hits its peak and begins to slide. The small investors then hang on, hoping their stocks will recover. Finally, they'll give up and sell—just when the market hits bottom, and a rally is ahead. (Small investors were consistent sellers through at least the early stages of the 1982 rally.) *Barron's* magazine publishes figures on odd-lot trading, and your broker can keep you posted.

Watch the ratio of stocks advancing against stocks declining, and of stocks hitting new highs for the year against stocks hitting new lows. Both offer clues to the market. A growing bulge between advancing and declining stocks and between new highs and new lows, is a signal of strength in the market. A narrowing of the gap between advancing and declining stocks and new highs and new lows is often a sign the market is peaking—running out of steam, and poised for a slump.

Watch the stocks that are hitting new highs. Early in a rally, it will be the old, familiar names—the blue chips and the solid growth stocks. Late in a rally, the names will be less familiar. The old favorites have had their fling, and now the traders on Wall Street are looking for fresh talent. The more frenzied this search for fresh leaders for the rally, the more certain it is that the rally has just about run its course. Read the published lists of most active stocks each day. Begin to worry if day after day more than half the stocks on that list are unfamiliar to you.

Which Stocks to Buy, When

There's a season for almost every stock in the market—some when the market is strong, and some when it's weak.

There are stocks that are tied closely to interest rates. They'll tend to rally at the first sign of lower rates, and they'll slump at the first sign of higher rates. Into this class fall banks, savings and loan associations, insurance companies, makers of building materials, builders, and—because they're the biggest borrowers around—the utilities.

There are stocks that tend to be relatively immune to the economic cycle. They may not show all that much vigor in market rallies, but neither will they fall as far when the market is sinking. Because their earnings tend to hold up through bad times, they frequently command fairly high p/e's. We eat in good times and bad, so the food processors fall into this category. We get sick in good times and bad, so companies related to health care (drugs, hospital supplies) also fall into this category. Cosmetics are one of the last things we cut back on when times get hard. Brewers usually do well in recessions, because we switch from more expensive beverages to beer.

Then there are the cyclicals. These are stocks that ride the economic cycle—badly depressed when the economy is depressed, and quick to revive as the economy revives. They will tend to rise in the early stages of market rallies and fall as the market first begins to falter. That makes them most interesting at the bottom of a recession—which is when you buy—and least interesting at the top of a recovery—which is when you sell. The cyclicals include capital goods (machinery, computers, etc.), consumer goods (furniture, appliances, etc.), automobiles, steel and other metals, farm equipment, oil and other energy companies, airlines, truckers, railroads, and retail stores.

Then there are the superstars—stocks that because of uniqueness or superiority in some key way have attracted the special attention of the big institutions that buy in bulk. IBM was the superstar of superstars for years, and it was a longtime Wall Street adage that nothing good ever happened to anyone who sold IBM. There isn't the growth in big computers there was a generation ago, and IBM has more rivals in more parts of its business. Yet it still has a special place in the hearts of big investors. Eastman Kodak has had a few rough years, but still is regarded as a success in just about all that it tries.

Some stocks have had their superstar status taken away. Citicorp, the giant bank holding company, was a superstar a decade ago, when it was the supreme innovator among banks. Other banks have closed the gap, and Citicorp's earnings have had their ups and downs. Earnings problems knocked Sears Roebuck, Xerox, Polaroid, and many others off the list. The world oil glut, and problems in the non-oil part of its business, knocked Exxon off the list. The oil glut has done the same to nearly all energy companies.

The trouble with superstars is that, in Wall Street terms, they're almost always "fully priced." In other words, they go at high p/e's.

Start with the "500"

If you're a novice in the market, confine yourself to the 500 stocks that make up the S&P 500. They're the stocks with the established track records, and the ones the Wall Street analysts cover most closely. Among the 500 is every kind of stock you can think of. These stocks seldom offer spectacular gains —unless the market itself is going through a spectacular gain. Neither are they likely to post spectacular losses—unless the market is going through a spectacular slump. When that happens to the market, you're not supposed to be around.

With 500 stocks to think about, you have your work cut out for you. You have still more work to do as you gain experience and begin reaching out beyond the 500.

Reach Out to the World

Everything that happens in the world is grist for your mill. Every newspaper or magazine article about a company or an industry will contain clues about stocks to avoid and stocks to buy. You're always on the lookout for turnaround situations —a company or a whole industry, which has had a run of bad luck, but which now seems on the verge of turning around.

The auto industry clearly improved its fortunes in 1982 by getting the United Autoworkers to accept wage-and-benefit concessions, which reduced costs and which should enhance industry profits.

You're always buying the future, and the darker the present is for some company, the brighter its future could be, under the right circumstances. As things got better for Chrysler in 1982, its stock exploded in the market—from $3 to $29 a share. That Chrysler was still alive was reason for shrewd investors to buy its stock as a speculation. A more-telling clue came in August of 1982 when President Reagan invited Chrysler Chairman Lee Iacocca to be at his side as he pushed for congressional passage of the tax hike bill. Presidents don't go out of their way to tie themselves to losers. White House sages had obviously decided that Chrysler had turned around—and that it was politically safe to have the President appear with Iacocca.

You're not necessarily buying, so you can hold on until the company does turn around (which it may not do, anyway). You want to ride along as speculators run the price up in hopes that the company will turn around.

Be alert to all that's happening in the world that might make a difference to some company or some industry. What are the economic trends that people are talking about? The population trends? What new products are appearing? Who has the hot new game, or the latest fad item?

By reading and listening, you'd know we're going through a modest baby boom in the country. The percentage of the population under five years of age shrank between 1970 and 1980. It's expected to increase by 20 percent between 1980 and 1990 (all of which I learned from a newsletter that came my way).

That should benefit companies that make products for the young—from manufacturers of toys and children's clothing, to makers of cribs and carriages and the other things that infants use, to makers of baby food and breakfast cereals. (Sure enough, another item landed on my desk telling me that makers of juvenile furniture had enjoyed their best year on record in 1981, recession or not.) You'd also expect it to benefit an Eastman Kodak and a Polaroid, as more doting parents take pictures of the kids.

The elderly—sixty-five and over—will increase in number faster than the general population. Between Social Security and pension plans, the elderly are better heeled than ever before (a fact I learned from reading a report from a bank). That should help makers of drugs and hospital supplies, hospital management companies, and providers of other products and services to the elderly.

A report from an investment advisory service told me we spent $287 billion on health care in 1981—15 percent more than in 1980. More than 11 cents of every dollar spent in our economy now goes into making and keeping us well. And health care is one area in which prices are going up as fast as ever (which I know from reading the monthly report on consumer prices). That obviously should benefit everyone connected with health care.

Narrowing the Field

At one time or another, I've read nearly all the high-priced tip-sheets sold to investors, and I can't say I've ever found any of them to be consistently useful. Your broker will have plenty of material for you to read, and magazines like *Forbes* and *Barron's*, which are mostly for investors, will have more. Standard & Poor's has an array of investment advisory material, including a weekly stock market letter, called the *Outlook*. It tends to be sound and conservative, rather than brilliant and daring, but it's worth looking at.

For every stock you buy, keep tabs on a dozen companies —stories clipped from magazines, financial reports found in the back of *The Wall Street Journal*, and analysts' reports from your broker. When a company really catches your eye, check out its background in the financial reports from Standard & Poor's. Get an annual report and study it. You're always on the lookout—honing your economic sixth sense—learning how to study companies and select stocks.

You want companies that have maintained a reasonable level of growth, in good times and bad. Except in the depths of recession, the company should have increased sales by 10 to 15 percent a year, and, even in recession, there should be no precipitous slide in sales. The company must be able to translate sales into profits. Ideally, the company should be increasing its pretax profits by at least 10 percent a year, on average. It might stumble a bit during a recession, but it should recover quickly. And the company should consistently be able to outperform other companies in its industry.

The company must be financially sound. It should have no more than 20 percent of its capital in the form of debt. A debt level higher than that means money that would otherwise be plowed into future growth must go to pay off debt. The company should have at least $2 of current assets for each $1 of current liabilities—showing that it's keeping itself financially sound. You want a company with at least a BBB credit rating (from Standard & Poor's) and Baa (from Moody's).

You want a company as immune as possible to foreign competition. You want its products to be regarded as superior to those of its competitors. Unless you're buying for income, you want a company that pays a modest dividend—or no dividends at all—and that plows its money back into growth. You want that promise of future growth, because it's that growth someone will buy from you for more than you paid for the shares.

The kicker, of course, is that you want the stock for the lowest possible p/e—under 10 if possible. The higher the p/e, other things being equal, the more likely it is the stock has already gained as much as it's likely to gain near-term.

Don't automatically assume that others have discovered a stock before you have. You start with the S&P 500 stocks because those are the ones the analysts cover—and they're about the only stocks that analysts cover. For every stock that the institutions buy, there are a dozen stocks that institutions can't touch, because there aren't enough shares out, or because the company just isn't big enough.

It's every investor's dream to find the IBM of the future—the small, fledgling, superstar company that will someday grow to great size. And those kinds of companies still exist. The late 1970s and early 1980s were hardly the best of times for American business. Yet between 1977 and 1981, Apple Computer increased its sales by 43,000 percent and its profits went from $42,000 to $40 million.

It's not impossible you'll find such stocks. There are always new companies first selling stock. Standard & Poor's says that while its 500-stock index fell by 2½ percent in the first eight months of 1982, its index of new issues was up 10 percent, and from March through August, the gain in those new issues was 40 percent.

Understand, though, that the odds are against you. You can't buy everything that comes to market, and you certainly don't have the time to research each new issue for its potential, which can change overnight. (Fledgling energy issues were all the rage until we developed an oil glut, at which point most new energy stocks went into the tank.) Apple was already off and running before the average person—before the average Wall Street analyst, for that matter—even knew there was such a thing as a microcomputer. For every Apple, a dozen companies in the microcomputer field have already folded.

Watch and listen, and you may get lucky. The longer you work it, the more your economic sixth sense is likely to pick up the spore of a promising young company—a potential superstar of tomorrow.

Structuring Your Portfolio

The more stocks you own, up to a point, the better off you are. With diversification, you're protected against the possibility that a drop in a single stock will wipe out your capital, and you have more chances to pick a winner. Yet, if you own too many stocks, you can't own enough of any one of them to make a real killing if it goes up. If you can't buy at least 25 shares in at least four different stocks, you're better off in a mutual fund. If you hold more than 10 stocks, you're spread too thin. You'll have trouble keeping track of all you own—and you won't own enough of any of them to really pull off a nice gain.

Beware of stocks in which the institutions hold big positions. Heavy institutional buying can pull a stock's price up—but heavy selling can hammer it down in a hurry. There's a herd mentality among those who manage money for institutions (another sure sign of "expertitis"). When one sells, all sell. Some analysts suggest avoiding any stock in which mutual funds hold more than 10 percent of the outstanding shares. That may be too confining for you, but avoid any stock in which the funds hold more than 25 percent.

You aren't investing in any stock for life—a stock to be bought now and kept until you're old and gray, and then passed along to the grandchildren. Times change—very quickly these days—and today's winner may be a stock that tomorrow you wouldn't touch. As in any other market, get your profit (or swallow your loss) and get out.

When you buy, always have in mind a price at which you'll

sell—that price representing a reasonable return on your money. A 20 percent return over a year (taxed at capital gains rates) would be excellent. Set a floor on how much you're willing to lose. If the price of the stock should drop 10 percent, sell. You can place a "stop-loss" order with your broker. The stock will then be automatically sold for you when the price has fallen to the designated level. You can similarly place a sell order, so the stock is automatically sold when you've earned from it what you hoped to.

Never fall in love with a stock so that you ignore its faults and see only its virtues. These are cold-and-hard business decisions. A company may be the sole support of your favorite charity, or it may make a product you've used all your life. Just pay attention to what the stock is doing in the market. If it's making money for you, or if it shows promise of making money for you, keep it. If it doesn't, sell it.

You can buy stock with as little as 50 percent of the purchase price—buying on margin—and borrowing the rest from your broker. The 50 percent rule is set by the Federal Reserve, and it's in contrast with the twenties when 10 percent cash was more common. It was that pyramid of debt, as much as anything else, that dragged down the market, and hurt so many investors, during the Crash.

It's still a chancy business. You're paying a comparatively high rate of interest to borrow that money. Should the price of the stock fall, the broker will demand that you put up more cash to make up the loss—meeting a margin call. You're doubling your purchasing power, which is good, but you're cutting your potential for profit, with the interest on the borrowed money, and you may have to toss away more of your capital after a falling stock, which is bad.

The final rule is not to be so enamored of the stock market that you ignore your economic sixth sense when it tells you to get out. It's a heady business, trading stocks, and there's always that temptation to hang around just a little longer, to fatten your profits. You don't have to get out exactly at the market's peak; it will be a while before the market begins to slide. But you do want to come as close to spotting that peak as you can, and you want to be out of the market within three months after the peak. By that time, inflation is going strong, interest rates are climbing, and you can jump back into cash —diving back into your hole—with your profits from the stock market, and with a nice return on your cash to comfort you until the indicators again tell you it's time to buy stocks.

You've lived through one-half of the market cycle—the upswing. You don't want to be around to watch the other half—when the market turns down, sweeping away all those not wise enough to be gone in time.

Guidelines for Action

Shun all maxims and folk myths about the stock market and stick to the basic rules.

To say it again, buy stocks when the economy is emerging from recession, because that's when the stock market is most likely to rally. Think about selling when the recovery is in fullest flower, because a decline in the market is inevitably ahead.

Prolonged periods of rapid growth in the money supply (5 percent and more) and of rapid growth in wholesale prices (also 5 percent and more) are always dangerous for the stock market. Nowadays, this is especially true, given our inflationary history.

At first, stick to the standbys—the 500 stocks on the Standard & Poor's list. You won't win big—but you won't lose big.

When you get beyond that—read and listen to everything in seeking out stocks that will provide the choicest gains.

CHAPTER 9

Options and Futures: Daring Money Tactics with a Conservative Twist

The way the economy looks today, you must think about stocks and bonds, because that's where the gains are, and capital gains are what you're after.

You might buy stocks or bonds, or you might play both markets—as fast and as furiously as you like—without owning a share of stock or a single bond. Once you know how, you may do better if you don't own stocks or bonds than if you do.

You'd use the new markets in financial options and financial futures, in which you play stocks and bonds at a distance—and, if you're fortunate—at a profit.

Both markets give you a chance at lush profits on a modest cash investment. Both let you bet on rising or falling stock or bond prices, with a chance to profit no matter which way the markets go. Both markets can shield you against loss on stocks and bonds you own. In options, you know the instant you buy in, the most you can lose on any trade—and you never have as much at risk as if you bought the stocks or bonds outright.

The pace is frantic, and both markets are so new even the professionals don't know all the wrinkles. It's not for novices: You move to this stage after you've had firing-line experience in stocks and bonds. But neither are options or futures as mysterious as they appear. Both are useful weapons as you build and protect your capital in an uncertain world.

Both markets are spewing out new variants faster than you can count them. To bring you up to date, there are stock options, which date back to 1973, and interest rate futures, which date back to 1975. Stock-index futures came along in 1982, followed by options on interest rate futures and options on interest rates. Then came options on stock-index futures, and then stock-index options. There could be more by the time you read this—the imaginations of those in the markets knowing no bounds.

It all sounds baffling, but note: For all the variants, there are, at the heart of it, just options and futures. We'll ease our way into both markets, learn some basic strategies for options and futures, and then we'll get to their myriad offspring.

Starting with Options

The original option was a stock option, so we'll start there. You're betting on the stock market when you buy a stock option, but at one remove. You're not buying or selling stock: You're buying the right to buy or sell stock at a set price, if you want to.

There are two kinds of options—puts and calls.

CALL OPTION. A contract allowing you to buy 100 shares of a given stock at an agreed-upon price, within a nine-month period, which is the life of the option. On the other side of the contract is the seller of the option who must *sell you* the 100 shares of that stock at the agreed-upon price during the nine-month period.

You pay a price for this option, which is called the premium.

You don't have to exercise the option: You don't have to buy those shares at the agreed-upon price. If you do exercise, the contract requires the seller of the option to sell you the shares at that price.

You'd exercise the option if the price of the stock went up in the market. The option, for example, is for 100 shares of Universal Overshoe at $10 a share. If you choose to exercise the option, the person who sold it to you must sell you 100 shares of Universal Overshoe at $10 a share at any time during the nine-month life of the option, from Day 1 to Day 270.

If the price of Universal Overshoe shares went to $20 a share in the stock market, you would exercise the option to buy the stock at $10 a share. You have paid $1,000 (100 shares times $10 a share) for stock which could be sold immediately in the market for $2,000 (100 shares times the market price of $20). If the stock did not move up in the market, you wouldn't exercise the option. At the end of nine months (the life of the option), it would expire, and you would be out the premium you paid for the option. But the premium would have cost you less than 10 percent of what you would have paid to buy 100 shares of Universal Overshoe in the market. If you had bought the stock outright and the price didn't go up, you'd be out a lot more than you paid for the option.

PUT OPTION. The reverse of a call option since it is a contract that requires the person on the other side (the seller of the put option) to *buy from you* 100 shares of a given stock at an agreed-upon price, within a nine-month period.

As with a call, the price of the put option is the premium, and again, you don't have to exercise the option if you don't want to. If you do want to exercise it, the seller of the put option must buy the stock from you at the contract price.

You'd exercise the option if the price of the stock fell in the market. Again the stock is Universal Overshoe, but the option is for 100 shares of Universal Overshoe at $20 a share. Universal Overshoe stock falls to $10 a share in the market. You could buy the shares in the market for $1,000 (100 shares times $10). The seller of the put option must buy them from you for $2,000 (100 shares times the option price of $20).

If the price of Universal Overshoe stock goes up in the market, you wouldn't exercise the option because the most you can get from the seller of the option is $20 a share. Because you don't exercise the option, the premium you paid for it is simply lost. But you didn't pay all that much for the premium, and you might have made a very handsome profit on that small investment had the price of Universal Overshoe stock gone the other way.

In both of these examples, I have you exercising the option or allowing it to go to the end of its nine-month life and then expire. In most cases you would do neither. Options are traded just as stocks are traded. You can buy an option at any point during its nine-month life. You could sell it to someone else just as soon as you started making a profit—or as soon as you lost as much money as you cared to.

There are plenty of options to choose from—with options on some 400 stocks traded on the Chicago Board Options Exchange (an offspring of the Chicago Board of Trade), and the American, Philadelphia, and Pacific stock exchanges.

That's options in a nutshell—starting with stock options. If you can trade options on one stock, you can trade them on many stocks. And if you can trade options on stocks, you can trade options on anything that is traded: bonds, gold, bubblegum cards, anything.

And a Look at Futures

Trading in futures (more precisely, in contracts for future delivery) is far older, and the Chicago Board of Trade is approaching its 150th birthday.

There are the traditional futures contracts in corn, wheat, copper, sugar—traded on commodity exchanges around the country, of which the Board of Trade is the biggest. What's new in the market is that instead of trading only physical commodities—things you can touch and pick up—the exchanges now also trade more abstract commodities: interest rates, the value of a group of stocks. But if the nature of the commodity is different, the way it trades isn't.

When you enter into a futures contract—no matter what the commodity—you contract to buy (if you're on the long side) or sell (if you're on the short side) a set quantity of that commodity at an agreed-upon price at the end of a set period of time.

Exchanges set the basic terms of each contract. It's always for 18 months with a new 18-month contract started every month or two. There's always a fixed quantity of the commodity in a contract: always 5,000 bushels of corn, always 25,000 pounds of copper. The one variable is the price of the contract. Once the contract is created—once the clock starts ticking on those 18 months—the price of the contract begins to fluctuate on the exchange floor, according to what people think 5,000 bushels of corn or 25,000 pounds of copper will be worth in 18 months.

The price quote, which you'll find in the newspapers, is for one unit of the commodity—one bushel of corn, one pound of copper. You multiply the price by the number of units in the contract—5,000 bushels corn, 25,000 pounds copper—to get the price at which your contract is trading on a given day. You seldom put up more than 10 percent of the contract price in cash, giving you the same sort of leverage in futures as the low price of an option gives you in the options market.

You may hold the contract for the full 18 months, but you don't want to own 5,000 bushels of corn or 25,000 pounds of copper: You want to make a profit. As with an option, you'd sell once the price of the contract went up enough to give you a profit—or fell enough to cost you as much as you cared to lose.

As interest rates began heating up, the exchanges came up with "financial futures," starting with contracts in which you bet on interest rates by betting on the future price of Ginnie Mae passthroughs, Treasury bills, and Treasury bonds. When those were a hit, the exchanges, early in 1982, came up with the stock-index future. Instead of betting on the future price of corn, or copper, or a Treasury bond, you bet on the future level of a stock index: the Value Line composite index of 1,700 stocks (from the investment advisory service of the same name) at the Kansas City Board of Trade, the Standard & Poor's 500 at the Chicago Mercantile Exchange, and an index of 1,500 New York Stock Exchange stocks at the New York Futures Exchange (a unit of the Big Board).

If the stock index moves as you hope it will (if the stocks that make up the index move as you hope they will), you make a profit. If they don't you lose. As with any other commodity, the contract price is steep—$500 times the latest quote for the index ($500 times 134, or $67,000 for the S&P 500 on one recent day). But as with any commodity, you seldom put up more than 10 percent in cash.

The Newest Markets

Late in 1982 the walls simply came tumbling down—a torrent of new products based on options and futures.

First, the commodity exchanges began offering not merely futures but options on futures. Instead of buying a futures contract (on so many pounds of sugar, or so many Treasury bonds, or so many slices of a stock index), you could buy an option to buy the contract, if you wanted to, at an agreed-upon price, during the nine-month life of the option.

With the commodity exchanges offering not only stock-index futures but also options on stock-index futures, the options markets—the Chicago Board Options Exchange and the American Stock Exchange—quickly countered with options on stock indexes. Instead of an option on a single stock it's an option on the performance of many stocks—100 on the CBOE, 20 on the Amex. Since there's no single stock to buy if you exercise, everything is settled up in cash.

There seems to be no end to it—zillions of new instruments, each with its own risks and rewards; each with its own appeal to investors; each with its own complexities. But again note: All still are just variants of those prolific progenitors, options and futures.

The two markets do differ in some very important ways. In options, you have only the option of taking possession of something; in futures, you contract to take possession. In options you can't lose more than your original investment—the cost of the premium. In futures, as you'll see, you can lose lots more than your investment. There are tax differences between the markets. You never stay long enough in either market to pay taxes at the capital gains rate. Your gains in options are taxed as ordinary income (at rates up to 50 percent). Your gains in trading futures are taxed at a special rate (where the maximum bite is 32 percent).

Digging into Options

Newcomers to options are taught the real estate analogy. You offer me an acre of land for $10,000. I want to think it over, so for $1,000 you sell me an option that lets me buy the land at any time in the next 30 days for $10,000. If they strike oil on the land and its value goes to $1 million, you still must sell me the acre for $10,000 during the next 30 days. If I decide to buy, it's mine for $10,000. If I don't buy, I'm out $1,000—but that's only one-tenth of what I'd have paid had I bought the land and then decided I didn't want it.

The life of an option (stock or otherwise) is always nine months, with a new option, running for nine months, created every three months. There's always an array of different exercise prices for each option (again, stock or otherwise). And there are always markets in both calls (an option to buy) and puts (an option to sell).

By looking at the stock tables, you can see the price of Exxon shares on the New York Stock Exchange. By looking at the option tables, you can see quotes for all the different Exxon options available. You can buy or sell an option as quickly as you can a stock—through your broker, paying a commission just as on a stock.

Take a day in June of 1982. Exxon shares closed at 27⅞ ($27.87) each on the New York Stock Exchange. On this day, the Chicago Board Options Exchange offered 18 different Exxon options: call options to buy Exxon at $25 a share, expiring in July, October, and January; call options to buy Exxon at $30 a share, also expiring in July, October, and January; and call options to buy Exxon at $35 a share, also expiring in July, October, and January.

There were comparable put options, to sell Exxon at $25, at $30, and at $35 a share—in every case with July, October, and January expiration dates. And there was a different price quote for every one of those 18 Exxon options.

For $25 you could buy the July 30 Exxon call option—

allowing you to buy, if you chose, 100 shares of Exxon at $30 a share at any time between now (mid-June) and late July. No matter how high Exxon shares go on the NYSE, the seller of your option must—if you ask—sell you 100 Exxon shares at $30 each, at any time from this instant until the contract expires in late July.

The newspaper lists the price of the option at 25 cents. That's the per share price. Since an option is always for 100 shares, that 25-cents-a-share comes to $25 for the option. That, and a modest commission, is all you pay to buy the option. For $25, you're betting on what 100 Exxon shares will do in the market—shares which, if you bought them outright, would have cost $2,787.

The price of the option is cheap because it's near expiration, and while the exercise price is $30 a share, Exxon shares sell for $27.87 each. Unless Exxon shares go above $30 in the few weeks left before the option expires, there'd be no point in exercising the option, because you'd lose $2.13 per share. In the jargon of the market, the option is out of the money.

But you have other choices. For $275 ($2.75 times 100) you could buy the January 30 Exxon put option. That requires the seller of the option to buy—should you demand it—100 Exxon shares from you at $30 a share, at any time between this moment and late January of the following year. The price is higher, because this option is very close to being in the money. You could buy Exxon shares at $27.87 and the person on the other side of your contract must buy them from you at $30 each.

The economics still aren't exactly right. You paid $275 for the option, and you'd pay $2,787 to buy the shares, plus a little more in commission—say $3,100 in all. And you'd get only $3,000 for those shares if you exercised the option. Still, it's getting close to the breakeven point; this is June and a lot can happen between June and next January.

Or for $337 ($3.37 times 100) you could buy the July 25 Exxon call option. By exercising that option, you could buy 100 Exxon shares at $25 each. This price is the highest of all because Exxon shares are several dollars above $25 in the market—right at the point where exercising the option begins to make financial sense. This option is very much in the money.

There's a different price for each of those 18 Exxon options—each based on the likelihood that Exxon shares will move (or not move) to a given price level by the time the option runs out.

Four Strategies for Options

Say that I truly believe that the price of oil is about to shoot up and that Exxon shares will go higher on the news. I could buy 100 shares of Exxon at $27.87 each, or $2,787, plus a broker's commission of $100. I would have put my money where my mouth is to the tune of $2,887, including commission. Should Exxon stock reach $35, I might be tempted to sell out. I'd get $3,500 for my 100 shares, less a broker's commission of $100. I spent $2,887 and got back $3,400—a profit of $513 after all commissions.

But my $2,887 was tied up for that period, and it couldn't be used in some other fashion. Also, my Exxon shares could have climbed just a few cents a share, or they could have fallen. Instead of a $513 profit, I might have made a $5.13 profit—or I might have lost $513.

Or I could have used the options market. Look at four basic options strategies, starting with:

STRATEGY 1. I'm bullish on Exxon, but instead of buying Exxon shares outright, I buy the Exxon July 30 call option for $25, plus a $5 commission. I have $30 at risk, rather than $2,887. Say that Exxon does hit $35 a share by the end of July. For $25 plus $5, I've bought a contract obliging you to sell me 100 Exxon shares at $30 a share at any time before the contract expires in late July. When the market price of Exxon hits $35, I exercise the option. I give you a check for $3,000 (100 times $30) and you give me 100 Exxon shares. Before the ink is dry on that check, my broker sells the Exxon shares for $3,500. He takes a $100 commission, and gives me $3,400. I paid $3,000 for the shares and $25 for the option, plus commissions. And I have a $370 profit on a cash investment of $30 (the cost of the option plus commission). The money I saved by not buying the Exxon shares outright has been at work for me in other profitable ways.

Even if Exxon shares hadn't gone to $35, I still would have made a modest profit once the price got over $32. Anything below $32 and it wouldn't pay to exercise the option, and I'd be out $30 (as I would be in real life, as opposed to the world of hypothetical examples. Exxon shares closed July, 1982 at $26). But that $30 would be the extent of it—the most I could lose on the transaction. As a winner, I could get back five times my $30, 100 times my $30—the sky's the limit. From the day I bought the option, I knew I couldn't lose more than $30.

A put option is the mirror of a call option. Instead of buying an option in hopes that prices will go up, you buy in anticipation that prices will go down. And that brings us to:

STRATEGY 2. On this same day in June, I buy an Exxon 25 put option expiring in October, for just $25. That, again, is 25 cents for each of the 100 shares in the option, plus a commission. The seller must always be ready to buy 100 shares of Exxon from me at $25 a share between now (mid-June) and the following October. It wouldn't make sense at the moment. I'd be paying nearly $28 a share for Exxon in the market so someone else could buy them from me at $25.

But I fear the world oil price will soon plunge—carrying Exxon shares down with it. I prove correct, and Exxon shares fall to $20 on the Big Board. I buy 100 shares at $20 a share—$2,000 in all. I then exercise the option, requiring the other party to buy those shares from me at $25 each, or $2,500. I paid a modest commission to buy the option and a larger commission when I bought the 100 shares in the market. Still, I've made about a $400 profit on my $30 cash investment.

Again, it might not have worked out that way (and it didn't since by October 1982 the rally had lifted Exxon shares higher). Still, I couldn't be out more than $30 in cash—the cost of the option plus the commission.

You can become a seller of options (known as a writer of options). You'd do that to turn an extra profit from shares that you own. And that takes us to:

STRATEGY 3. Believing that oil companies are the wave of the future, you buy 100 Exxon shares at $28 a share. You're counting on a higher price for Exxon to turn a capital gain for you. To earn a little more from those shares, you write (sell) an Exxon 30 call expiring the following January—roughly six months from now. The premium on that option is $125—$1.25 per share times 100 shares. The price would have to go to at least $32 a share before the buyer of that option would exercise it—requiring you to sell your Exxon shares at $30 a share. If the price doesn't go above $32 during the life of the option, the option won't be exercised and you keep the $125 premium—a little extra on your holdings. And you still own the Exxon shares.

Say that Exxon stock does move. At $32 a share, or close to it, the buyer of the option exercises it. You must sell your 100 shares at $30 a share. You've given up all the gain you might have made as Exxon stock went beyond $30, because you must sell at $30. But you have the gain on the difference between what you paid for the stock and the $30 you got when you sold. And you got $125 for writing the option. That's still not a bad profit. You'd have done better if the option didn't require you to sell at $30, but you didn't do badly.

If you own stock, and the market seems likely to fall, you use an option to hedge against loss, which takes us to:

STRATEGY 4. You own Exxon shares and you live in dread that the price will fall. You could sell out, and put your money someplace else. Yet there's a chance you're worrying about nothing. Exxon shares may not fall, in which case you let cold feet chill your chances for a profit.

You buy a put option—obligating the seller to buy your stock at the option price, no matter what happens to the market price of the stock. Say you buy the Exxon 25 put, expiring next January. The price is $50 for the option. If the price falls, you've put a floor under how much you can lose. No matter how low the market price goes, someone must buy those shares from you at $25 a share. You've bought peace of mind for $50. If the price goes up, you're out the $50 premium, but you make a nice profit from the higher market price for Exxon shares—a profit you couldn't have made if you'd sold the shares.

Our four strategies will work out this way:

1. You buy a call, betting on higher stock prices.
2. You buy a put, betting on lower stock prices.
3. You sell a call, to earn more from stock you already own.
4. You buy a put, to hedge against a decline in stock you own.

Some Rules for Options

Ignore options until you understand the stock market. Even when you think you understand the options market, do only paper trades for a few months—make-believe plays in options. Pick out a few dozen stocks and buy and sell some make-believe options. Chart your progress day by day and see if you're making any make-believe money. If after three months of paper playing you aren't winning on at least one option out of five, maybe you just don't have a feel for the market.

The options market is based on the stock market—but it isn't the stock market. The pace is faster, and time horizons are shorter. An option will run for nine months, but 90 percent of the time you won't ride it to the end. The stock may go up enough in price to warrant exercising the option. Or the price of the stock (and hence of the option) may go up a little, and you sell and take your profit. Or the price may fall, at which point you sell and take your loss.

Greed kills in any market, and that's certainly true of options. You have big bucks tied up when you buy stocks. You don't have much cash on the line in options, and it doesn't take much of an advance to produce a decent return on your money. You'll win far more often if you settle for lots of small gains, instead of hanging in, hoping for a big kill. Set a profit goal before you buy, and place a stop-order with your broker to sell at that price. Set a limit on the loss you'll take, and use a stop-order to make sure the option is sold if it falls to that price.

Recall that an option that clearly isn't going to make it to the exercise price is "out of the money." That's where you'll be if you hold on too long. Sometimes an option will come back into the money, but don't count on it. The closer to the expiration date an out-of-the-money option goes, the lower its price will drop, and the more you'll lose. The instant an option loses half its value—you paid $50 for it and the price is down to $25—take your loss and get out.

Don't buy an option just because it's cheap: It's cheap for a reason. The cheapest options are those farthest from the exercise price and closest to expiring. Buy an option with more time to run, and with an exercise price that's in the money. You'll pay more, but your chances of turning a profit are greater. Even if you must sell at a loss, you might still get something for your option, if you sell before it falls completely out of the money.

Introducing Stock-Index Options

The obvious drawback to the options market—just as it's a drawback to the stock market—is that you need to pick a single stock from among the universe of stocks. That's why people buy mutual funds: their money is invested, by professionals, in an array of stock. If you could buy an option on an array of stocks, instead of on a single stock, your task would be far easier. Instead of buying an option on Universal Overshoe—your money riding on the fortunes of Universal Overshoe stock in the market—you could buy an option on dozens or hundreds or thousands of stocks. Then, all you'd have to do to win would be to decide whether that array of stocks was going to go up or down in the market.

That's the point of stock-index options. (It's also the point of stock-index futures and options on stock-index futures, which we'll get to in just a bit.) You are buying an option on a universe of stocks. Instead of betting on whether the price of a given stock will move to a certain level, you're betting on whether a stock index will move to a certain level. You're no longer betting on one stock, you're betting on many stocks: on so many stocks that it simply becomes a matter of guessing which way the overall market is going.

The rules and strategies are the same, whether you're betting on one or many stocks. You're not likely to win as big betting on an index of stocks as you might by betting on a single stock—just as you're not likely to win as big buying shares of a mutual fund, as by buying a single stock. But you're likely to win more often betting on a stock-index than betting on a single stock. When you get a market rally, the magnitude of the 1982 rally, even a bet on a stock index would reward you beyond your wildest dreams.

The basic strategies in stock-index options would be buying a call option on an index (betting on a gain in the market) and buying a put on an index (to bet on a decline in the market, or to hedge against a decline in the market).

There's no individual stock to change hands when you bet on an index. When the option is exercised, you settle up in cash. If the value of the index you're betting on moves sufficiently above the exercise price, you'd exercise the option, and the person on the other side would simply give you some money.

One peril to the market in stock-index options right now is that it's such a new market that you don't know all the ins and outs. Even the professionals in the market don't. It takes at least three years to work out all the bugs in any new market, and the markets in stock-index options are so new you can't know what all the quirks are. Watch these new markets, talk them over with your broker, but approach them very gently for a while.

Inside the Futures Markets

The first trading in stock indexes was in the futures market, and the futures market also offers you ways to play the stock and bond markets at a remove.

As with options, you command a substantial investment with a fairly small amount of cash. As with options, you can win big relative to what you have at risk. As with options, you can—by tailoring your moves—win when the markets are rising and when they're falling. You can use stock-index futures to hedge against loss on stocks you already own, and interest-rate futures to hedge against loss on bonds you already own.

When you win, your tax situation is better with futures than with options, since the maximum tax on a gain in options is 50 percent, while it's 32 percent in futures.

A crucial difference is that, unlike the options market, where your loss is always limited to the cost of the option, you can lose a lot more than your original investment in futures. On that basis alone, it's a far riskier game than options. There is the still-newer game in options on stock-index futures, in which the risk is greatly reduced. Still, the futures market—just like the options market—is for veterans who've learned about stocks and bonds firsthand and are now ready to branch out. Neither market is for beginners.

We'll approach futures trading by looking at the basic market first—starting with a contract in a more traditional commodity, copper. Then we'll get into stock-index and interest-rate futures. Finally, we'll get into options on stock-index and interest-rate futures.

Copper trades on the New York Commodity Exchange—known as the Comex. The standard contract is for 25,000 pounds. Contracts run for 18 months and there's a new copper contract started almost every month. On this day—in mid-June of 1982—there are 13 copper contracts trading on the Comex: one expiring in a few days, and others running far off into the future. The price quote is in cents per pound and you could buy the nearest contract (the one expiring soon) for 57.9 cents a pound. The most distant contract (expiring in about 18 months) costs 74.4 cents a pound. Since each contract is for 25,000 pounds, that comes to $14,475 for the nearest contract and $18,600 for the most distant.

There's always a "spot" price for every commodity—the price at which the commodity is selling for that very day, in what's called the "cash" market. On this day the spot price of copper is about 58 cents. The 57.9 cent price for the nearest contract means that no one expects the spot price to go any higher in the next couple of weeks. The 74.4 cent price for the most distant contract, means that people believe the spot price will climb that high over the next 18 months.

You'll put up about 10 percent of the contract price, which

is really a performance bond to ensure that you'll live up to the terms of the contract. Depending on which side of the contract you're on—long or short—you agree either to buy 25,000 pounds of copper at the contract price (long) or sell 25,000 pounds of copper at the contract price (short) when the contract expires. Your broker can handle the details through either his own firm or a firm that specializes in commodity trading. Still, it's an art form, and you probably want a broker who deals only in commodities, for the specialized knowledge he'll bring.

You believe, on this date, that the world economy will improve soon and that copper must soon recover from its depressed state. You further believe this will happen by the following January (this being June), so you buy a copper contract expiring the following January. The price is 63.35 cents a pound. At 25,000 pounds, that comes to $15,837.50, of which you put up about $1,600 in cash. You've contracted to buy 25,000 pounds of copper for $15,837.50 come next January. On the other side of the contract—the short side—is someone who must sell you 25,000 pounds of copper for $15,837.50 late in January of the following year.

Let's say copper does recover; instead of selling for 58 cents a pound in the spot market, as it was when you bought the contract, it's selling for 75 cents a pound the following January. Now those 25,000 pounds of copper are worth $18,750. You paid only $15,837.50 for the contract, so you've made a profit of $2,912.50 (less some commissions). Since you put up only $1,600 in cash, you've nearly doubled your money in six months. And your tax bite is a maximum 32 percent.

It could have gone the other way. Instead of going to 75 cents a pound, copper might be 50 cents a pound in January. You paid $15,837.50 for a contract which is now worth only $12,500. You might take your 25,000 pounds of copper and hold it for a while, hoping the price will climb. You wouldn't have to keep it in your backyard: you'd get a receipt showing that you own 25,000 pounds of copper in a warehouse someplace. More likely, you'd sell the copper immediately for what you could get for it ($12,500), take your loss ($3,337.50) and hope to make it up someplace else.

In fact, you'd never let it go that far. You'd sell the contract as soon as you made a respectable profit, or to limit your loss as soon as the price went against you.

Spot copper was 58 cents on the day you bought your contract. The price of copper in your January contract is 63.35 cents. Should spot copper go to 60 cents in a week, investors will assume the price will be higher still by January and they'll bid the price of January copper up by roughly 2 cents. At 63.35 cents, your 25,000 pounds of copper was worth $15,837.50. At 65.35 cents, it's worth $16,337.50.

By buying the contract for $15,837.50 and selling it a week later for $16,337.50, you've turned a $500 profit on a cash investment of $1,600 (diluted only by some commissions).

But say that copper—58 cents in the spot market when you bought—falls to 56 cents during the next week. With spot copper down, the price of January copper falls as well—to 61.35 cents a pound. You paid $15,837.50 and at 61.35 cents a pound, your contract is worth only $15,337.50. You've lost $500, and while you might wait around, hoping for the price to go higher, it's going to cost you. That's because each night every contract is "marked to the market" with the exchange it's traded on.

Thanks to margin, you control about $16,000 worth of copper with $1,600 in cash. That's your "initial margin"—that good faith money you put up to ensure that you live up to your end of the contract. For every contract, there's also a "maintenance margin"—which is around 80 percent of the initial margin. You always must have at least that much cash on the line, to make certain you really do live up to the terms of the contract.

Now the value of your copper contract has fallen by $500. To make up that loss, your broker will take $500 out of the cash you put up and send it along to the exchange—thereby marking you to the market. If that $500 drops you below the maintenance margin level, your broker will take what he can until you hit the maintenance margin level, and he'll demand the rest, in cash, from you. Should the value of your contract fall another $500 the next day, your broker will be back for another $500 in cash. The more the price of copper falls, the more cash you have to put up. You put up $1,600 in cash to start out, but each margin call adds to the money you have on the line. Miss a margin call, and the broker will sell your contract, and you lose it all.

Should it go the other way, each day's gain in the value of your contract will go into your account that night—there for your taking.

Playing the Futures Market

Watch the market, minute by minute. When the price moves up, even a little, grab your profit and run. When the price falls, even a little, swallow your loss and get out, before the margin calls hit. A penny a pound increase on 25,000 pounds of copper still comes to $250, on a cash investment of $1,600.

And that penny-a-pound can come in a day or less. On the day I'm writing this, January copper lost 2.15 cents a pound in just a day. Had you bought that morning, and put up $1,600 in cash, your broker would already be hitting you for another $537.50—unless you sold out around lunchtime. Had you been on the other side—the short side—you could buy back a contract for $537.50 less than you sold it for—which would be pure profit to you.

The pace in the futures market is even more hectic than in the options market, which is hectic enough. And stocks tend to move rationally—in response to changes in the economy or in interest rates or to something fundamental about the company. Commodity prices respond to all of the above—and to much more—the weather, hints of a coup in some far-off land, rumors of impending war, etc.

The gospel is that even veteran commodity traders lose on nine trades of every 10—counting on a huge win that more than makes up for all the losses.

Introducing Stock-Index Futures

Now, all the thrills and chills of commodities have been wedded to all the thrills and chills of the stock market, through the stock-index future. A stock-index future is both very much like—yet quite different from—virtually all other commodities.

There's a standard contract with a standard quantity ($500 times the stock index) and each contract runs for 18 months. But there's nothing physical to change hands: not 25,000 pounds of copper or 5,000 bushels of corn. Even interest-rate futures involve something tangible: $100,000 in Treasury bonds, or $1 million in Treasury bills. Should a stock-index future run to maturity, you'd have to settle in cash, because the contract is based on an abstraction—an index of common stock prices.

When you invest in the stock market, you buy one stock at a time. A stock option involves a single stock. When you buy a stock-index future (as with a stock-index option), you're buying a universe: the 1,700 stocks that make up the Value Line index; the 500 stocks that make up the S&P 500; the 1,500 stocks that make up the New York Stock Exchange index. You don't have to worry about picking the right one or two stocks from among all stocks: You only have to guess right about whether the market will go up or down, which is no small advantage (shared, of course, with stock-index options).

As with all commodities, the price of a contract is high—$75,000 when the S&P 500 is at 150. But you'd only put up about 10 percent of that in cash. There are standard delivery months—March, June, September, and December, but you'd be no more likely to run to the end of a stock-index contract than with any other futures contract. You'd be in and out, playing for a small, quick profit, or getting out after a small, quick loss.

Playing the Market

You're bullish on stocks. On this day in June, the price of a December contract in the Value Line index is 116.50, which times $500, is $58,250. You buy the contract, putting up about $6,000 in cash: contracting to "take possession" of 500 slices of the Value Line index six months from now for $58,250, from someone who must sell you 500 slices of the Value Line index at that price.

A week after you buy, the market moves higher and the Value Line index is now at 118.50. That, times $500, is $59,250. You've made a $1,000 profit, at which point you sell. Had the market—and the Value Line index—fallen, you'd be in the same trouble you'd be with any other commodity—margin calls. More likely, you sold as soon as the index began to slip, taking your loss and moving on.

If you were bearish on stocks, you'd sell a stock-index contract. Now you're the one who sells, not the one who buys. You must deliver 500 slices of the Value Line index at the contract price to the person on the other side of the contract, who must buy them at the contract price—which again is $58,250 ($500 times the Value Line index at 116.50). It's all just play money at this point. You don't get $58,250—or any money at all—for having sold the contract. In fact, long or short, you must put up margin to make sure you live up to your end of the bargain, which is to deliver or accept those 500 slices of the Value Line index when the contract matures.

Say the market does slump, and when the contract runs out in December, the Value Line index is at 110. The contract is worth $55,000 but the person who is long must pay you $58,250 for it. You've turned a $3,250 profit in six months on a cash investment of $6,000, which isn't bad.

But you wouldn't stay in to the end. You'd get out as soon as you had a profit, or began showing a loss. Say that a week after you buy, the Value Line index is down to 114.50, which times $500, is $57,250. On paper, at least, you got $58,250 when you sold that contract. A week later, you can buy it back at $57,250—and that $1,000 profit is real money, which you keep. Should the index begin climbing, you'd get out in a hurry, because now you have a contract price that's above what you sold it for. You're losing money, and losses in the futures markets mean margin calls.

As with options, you take your profits when you see them, and you get out fast when you start losing. In fact, you get out even faster than in options, because you don't have margins calls to worry about in the option market. Before you go in, you set a profit goal and a loss limit, and you place sell orders with your broker to make sure you get out when you want to. And if you don't have a very clear feel for which way the underlying stock market is likely to go, you don't get in at all.

Using the Market to Hedge

So far, we've talked about gambling—speculating in futures. The second function of a futures market is as a place to hedge against loss on your investment, much as can the right sort of play in options.

Take a traditional commodity first. The company is the Oil & Vinegar Salad Dressing Company, and the oil it uses is soybean oil. It must buy 100,000 gallons of soybean oil in the spot market when the crop is harvested in the fall, and it fears the price of oil will be higher in the fall than it is now. So it buys a couple of soybean oil contracts that will mature in the fall when the soybean crop is harvested. If the spot price oil goes up, it will pay more for the oil it needs. But since the price is higher, so is the price of its futures contracts. The higher price of oil is offset by the profit it makes on its oil contracts.

Or maybe it already bought the oil at a stiff price, and it's afraid that a subsequent drop in price will depress the price of salad dressing. So it will sell a couple of soybean oil contracts. Should the cash price of soybean oil fall, so would the value of its inventory. But so would the price of the soybean oil contract. It would buy back the contract for less than it sold it for, and the profit would offset the loss on the value of its inventory.

A hedge in stock-index futures works the same way. What you're hedging is the value of stocks that you own.

You hold a portfolio of $50,000 worth of common stocks, and you fear the market is about to fall. You could sell out, but if you're wrong, you've sold stocks you should have held. So you sell a stock-index future. If stock prices fall, the value of your portfolio falls with it. But you buy back your contract for less than you sold it for, and that offsets much of the loss on your stock portfolio.

If you were wrong, and the market moved higher, you'd

take a loss on the futures contract you sold, but the gain in your portfolio should make up for the loss on your contract.

You get a break when you hedge. Your broker will let you in for about half the margin required if you weren't hedging. Even a promise to buy the stock in the future may qualify you for hedging margin.

Interest Rate Futures

The rules, risks, and rewards in interest-rate futures are about the same as in stock-index futures, except that the market has been around longer.

There are contracts in Treasury bills and bank certificates of deposit (each contract for $1 million), and Treasury bonds and Ginnie Mae passthrough certificates (each contract for $100,000). You'll seldom put up more than $3,000 in cash.

As in any futures market, you can simply gamble on interest rates, betting that rates will go down (and prices up), or betting that rates will go up (and prices down). If you're betting on long-term rates, buy either the Treasury bond or the Ginnie Mae contract. If it's on short rates, buy either the Treasury bill or the certificate of deposit contract. You're speculating, pure and simple, but with less money than if you went into the market and bought bonds. And your money is going a lot further, since $3,000 or less will control $1 million in Treasury bills, or $100,000 in Treasury bonds.

You're absolutely certain that rates have gone as high as they can. The economy is at a dead halt, and the Federal Reserve must surely help out by driving interest rates down, before the economy falls into depression. (A very reasonable assumption, since that's actually what happened in the summer of 1982.) You might back up that belief by investing $10,000 in the bond market—buying an assortment of government and corporate issues. When rates fall, the prices of those bonds will go up, and in short order you'll have made a dandy profit.

Well, the Skid Rows of America are populated with people who knew, in their heart of hearts, that rates were about to fall—except they didn't.

So you gamble—not in the bond market, but in the futures market. Say it's the summer of 1982 and you expect that break in rates to come very soon (as indeed it did). There's a Treasury bond contract, traded on the Chicago Board of Trade, maturing in September of 1982. You put up $3,000 in cash and buy a contract covering $100,000 worth of Treasury bonds. Those bonds carry an 8 percent rate—laughably low in this day and age—and so the price of the September contract has been adjusted accordingly to a hair under $62,000.

You're soon proven correct and rates fall, and as rates fall, prices go up—including the price of your bond contract. You "paid" $62,000 and by September the price of the contract is $68,000. Depending on when you sold, you made up to $6,000 profit on a cash investment of $3,000. The money that you didn't use to buy bonds was earning more money for you in other markets.

As always, you might have guessed wrong. Say that rates didn't fall after all and you lose on your Treasury bond contract. But you didn't lose as much as if you had spent $10,000 buying bonds.

And you can hedge against falling prices by using interest rate futures.

Say you really did it: You jumped into the market and bought $10,000 worth of corporate bonds, in anticipation of lower rates and higher prices. Just to be safe, you hedged your bet by selling a Treasury bond contract. The price is still the same—$62,000. Because you own the bonds, you're not a speculator, you're a hedger, and your margin is now a good deal less than $3,000.

Should rates rise, instead of falling, you lose on the bonds you bought. But the price of the Treasury bond contract falls and you buy it back for less than you sold it for, and that profit offsets much, if not all, the loss on your bonds. It gets a little dicier if rates do fall. Prices are going up and you're making a profit on your bonds. But the price of your futures contract, which you must buy back to close out the contract, is also going up, and you're losing there.

As soon as rates begin to move down, sell out the futures contract to limit your loss there, and hope for more than enough profit on the bonds you own to offset whatever loss you suffered on the futures contract.

The Newest Options in Town

All of this brings us to the newest of the new: all sorts of new options—on stocks and interest rates—plus options on futures—stock-index and otherwise. We're still dealing with just options and futures, but my how they've grown.

Things are happening so rapidly in the market that I simply can't be sure all that will be available by the time you read this. Each new market will be reported on in the press, and your broker is paid to keep tabs on each new investment wrinkle. If you think your broker isn't keeping up with all that's new and exciting in the financial markets, maybe you need a new broker.

Briefly, in October of 1983, there were:

1. Options on stock-index futures, based on the New York Stock Exchange index, and on the 500-stock index of Standard & Poor's.
2. Options on stock indexes, from the CBOE and the New York and American stock exchanges.
3. Options on Treasury bonds, from the CBOE.
4. Options on Treasury bills and notes, from the American Stock Exchange.
5. Options on Treasury bond futures from the Chicago Board of Trade.

Just remember that an option is an option, whether it involves 100 shares of one stock or a whole stock market index or a Treasury bill. There are both puts and calls, the option runs for nine months, and you can exercise it or not as the spirit (and the performance of the underlying market) moves you. The price you pay is still the premium—and, as in all options, the most you can lose is the premium. Further, the premium on an option will always be less than the cash you'd have to put up on a futures contract.

Assume that still more options will come along—on physical commodities, on more stock indexes, on parts of stock indexes, on everything you can think of.

It is still the options market—no matter what the option is based on. Instead of buying a futures contract outright—July grape jelly at $1 a pound—you'd buy an option to buy the grape jelly contract. Should the price of grape jelly futures in the market go high enough, you'd exercise your option to buy the contract at $1 a pound. Then you'd immediately sell the contract—at the latest price of, say, $1.25 a pound—and pocket your profit.

If you bought grape jelly futures outright, and the price went against you, you might lose all your money, plus more, to meet margin calls. By buying an option to buy grape jelly futures, the most you could lose would be the price of the option.

There still are no guarantees in any of these markets. You can limit your loss with an option, but that's a long way from guaranteeing that you'll win anything. You're betting that something will happen in a market in a given period of time: until the option or futures contract runs out, or until you've made or lost as much money as you care to. All markets are crap-shoots: They may go as you want them to, and they may not.

You increase your chances of winning when you buy a stock-index option, or an option on a stock-index future, as opposed to buying a straight stock option. You're betting on the broad movement of the market rather than on one stock. But you're unlikely to make as big a profit as you might if you bet on one or two stocks and those stocks did well. Among all the stocks that go into an index, some will do well and some won't, and the performance of the index will reflect this.

As with any investment, you can guess wrong—and lose. You can guess right on the direction of a market but guess wrong on the timing—and lose. You can guess right on the direction and the timing and still not turn a big enough profit to make it worthwhile to exercise the option. You're not losing as much as if you had a futures contract, but you are losing. In the early days of the market, the premium on an option on a stock-index future was running substantially higher than the premium on a plain, old stock option. The higher the premium, the more it takes to make a profit.

The more sharply honed your economic sixth sense has become, and the more experience you've gained in the investment markets, the better you'll tend to do. You'll do much better if you take small profits and run with them than if you hang on for that extra dollar or two. Options require careful watching, and when it's an option on a future, you're obliged to watch two markets at the same time: what the option is doing, and what the underlying market is doing. That's a lot of watching to do, and you have to be willing to do it, to play these markets.

Time may establish more distinct differences between stock-index options and options on stock-index futures. With either, you're getting a tolerably conservative run for your money: betting on the overall direction of the stock market (or of interest rates) rather than buying stocks (or bonds) outright, and rather than buying a stock option. And there's the limitation on your loss that an option provides.

Buying a call (on a stock-index option, an option on a stock-index future, an interest-rate option, or an option on anything at all) would be the speculative strategy. You're betting on a move in the underlying markets. Buying a put would be the defensive strategy—trying to hedge against loss on stocks or bonds you already own. You'd turn offensive early in a rally, and defensive as the market began to turn down: speculating on rising prices when the markets are moving up, and on falling prices when the markets start to turn down.

You always rely on your economic sixth sense to tell you when to go on the offensive and when to turn defensive. But that's investment strategy: when to commit your money to stocks and bonds, and when to hide out in cash. Right now, we're talking about tactics. Once all these markets get shaken down, and as you hone your skills in these markets, they can make a lot of tactical sense.

Guidelines for Action

Once you know about stocks and bonds, take the next step up. Look at the newer markets in options and futures. You may do better, and you'll have less of your money on the line than if you buy stocks or bonds outright.

With options, you'll even know the most you can lose before you start playing.

Both markets demand close watching. Unless you're willing to do that, stay away.

Greed kills in all investment markets—but most of all in options and futures. Aim for lots of small gains: Hanging on for the big win can wipe you out.

Hedge your bets: several options or futures contracts, instead of all your money in one option or one contract.

The best all-time investment play (when you're ready for it) could be an option on a stock-index future.

CHAPTER 10

When to Try the Other Markets—From Gold to Old Masters

And then there's everything else: the broad universe of "other" markets that embraces nonfinancial futures, gold and silver, diamonds and other gems, art, antiques, and other collectibles from rare books to rare wine to Mickey Mouse watches.

As broad as this universe is, there's a common thread that runs through all of it, which is: Let the buyer beware.

All are high-risk markets, and most of the time, those risks are greater than you should take with your money. Except for commodity futures (and options on futures), all are traded in markets that are haphazard and unregulated, in which the sellers write all the rules, and you have to play by them. You couldn't tell a perfect diamond (graded D-flawless) from something not so perfect in a million years, but one will sell for three times the price of the other. Unless you take the time and trouble to learn all you can about a market, you'll always be a novice going up against professionals.

You can play any of these markets if you are experienced and daring enough. Or you can not play them at all: Simply buy a work of art, or an antique, or a bit of jade to have something handsome around the house.

But there are economic seasons for all these markets, and you must at least know about them.

Prices of all the industrial commodities—from copper to plywood—advance along with the advancing economy and they retreat when recession cuts into demand. The faster that prices advance, the greater the potential for profit, and the futures markets are at their hottest when the economy is booming, with enough inflation around to make it interesting.

Actually, as you'll recall from chapter 9, there are profits to be made in futures when prices are rising and when prices are falling. Economic instability makes for exciting—and potentially very profitable—commodity markets. That very instability, of course, makes for maximum peril to all but the most experienced. At least the industrial commodities are tied to the economy: The foodstuffs are tied to such things as the weather halfway around the world.

The other markets—gold, diamonds, fine art and the rest—whatever other functions they serve, have been "scary times" markets through the ages: the markets people turn to when superinflation or social unrest threaten the very fabric of the nation.

Stocks and bonds, and even our nation's currency, are just bits of colored paper—worth something only because a government or a corporation says they're worth something. Gold and diamonds and art and antiques are tangibles, and when times turn really scary—when the governments and corporations that issued the paper tremble—it's a comfort to have something tangible to cling to.

There are rules for surviving in these markets, and I'll provide them. But more than in any other markets, you're on your own. Your economic sixth sense may tell you when the economic tide is turning, but it won't tell you which young painter is tomorrow's Picasso, or how to forecast a freak storm that will turn a bumper crop into a disaster.

You need another kind of economic sense altogether to know what true values are in these markets. When times turn scary, there will be a stampede into all the markets, and sheer hysteria will push prices to lunatic levels.

Wealth beyond measure poured into all these markets in the 1970s, when inflation raged, and the stock and bond markets turned rotten. In just months gold went from less than $250 an ounce to $870, and silver from $7.50 to nearly $50 an ounce. Diamonds tripled in price, and coins, works of art, and collectibles of all sorts sold at record prices, and then were resold at still higher prices.

Then, in the 1980s, deflation hit and these markets all but collapsed. Gold fell back to $300 an ounce, silver to $10, and the price of top-grade diamonds fell 45 percent in 1981 alone. Prices of even the works of the Old Masters went tumbling, and billions of dollars of capital, put into these markets for safekeeping, were lost.

Think of these "other" markets as the Great Dismal Swamp of investing. There are profits to be made, and there's often the satisfaction of owning something beautiful. Prices right now are badly depressed in most markets, and you can buy at prices not seen in years. But you must feel your way cautiously, with a clear sense of where you're going and what dangers lie ahead. Before you enter one of these markets, pick a few specialties that interest you the most, rather than trying to master them all. Once you are in, you need a plan for getting out safely, before night falls and the creatures of the swamp devour you.

The Other Futures Markets

Understand, before you play, that financial futures (stock indexes, Treasury bonds, and the rest) are totally different from the other commodities because they involve things you already know a lot about—stocks and interest rates. Chances are you know next-to-nothing about any of the other commodities. You can limit your potential for loss, to the extent you can buy an option on a commodity. But that only minimizes your risk; it doesn't really change the fact that the commodities markets are super-high-risk markets in which you can lose a lot of money in a hurry.

You're not betting on the course of interest rates or the performance of an index of 500 stocks. You're betting on next year's corn crop, or on the political climate in Ghana, where cocoa comes from. If you guess wrong about what OPEC will do to the price of oil next year, an option on heating oil futures would only mean a smaller loss than if you bought a heating oil contract outright. You'll still lose money.

As far as the other commodities go, there are first the grains and oilseeds (corn, oats, soybeans, wheat, barley, flaxseed, rapeseed, and rye), and the Chicago Board of Trade is the big grain market. There's livestock and meat (feeder cattle, live cattle, hogs, and pork bellies), traded on the Chicago Mercantile Exchange. There are the foods and fibers (cocoa, cotton, orange juice, potatoes, and sugar), traded on the Coffee, Sugar & Cocoa Exchange, the New York Cotton Exchange, and the New York Mercantile Exchange. There are the metals and petroleum (copper, gold, silver, platinum, and heating oil), traded on the Commodity Exchange in New York, the New York Merc, and the Chicago Board of Trade. Finally, there are the woods (lumber and plywood), traded on the Board of Trade, and the Chicago Merc.

No matter what commodity you try, you're always betting on a change in the price—and the bigger the change, and the faster it comes, the better for you.

You're really trying to guess future levels of supply and demand, since these are the basic determinants of price. If there's likely to be too much of something, relative to demand, the price will probably go down, and if there's too little of something relative to demand, the price will probably go up.

You make use of your economic sixth sense to calculate the economic future since it's mostly the relative strength or weakness of the economy that determines demand. As the economy surges, we'll buy more of everything from copper to plywood. As the economy weakens, we'll buy less of everything.

You'll get plenty of help in determining the probable supply. The Department of Agriculture reports frequently and copiously on the probable supply of all major crops grown in America, and the probable size of our food-animal herds. There are comparable reports, from other government agencies and from private sources, on the likely supply of other commodities, from heating oil to silver. Your broker should have all these reports on hand, and most are widely reported in the press.

But if it were that simple, we'd all have made our fortunes in commodities.

Waiting for the Unexpected

Price movements are never absolutely random, but neither are they cut-and-dried. The keenest minds of our age might study all the available data and conclude that our prune crop will set records and that the price of prune juice will fall. Then the prune blight hits, the crop is mostly destroyed, and the price of prune juice—and prune juice futures—goes to the skies.

That's where the sex-and-violence—the great fortunes and the dashed hopes—come in commodities. You bet on what you believe are certainties and then you wait for the unexpected.

You're a hostage, not only to the fortunes of the economy, but also to Murphy's Law, which says that if something can go wrong it will go wrong. A sudden freeze in the South, a torrential rain in the Corn Belt, a war in Africa, can take the best forecasts and reduce them to waste paper.

The contract in frozen orange juice concentrate wasn't doing much of anything until the worst freeze in decades hit Florida early in 1982. Oranges froze solid on trees—each orange was hard as a baseball. Clearly, the situation had changed, and change makes for violent price movements, which make for big profits (and big losses). But how had it changed?

If the oranges were ruined, the price must go higher—and the prices on orange juice futures went sharply higher for a few days. But if the oranges could be picked quickly enough, they could still be turned into orange juice concentrate. They were picked quickly enough, and prices fell again.

The price of copper is affected by the level of economic activity—and your economic sixth sense can help you there. But it's also affected by how politically stable such countries as Chile, Peru, and the Philippines appear at any moment, since all are major copper producers.

Or consider the humble ear of corn, which we grow by the zillions in this country. We eat some as corn-on-the-cob, and some gets canned to grace the dinner tables of American families. The better off we are financially, the more corn we consumers will buy. If times turn hard, we'll buy fewer ears and fewer cans of corn.

But most corn isn't eaten by humans, but by livestock, to make them plump and edible. That takes you to that lesson from Economics 101, called the corn-hog cycle.

Say the weather is sheer perfection in the Corn Belt of the Midwest. The price of corn falls, because there's so much of it. Because it's so cheap, farmers will raise more hogs, since the corn they eat costs less. As they raise more hogs, the price of pork falls. Now we're up to our noses in piglets, each one eating corn as though there were no tomorrow. We're growing lots of corn, but the piglets are eating it faster than we can grow it and now the price of corn goes up. Because corn is so expensive, farmers raise fewer hogs and as they do the price of pork goes up. Now we have plenty of corn, but fewer piglets to eat it, and the price of corn falls again—and so on.

In the best of worlds, you'd simply trade the corn-hog cycle, based on the government's frequent forecasts of the corn harvest, and of our pig population.

But the weather isn't always sheer perfection in the Corn Belt. Sometimes it rains too much, and sometimes it rains too little, and we don't know today what tomorrow's weather will be. We don't raise corn just for our own use. We also sell it to other countries, and a massive demand from abroad can send our price higher, even with the best of harvests here. Russia, with a long history of crop failures, is a frequent buyer of American corn. But, the Russians being the Russians, we never know how much they'll buy until they buy.

All of the above—and more—goes into deciding which commodities to play and how to play them.

The Rules for Futures

The easier it is to estimate supply and demand factors, the safer you are. That argues for industrial commodities rather than foodstuffs because the use of industrial commodities (copper, lumber, heating oil, silver, etc.) is tied so directly to economic activity, while the foodstuffs bring in such additional complications as the weather.

Recovery, in 1983, revived all the markets for industrial commodities. You could, in fact, play these markets as you would stocks and bonds: buying in as the economy turns, and riding the markets up.

The danger is the same danger you find throughout the futures markets: the way you can lose your money in the day-to-day fluctuations in the market. You might wince if a stock or bond had a few bad days in the midst of an otherwise profitable advance, but it wouldn't really hurt you. In commodities, a few bad days in the midst of an otherwise profitable advance could wipe you out.

Finally, that such turns in the market can be predicted makes for steady, rather than spectacular, gains. Plungers in commodities play for the big, fortune-making gain, rather than steady gains. Plungers in commodities also tend to like high-stakes poker.

The other side of the market is that the more wild cards, the greater the gains you can make. Not many people will bet on higher copper prices during a recession, or on lower plywood prices when home building is fevered. They become dull markets, with limited potential for profit. The more unpredictable a market is, the greater the chance for profits—if you call it just right.

As with any market you're not familiar with, pretend-play for maybe three months—just paper trades—before you commit any money.

Play to whatever strengths you have: any specialized knowledge about any of the markets you've picked up along the way. It's easier to keep tabs on commodities with domestic sources of supply than those with foreign sources of supply. Keep your horizons narrow—sticking with just one commodity or one family of commodities so that you build an understanding of a corner of the universe—rather than trying to understand it all.

Read all you can, starting with the daily commodity column in *The Wall Street Journal*, plus whatever is written about commodities in the other publications you read. There are plenty of books on the subject. Ignore the fancy theories about trading commodities they offer and concentrate on intensifying your feel for the market.

If you're going to speculate in commodities (and everyone who's in the market is a speculator), you must have a broker who specializes in commodities. You want someone with a lot of specialized knowledge, and with access to the available research material (and who understands what the material really says). If you plunge into commodities, you'll spend more time with your broker than with your spouse.

Price movements are narrower the closer a contract comes to expiring, and wider the further it is from expiring. It's hard enough guessing the likely interplay of supply and demand a few months from now. Forget about trying to guess the economy 18 months from now. Stick with contracts that have between one and six months to run. Price swings won't be as wide, but you'll sleep better.

However you feel about going short in any investment—selling now in hopes of buying back at a lower price in the future—you have to do it if you're going to be in commodities. Short selling is a sometimes thing in the stock market—the exception rather than the rule (and not for you at any time). In commodities, every contract involves someone on one side who is long, and someone on the other side who is short—making it the rule rather than the exception. When you go long, you're betting on higher prices. When you go short, you're betting on lower prices—and we'll surely have a lot of ups and downs in prices in the eighties.

Always place stop orders with your broker before you go in—instructions to get you out when you've made the profit you've been aiming for, or to get you out fast if the price begins to run against you. The same marking to the market—and all those margin calls—hits in nonfinancial futures, just as in financial futures.

Minimizing the Risk

If commodities appeal to you, you can limit your risk by trying options or futures as they become available. As I write this, there are only options in Treasury bonds, sugar, and gold. By the time you read it, there should be lots more.

Once again, you're not buying or selling the actual futures contract, but an option to buy the contract (if it's a call option) or sell the contract (if it's a put option) at an agreed-upon price, at some point during the nine-month life of the option. Your loss is limited to the premium you paid for the option (which will be less than the cash you'd put up to buy a futures contract outright). You can ignore the minute-by-minute fluctuations in the underlying commodity and exercise the option only when it makes sense to do so. There are no margin calls to worry about, so you never have to worry about losing more than the premium you paid on the option.

Even commodity options only minimize the risk; they certainly don't eliminate it. You can guess wrong on direction or on the magnitude of price swings and lose time after time. When you play the futures market outright, it's hazardous in the extreme. When you're in the market, you must watch it minute by minute. In no other market can you lose as quickly as you can in commodities. A half-baked rumor can send the price tumbling, and you can lose your stake before the rumor is shot down. And no other market seems to be as susceptible to half-baked rumors as commodities. There's the "the president is sick" rumor, which seems to sweep the markets about once a week. There was the "Saudi Arabia is cutting the price of oil" rumor which hit the markets over and over again in 1982. One day in 1982 a German oil company reported a big loss. In a twinkling, speculators twisted that into "Germany's biggest bank has failed," and prices in the precious metals markets went crazy. They're silly rumors, but each cost a lot of people a lot of money. You might have the most perfectly honed economic sixth sense in the world, but that kind of rumor could still cost you plenty.

You can also minimize your risk by going into a commodity fund, which functions like a mutual fund that invests in stocks or bonds. You put up your money—typically $5,000 to get started—and the fund takes your money, and that of other investors, and spreads it out in a number of different commodities. You gain professional management, and you gain from having a more diversified array of commodities than you could hope to manage on your own.

There are perhaps 1,800 of these funds (or pools, as they are mostly called). Some are big, widely advertised, and offered by big brokerage houses. Some are small, with just a few participants. Deal only with a pool that's registered with the Commodity Futures Trading Commission, the government agency that regulates the commodity markets, and with a pool offered by a name that you recognize.

One advantage of pools, is that you're spared the bane of commodity plungers—margin calls. You can't lose more than you've put up. The drawback is that, with the pool in so many different commodities, you aren't likely to ever get the really big win that commodity players cherish.

The Perils of the Other Markets

As for the other "other" markets, understand the extent to which you're on your own, without rules and regulations to protect you, and with no real help to be expected from your economic sixth sense.

This isn't true when you trade gold and silver futures, or buy the shares of mining companies. It becomes more true as you get into the so-called bullion coins (Krugerrands and the others, bought solely because of their gold content). It's totally true when you get into numismatic coins (bought because their relative rarity makes them interesting to collect). And it's absolutely true of all the rest: Art, antiques, collectibles, and gems.

You buy from a private party or from a dealer, and while the seller may be perfectly honest, he or she may instead be the biggest crook that ever came down the pike. A dealer who may be scrupulously honest with a longtime customer may regard you as the sucker who's going to pay that month's rent. You pay what the seller charges, with only whatever knowledge you bring to the scene to tell you if you are getting a good buy or if someone is trying to take you. The item in question may be as described or it may be a fake. Unless you're an expert, or are prepared to pay for expert (and therefore costly) advice, you won't know until it's too late.

When you want to sell, you wait until a buyer happens along, and if you need money in a hurry, you take what you're offered. If the economy and inflation have slowed, you can wait forever and a day for a buyer. If you've bought something that has gone out of vogue, you may only find a buyer if you cut the price to next-to-nothing.

All these markets are subject to fads, and what's hot one year can be ice-cold the next. Even if you know all there is to know about a subject (Old Masters paintings, English silver, Chinese ceramics), you can never be sure how long something will stay in vogue.

So many people look upon precious metals and precious gems as safe havens in times of uncertainty, that you'd think they'd be the most stable of markets. When diamond prices crashed in 1981, not only the amateurs, but the market professionals, got slaughtered. The 1980 crash in the price of silver caught one of the richest families in America—the Hunts of Texas—by surprise, and the losses of brothers Nelson Bunker Hunt and William Herbert Hunt may have topped $1 billion. When gold plunged in 1980, the great banking houses of Europe and the oil sheiks of the Middle East lost billions.

Still, the more you know, the better you'll do in any of these markets, whether you're buying to decorate your home or buying as a hedge against bad times.

The Precious Metals

Gold and silver split the difference between the commodity markets and the "other" other markets, and you can play both all those different ways: speculating in futures, in options on futures, in options on gold, buying gold and silver-mining shares, buying bullion coins, and buying numismatic coins. You can invest in mutual funds that invest in gold. You can buy bags of silver coins. You can buy gold certificates from banks and brokerage houses, showing that while the gold is stored elsewhere, you own it.

You can do all that, but do you want to?

Buying precious metals as a speculation is a new thing. For eons, both silver and gold were money—their prices rigidly fixed by governments. For 100 years, the U.S. fixed gold at $20 an ounce, and for 40 years more it fixed it at $35 an ounce.

You bought gold and silver as bulwarks against chaos: if you thought the currency was about to collapse, if there was an invader at the gates. Gold is among the heaviest of elements, and you can cram a fortune in gold into a shoebox.

We fixed the price of silver until the late 1960s and the price of gold until 1973. Then, with the price set free and with inflation thundering all about us, the price of both went crazy, gold going from its fixed price of $35 an ounce to $870 and silver from its fixed price of under $2 to $50. And then inflation cracked in the face of back-to-back recessions, and the price of each crumbled.

If you want to buy a little gold as a hedge against bad times, you can buy a couple of Krugerrands and put them into a safe deposit box. When it comes to gold and silver as speculations, it becomes a far more complex matter.

Both are widely used in industry, and the price of each will in part reflect the level of world economic activity. Each is bought as a shelter against economic and political storms, and the higher the level of world economic and political tensions, the higher the price of each will tend to go. Finally, each is frequently bought with borrowed money, and high interest rates tend to depress the price, while lower interest rates will tend to inflate it.

Put all of that together, and you get extremely erratic markets. Having hit $870, gold fell to $300 in the early summer of 1982. Then between the war in Lebanon, martial law in Poland, and the ebb and flow of interest rates, the price quickly shot to $500 an ounce, then slipped to $400, and then churned violently.

Assume that to the extent that interest rates generally go lower, and the world economy revives, the prices of gold and silver will tend to move higher. Assume also that there will be enough crises around the world to keep the price of each from falling too sharply. That argues for gold and silver. But short-run fluctuates are so violent that the futures markets are probably just too perilous. When you buy gold-mining shares, you're betting as much on the stability of the South African regime (South Africa being the biggest producer of gold) as on any other single factor. Metallic gold pays no interest and must be safe-guarded at your expense. And that argues against both.

If you are buying gold as a hedge against hard times, buy only metallic gold. You can buy gold certificates, but you're buying gold in case times get hard enough to drag down the giant banks and brokers that offer them.

Gems, Precious and Otherwise

Diamonds and other precious gems went up in price as rapidly as gold—and for the same reason. They were seen as perfect shelters should inflation destroy our money and our economy. For most people, diamonds were an even more traumatic investment than gold.

Gold is gold, and you don't buy it until a government or a bank has certified it as absolutely top quality. To tell a top-grade diamond from a piece of junk requires expert analysis. Even experts will disagree on whether a diamond is top quality or just a bit off the mark, and the difference in price between top grade and just below is many thousands of dollars. The same holds true for rubies, emeralds, and sapphires.

You probably wouldn't get sold a mislabeled diamond if you went to a top name in the business. But as the price of gems rose, the market filled up with less-than-top names selling in a high-pressure way to people who knew nothing about diamonds. Plenty of junk diamonds sold at inflated prices—at which point prices broke and everyone in the market took a bath.

For most buyers of diamonds, and the other precious gems, it was a mug's game anyway. All the talk of fabulous price gains really applied only to top-quality, "investment grade" diamonds—one carat and bigger. Prices of smaller, lower-quality stones went up by much less (but also fell by much less when prices broke). Unless you had $40,000 or $50,000 to spend, you never saw an investment-grade diamond, and never had a shot at big gains. As an outsider, you paid the full retail price when you bought and got the wholesale price when you sold. There's no organized trading market in diamonds, and you get whatever a dealer or a jeweler offers you for your stone.

There are plenty of semi-precious gems (opal, topaz, tourmaline, tanzanite, amethyst, and many more) with much lower prices. But grading standards for these stones are less precise than for diamonds—increasing the risk that you'll be stuck with a stone of lower quality than billed. Most of these stones go into jewelry, and while a diamond may be forever, fashions in semiprecious stones can change quickly. Here, too, when you buy, you'll pay the retail price, and when you sell you'll be paid the wholesale price.

It's more a market for the smaller investor because prices are lower. Should inflation explode again, prices of most semiprecious stones would probably increase substantially. Consider it on that basis—as an inflation hedge, should that again become necessary. But keep your stake in the market fairly small. Buy a few high-quality stones, a carat each or bigger.

And the "Other" Other Markets

There remains the whole, vast area of "exotic" investments—the common thread being that people collect them for fun and in hopes of a profit. There used to be a fine publication (now gone) called *The Collector-Investor.* In its January 1982 issue, it listed these broad areas: antiques, arms and armaments, art nouveau and art deco, rare books, classic cars, clocks and watches, coins, esoterica, folk art, furniture (American), furniture (European), gemstones, glass jewelry, musical instruments, native American Indian art, Oriental art, Oriental carpets, paintings (American), paintings (Impressionist and Post-Impressionist), paintings (modern), paintings (Old Masters), photography, porcelain, prints, sculpture, silver, and stamps.

And if you don't think people are serious about this sort of thing, the magazine further listed some prices paid for items in 1981, which wasn't a particularly banner year for collectibles. What about $95,000 for a gold-inlaid Parker shotgun; a half-million for an armor-plated 1940–model Mercedes; $12,000 for the ruby slippers that Judy Garland wore in *The Wizard of Oz*; $5,000 for a letter from Greta Garbo; $2,000 for a Mickey Mantle baseball card; and $1 million for a 1715 Stradivarius violin.

There's something for every taste and pocketbook in this market, and you can just buy things because they're beautiful or rare or both, as well as in hopes of capital gains. You can frequent the ritziest galleries and auctions, but you can also find treasures at a garage sale. Collectors of different things meet frequently, and you can swap what you have for something that someone else has.

Prices for some things held up well even during the 1981–82 break. The markets for gems, Chinese porcelains, and Old Masters paintings were ravaged, but the markets for modern paintings and antique furniture fared much better. The market in rare books actually rallied when other markets were tumbling—as, oddly enough, it did during the Depression. And there's plenty available in the rare book market for under $500.

Whether you buy for pleasure or profit, you must remember the fundamental rules of all these markets:

1. Don't buy anything unless you know what you're doing or are willing to learn. Do your homework—or stay home.

2. Buy it only if you really like it, because you may not be able to sell it without taking a big loss—and, in some cases, you won't be able to sell it at all.

3. Don't buy until you have a feel for values in the market. Value is relative, but the more overpriced something is, the less room there is for further appreciation.

Pick your areas—one or two—and read all the available literature. There are plenty of books about every piece of the market, and each piece of the market has its newsletters and periodicals, with plenty of representative prices.

Befriend other collectors in your field. Go to museums at which the items you cherish are displayed. Learn who the better dealers are in your field and visit them—studying their wares, learning about prices. The more you can convince a dealer that you are a shrewd, knowledgeable individual, the better you'll be treated.

Before you buy in, learn all you can about how you're going to get out.

Will the dealer buy the item back from you, or must you find a buyer yourself? Will the dealer buy something outright, or will he take it only on consignment—displaying it and selling it when a buyer happens along, with nothing to you until it's sold (and with you and the dealer splitting the price when it is sold)?

There are items in every category available at modest prices. The markets in photographic prints, art prints, coins, stamps, books, and many more, are filled with items available for just a few hundred dollars. But the less you spend, the less likely you bought something that will show much appreciation. Buy one piece of something good—as much as you can afford—rather than dribs and drabs of cut-price items.

You're always on safer ground when you stick to things that are precisely catalogued and priced. There are books that list every coin and stamp likely to come your way—with a precise description and a price for each. You and the dealer may quibble over whether a coin is mint condition or a little worn. By and large, though, you'll know what the going price is when you buy in, and you'll keep close track of prices while you own the coin or stamp. The more you get into uncharted waters—the works of young artists, for instance—the more the price is set by the seller at whim.

Visit auctions, but stay out of the bidding until you know enough about the field to bid intelligently—and until you feel you can handle the frenzied pace of an auction. You can often pick up bargains at auctions—if the heat of the moment doesn't cause you to do something ill-advised. Until you really get the feel of things, you're better off buying in someone's showroom, after patient study, and with a chance to ask all the questions you want.

There isn't a precise correlation between inflation and prices in these markets. You can assume price appreciation won't be great unless inflation does come back. But that's when you want these markets the most. But you also want to be as close to the front of the parade as you can get—a shrewd investor who saw the signs early and acted upon them, not just another greater fool who came along late.

For now, buy for pleasure, and buy because prices are way down in most of these markets. Should your economic sixth sense warn you that inflation is flaring up, then you can move in earnest. Should inflation flare again, then you can be sure there will be plenty of people just behind you—also seeking shelter against scary times, but slower off the mark than you are.

Guidelines for Action

There are markets in everything under the sun—from corn futures to Old Masters paintings to diamonds to gold.

You might buy a work of art to have something nice to hang on the wall. More likely, you'll turn to these markets because they deal in tangibles and you no longer trust stocks or bonds or even paper money.

Unless or until you gain knowledge and experience, you're a rank outsider in all these markets. The theme that runs through all markets is: Let the buyer beware.

If you try these markets, learn all you can before you enter.

Favor markets where items are catalogued and priced (coins and stamps over the works of young artists).

Remember that gold is a hedge against hard times—not an investment. Approach semi-precious gems with caution—and don't approach the precious-gem market at all (ever).

CHAPTER 11

The Newest Wrinkles in Tax-Proofing Your Money

There comes, early in May each year, a holiday with special significance for all of us. The Tax Foundation, in Washington, calls it Tax Freedom Day. It's the day the average American starts working for himself—having worked all the days of the year until then to pay all the taxes that governments impose on us.

That's another way of saying that for the Average American, one-third of every penny earned each year goes to pay taxes. Unless you can do something about that, you haven't even started to take charge of your financial future.

The federal government takes up to 50 cents of each dollar you earn from your job. Your state takes some of what's left, and your city may take some more. The federal government takes up to 50 cents of each dollar of dividend income, with only the first $100 ($200 for a couple) free from taxation. It takes up to 50 cents of every dollar of interest income, and the $100–$200 exclusion applies only to dividends, not interest. Your state may also take a cut of interest and dividend income. And that doesn't count sales taxes, property taxes, excise taxes, gift taxes, estate taxes, and more.

The 1981 tax law changed some things. The maximum tax rate is 50 percent, instead of 70 percent as it used to be. We all pay taxes at lower rates. It used to take $60,000 in taxable income to put you in the 50 percent bracket. It's $109,400 in 1983 and it will be $162,400 in 1984 and after. The maximum rate on capital gains was cut from 28 to 20 percent.

In some cases, though, the 1981 law made things worse. Before, you got the first $200 of interest *and* dividend income free from taxes ($400 for a couple). Now it's $100 ($200 for a couple) and it applies only to dividends. After 1985, the first $450 of interest income ($900 for a couple), will be free of taxes, but that's in 1985. As the federal government eased its tax bite, states and cities intensified theirs. Then, having given us the biggest tax cut in history, in 1982 the federal government gave us the biggest tax hike in history. Among other things, the 1982 law severely limited the tax deduction on medical bills and casualty losses.

You can cheat on your tax return—underestimating income and overstating deductions and hoping your return will fall between the cracks at the IRS. It probably won't and you'll face hefty interest charges and penalties, and you could go to prison.

So you do what you can—using all your wiles and all the loopholes the law provides—to tax-proof your investments. You might hire a lawyer or accountant skilled in the tax laws. Once your taxable income reaches $35,000 (the 35 percent bracket in 1983), you're cheating yourself if you don't get expert help. (Some experts—doctors, dentists, and tax professionals—you just can't get along without.)

Unless your affairs are very complicated, you don't even need a lawyer or a CPA. There are "enrolled agents," who have passed an IRS examination and who are allowed to represent you before the IRS. Tax help should cost less than $1,000 for your first year and maybe two-thirds of that for each future year, and you should save more in taxes than you pay. What you pay for help is a tax deduction.

Whomever you hire, don't wait until the last minute. Tax professionals are at their busiest from January to April 15, and they won't have much time for you. Look for someone in May or June. Tax people have time free then, and there's plenty of time to do the planning that can save you money on the current year's taxes—as opposed to just filling out a return for the year that's past. A couple of planning sessions around the middle of the year, and a session early the next year to prepare your return, should be enough.

Armed with one of the better tax guides, you can do a lot on your own. My favorite is J. K. Lasser's *Your Income Tax* from Simon and Schuster. The price in 1982 was a tax-deductible $5.95, and I used it for years before Simon and Schuster became my publisher. It runs 322 pages, crammed with advice on how to prepare your current tax return, plus a lot of tax-saving tips you can use to tax-proof your money in the future.

The Lasser guide (and many others) tells you all that counts as income, and all the deductions and tax credits you can take. A deduction reduces the part of your income subject to taxation: In the 30 percent bracket, each dollar of deduction cuts your tax bill by 30 percent. A tax credit reduces—100 cents on the dollar—the taxes you actually owe. It's worth reading all the fine print to make sure you aren't missing a trick.

The 1982 tax law, furthermore, greatly raised the cost of missing a trick. It did that by authorizing a 10 percent penalty on any "substantial understatement" of income tax. If you come up with strange and wonderful deductions that reduce your tax to substantially less than the IRS thinks you owe, it can nail you for those extra taxes—and for a 10 percent penalty besides.

Make sure you get all the deductions right. You can avoid that 10 percent penalty if you "adequately disclose" why you thought you were entitled to the deduction. You can also avoid it if you can cite "substantial authority," which usually means having an opinion from a tax professional.

We're not just talking about cleaning up a single year's return, but about tax-proofing your money over the years. Once you get beyond deductions and credits, think about the whole array of tax-avoidance tricks: municipal bonds, tax shelters, and—should you gain wealth enough—even your own tax-free foundation, with plenty of way stations in between.

Reading the Law

The 1981 law made things easier for you in some important ways:

1. It turned the Individual Retirement Account (IRA) into an important-tax saving vehicle for everyone.
2. It more than tripled the amount you can give away each year without paying taxes on the gift. One way to save on taxes is to give assets to other people, which passes the tax burden on the income from those assets from you to someone else.
3. It virtually eliminated estate taxes for most people.
4. It made certain tax shelters more appealing to more people.
5. It created the dividend reinvestment plan for those who invest in utility stocks. You escape taxation on up to $750 worth of dividends a year from a utility ($1,500 for a couple) if you reinvest those dividends in the stock of the utility.
6. It cut the capital gains tax rate to a maximum 20 percent from 28 percent—making it more imperative than ever that you invest in hopes of capital gains.

The lushest return on a money fund or a savings certificate; the highest rate on a bond; the fattest dividend on stock, will be taxed at rates up to 50 percent. Turn a capital gain, and the most the government can take is 20 percent. If you lose, the government will bear half the loss, up to $3,000 each year. The government is aiming a gun at your head and ordering you to invest.

Keogh Plans and IRA's

Thanks to the 1981 law, you can save money, and skip taxes through an IRA or its kissing cousin, the Keogh Plan. Each shelters income put aside for retirement (and the 1982 tax law further sweetened things for Keogh Plans).

Keogh Plans came first, allowing the self-employed, with no pension plans to fall back upon, to put something aside against retirement each year tax free. You could set aside up to $7,500 each year, and pay no taxes on that or on the income it produced until you retired. You'd pay taxes then—but the rate would presumably be lower than during your working years. For the average person, income—and so the tax bite—drops about 50 percent at retirement.

To give something to working people who weren't covered by a pension plan, Congress next approved the IRA. If you worked for someone but didn't have a pension plan, you could put aside $1,500 a year tax free, just as Keogh Plan money was tax free.

In 1981, Congress raised the maximum annual contribution to a Keogh Plan from $7,500 to $15,000, and in 1982 it raised it again. Starting in 1984, you can contribute up to $30,000 a year to a Keogh Plan, and starting in 1986, the maximum annual contribution will increase in line with inflation. In 1981, Congress also raised the maximum annual contribution on an IRA from $1,500 to $2,000, and it dropped all rules on who could have an IRA. You can have the most lavish company pension plan known to man (or woman) and still have an IRA.

Just to review the rules:

1. You can put up to $2,000 into an IRA each year for yourself, and up to $2,250 if you have a spouse who doesn't work. If you and your spouse both work, you can each put in $2,000 a year.

2. You pay no taxes on your annual contributions, or on the income the money earns, until you begin drawing on your IRA.

3. You can't withdraw IRA money until you're 59½ without paying a penalty, and you must start withdrawing it by the time you're 70½.

The government further said that financial institutions can pay any rate of interest they want on IRA accounts—and to stay competitive, institutions began offering very choice returns on IRA money. They also began making some very overblown promises. You were told that if you started young enough, you'd be a millionaire by the time you retired. So you would be—if your IRA money earned a high enough rate of interest through your lifetime. But that would imply so high a rate of inflation that your millions wouldn't stretch very far:

your IRA worth a million dollars, but a hamburger costing $100.

Whither Your IRA Money

There are only a few rules about where you can't put your IRA money. It can't buy life insurance, since money in life insurance builds up tax free each year anyway. You can't invest in precious metals or collectibles (art and antiques, stamps, coins, precious gems and the like). Both areas were deemed too volatile for money that's supposed to be there when you retire. You can buy stocks and real estate with your IRA money, but you can't buy them with borrowed money.

With all that money on the line, some pretty kinky ways of investing your IRA money have appeared: strange deals involving real estate, oil and gas drilling, and other things. Should the IRS decide what you've invested in doesn't belong in an IRA, your tax break goes out the window. If you're thinking of moving your IRA money beyond the normal range of investments, check it out with a tax professional.

Normal would include the offerings of banks, thrift institutions, insurance companies, (annuities, not life insurance), brokerage houses, and mutual funds. Banks, thrifts, and insurance annuities sell on the basis of pure yield, and you want the highest yield you can get, guaranteed for the longest period of time.

Something in a fixed-income security would seem nice—a top-grade corporate bond or a passthrough security from the Government National Mortgage Association. You'd have to tailor your bonds pretty precisely so they'd mature just when you need the money. You don't want to hit retirement with bonds still some years from maturity and selling at deep discounts in the market. Another problem is that bonds—and Ginnie Mae passthroughs, in particular—throw off lots of income, which must constantly be reinvested. You can't spend any of that income until you reach 59½. And, of course, each year you must buy anew, with the $2,000 you'll have to invest that year—which may involve more work than you really had in mind.

Brokers offer IRA plans, which involve investing your money and reinvesting the income on your money. Mutual fund outfits offer the full array of their funds: money market, stock funds, bond funds, income funds, growth funds. Almost all funds permit unlimited shifts, from one to another, with just a phone call. (IRA money can always be shifted from one institution to another: from a bank to another bank, from a bank to a broker, from a broker to an insurance company. Make sure the institution handles the transfer: If you come into possession of the money, even for a short time, you may have to pay taxes on it.) You can establish your own investment account with IRA money, so long as it's totally segregated from all your other investments.

Still, this is retirement money we're talking about, and you don't want to risk it. IRA money put into stocks or bonds can produce gains as well as income—but it can also produce losses, and instead of getting bigger, your IRA pool is suddenly getting smaller. This is money you don't want to gamble with.

Narrowing the Field

Bank deposits are insured (up to $100,000), and when it comes to IRAs and Keogh Plans, nearly all rules on rates, minimums, and maturities were scrapped on Dec. 1, 1983. You can get any rate for any maturity with any minimum that you can negotiate. Obviously, you want the highest rate for the longest period of time.

The newest thing in tax tactics is the "zero coupon" government issue, packaged by Wall Street banking houses, and given such colorful names as "tigers" (Treasury Investment Growth Certificates, from Merrill Lynch), and "lions" (Lehman Investment Opportunity Notes, from Lehman Brothers).

A zero coupon issue pays no interest. You buy it at a big discount and you are paid off at par, which is where the return on your investment comes.

There is no such security in real life. These Wall Street houses concoct their own, based on Treasury issues, and they can run from a few months to many years. Their biggest drawback to most investors is that, although you get no interest along the way, the IRS taxes you each year as though you did. Still, they pay a handsome return, and since all income from your IRA is sheltered until you dip into it many years in the future, the tax treatment of zero-coupon issues doesn't matter one little bit to you.

There are also zero-coupon corporate bonds. But you'll have to look harder to find them, and you're betting on the ability of a company to pay off far in the future, as opposed to the ability of the Treasury to pay off.

My own choice was an annuity from an insurance company that I've been doing business with for 30 years. It pays a competitive rate, adjusted every six months, and I have total confidence in the company's ability to survive. I wouldn't risk my IRA money in stocks or bonds or anything else that might lose value over time. The IRA is my ace-in-the-hole. I want it as immune as possible from economic slings and arrows, and I don't want to put the money into an area the IRS might challenge. So early each year, my $2,000 goes off to the insurance company to make another payment on the annuity.

If you opt for a plan at some brokerage house or mutual fund outfit, make sure you know what their fees are for the service: how much goes to you and how much goes to whoever has your account. With my annuity, every penny benefits me.

Many employers offer payroll-deduction IRA accounts. It's strictly a business decision. Where will the money be invested? How much will it earn compared with what other accounts are paying? How confident are you that your company will be around when you retire—and what would happen to your IRA money if the company folded or merged.

Put all you can into an IRA. The government isn't giving you the money tax free, but it's lending you money, interest free, for a long time. The Investment Company Institute—the trade group for mutual funds—reckons that $2,000 a year for 30 years, put into an investment yielding 12 percent, would produce $264,364. For someone in the 30 percent tax bracket, that same money in an IRA would produce $540,585, since everything is reinvested, and nothing is taken out to pay taxes.

The Market in Municipals

Once you get into the 30 percent tax bracket ($30,000 in taxable income in 1983, $35,300 in 1984 and beyond), think about municipal bonds—the traditional tax-avoidance vehicle of those with money. A municipal bond costs $5,000, but you can buy older bonds at a discount. There are municipal unit trusts that start for $1,000. There are municipal bond mutual funds, into which you can buy for $1,000, and shares cost $10 or less. There are tax-exempt money market funds that invest in short-term state and local government issues.

There are general obligation (g.o.) municipal bonds, which are repaid out of general tax revenues, and municipal revenue bonds, which are repaid from the earnings of some specific revenue-producing facility, like a toll road or a sports stadium. A general obligation bond is backed by the taxing power of the issuer, while a revenue bond is backed only by the ability of the facility to produce revenue. In the scheme of things, a revenue bond will yield a little more than a general obligation bond because it's a somewhat riskier proposition.

There are bonds issued by cities and states, and bonds issued by counties and townships. There are bonds issued by school districts and bonds issued by authorities created to do some specific thing (build a bridge or run an airport). There are long-term bonds, running out to 30 years, and there are shorter-term securities. There's a flood of new issues every year, and there are issues sold in the past and now available at discounts because rates have climbed (and prices fallen) in this market, as in all the bond markets. Either your broker works for a firm that brings municipal bonds to a market, or he can buy a bond for you from a firm that operates in the market. Banks are allowed to deal in general obligation bonds, and it's possible your bank does.

No matter who issued it or why, or for how long, all municipal bonds have this in common: The interest is exempt from federal taxation. The theory is that cities and states will sell bonds to finance such basic services as schools and sewers and streetlights, and that these basic services are so vital, they must be financed at the lowest possible cost. Nowadays, the money probably goes to build a domed sports stadium, but the tax exempt feature endures.

Municipal bonds are not exempt from state income taxes, and that could cut into your return. Most states, though, don't collect taxes when a citizen buys a bond issued within the state. It usually pays to buy close to home to avoid state taxation, if you don't have to give up more yield than the state tax would cost you.

The Special Rules for Muni Bonds

The interest on all bonds—including municipal bonds—is set when issued. As with all bonds, the price of older issues will fluctuate in the market to bring the yield into line with rates available on new issues. When rates are rising, prices of all older bonds—municipal and otherwise—will fall, and sometimes they'll fall sharply. But a special consideration affects the price of municipal bonds.

The interest on municipal bonds is exempt from taxation, but capital gains aren't. When you buy a bond at a discount, you're guaranteed a capital gain, because someday the issuer (you hope) will pay off the bonds at their face value. Because you're guaranteed a capital gain, you're also guaranteed having to pay a capital gains tax. To compensate you for that tax bill, the price of a municipal bond will be cut by a little more than the price of a comparable corporate or government bond. "Double-discounting," it's called, and when corporate or government bond prices fall, municipal bond prices will tend to fall more sharply.

When you buy any bond, you risk seeing the price fall. In municipal bonds you risk seeing the price *really* fall.

Because of the tax-exempt feature, a municipal bond will, before taxes, yield considerably less than a corporate or government bond. If a high-grade corporate bond is yielding 12 percent, a high-grade municipal bond will yield about 8 percent. It's the after-tax yield you care about. The higher your tax bracket, the higher the after-tax yield on a municipal bond. If you're in a lower bracket—under 30 percent—munis (as they're invariably called) don't make much sense, because you can get a better after-tax return elsewhere. Once you get beyond the 30 percent bracket, they start to make a lot of sense, because you're now being offered a higher after-tax return than you could get anyplace else.

The calculation is always the after-tax return on a muni—at your tax rate—against what you could get from a government or a corporate issue, or a money fund, or whatever. Every bond salesman will have tables showing the after-tax return, at your bracket, for what he's selling.

The other side of a municipal bond is that when prices rise, they *really* rise, since each advance in the price cuts into the potential capital gain, and that double discount melts away. When bond prices generally are rising, the municipal bond market can get pretty frenzied. Catching the turn—buying just as prices are turning higher—can be particularly rewarding in municipal bonds.

Still another consideration is that while municipal bonds are rated for quality by the big rating agencies, as corporate bonds are, the rating on a municipal bond is more tentative than the rating on a corporate bond. A company must keep its books in good order, those books must be audited by an independent certified public accounting firm, and the financial picture of the company must be made available to shareholders and investors each year in the annual report, and in documents filed with the Securities and Exchange Commission.

Local government bookkeeping can be haphazard. More cities and states now use outside auditors, but most still do the work themselves, and you're betting on the ability and the candor of those in-house auditors. The auditor of a city's books may be skilled and able, or he may be the mayor's kid brother. With 1½ million different municipal bonds out in the world, it would take more staff than any rating agency has to make sure that all municipal bonds are as they should be. The rating agencies were very slow to spot the worsening financial plight of New York City in the 1970s.

Safety First

That makes it all the more important that you have total confidence in whomever you buy municipal bonds from—bank or broker. There are so many bonds available that each firm will have just a representative sample available, and it may not be the same representative sample that the firm across the street has. You really can't comparison-shop, so you're betting your all on the quality of the bonds available at the firm you buy from, and you're relying very heavily on its recommendations.

Instances of default are still rare. New York City never defaulted on its debts; it merely put everyone on hold. You got another kind of security to replace the New York issues that were maturing and, of course, no one would buy a New York issue from you. If you wanted your money in a hurry, you were stuck.

When you buy a municipal bond, stick with quality—A-rated or better. If possible, buy only issues where the finances have been certified by an independent, outside auditing firm. Favor issues of states over cities (more taxing clout), and steer clear of all those local school districts, sewer districts, and all other unknown issuers. If you haven't heard of it, don't buy its bonds.

The financial problems of most cities and states in the urban North have been well publicized. Don't automatically assume that anything from the Sunbelt is a solid investment. Hyper-rapid growth has strained the finances of plenty of Sunbelt cities. Many of them have offered so many tax breaks to attract new industry that they're deriving very little in tax revenues from that growth. Unless you have good reason to believe otherwise, assume that a Sunbelt city is simply a city whose financial problems have not yet surfaced.

Some parts of the North—New England, for instance—have developed new industries to replace the dead industries of the past and have come back stronger than ever. In late 1982, when unemployment was rising in such Sunbelt cities as Houston, Dallas, Tulsa, and San Diego, the rate of unemployment in Portland, Maine, and on Long Island, New York, was only half the national average, and the jobless rate in Massachusetts was lower than the jobless rate in either Texas or California.

Don't buy bonds from any state where the unemployment rate is more than 20 percent above the national average. (The Labor Department, in reporting on unemployment nationally each month, also reports on unemployment state by state.) Buy from states where there's a diversity of industries, so if one industry falters, another can keep the state's economy going.

Favor general obligation bonds over revenue bonds even if the yield is a little lower. A state (or a city, for that matter) can tax itself to solvency, but a revenue bond lives or dies on the ability of the facility that it financed to make a profit. Hard times can hit even the most promising of revenue-producing facilities. We don't drive as much as we used to, and marginal toll roads and toll bridges aren't earning what they used to. Some face monumental repair bills that could strain their financial resources. A sports stadium is no better than the teams that play in it. If it's a marginal team—or even a solid team in a marginal sport—it can fold and the stadium can go dark.

Whenever possible, taking all of the above into consideration, buy as close to home as you can. Your bank or broker will know more about local issues than it will about a state a couple of thousand miles away. If there's a considerable local tax bite, it probably won't apply if you buy local issues.

Municipal Bond Strategies

For tax-free income, buy new issues or discount bonds. The yield should be at least 65 percent of the yield on a Treasury issue of equivalent maturity. At times, in recent years, the yield on municipals has gone above that level because price cutting in municipals has been so severe. If municipal bonds in general are yielding more than 65 percent of Treasuries, that's the way the market is behaving. If other municipal bonds are yielding about 65 percent of equivalent Treasury issues and the bond you're looking at is yielding more, you want to know why. A deliciously high yield on a bond may mean there's some danger in the situation you don't know about—all the more reason for sticking with quality and buying only from someone you know and trust.

For capital gains, buy a discount bond maturing in seven years or so. You have a tax-free return, plus a crack at capital gains. Again, when prices of municipal bonds fall, they *really* fall, and when they rally, they *really* rally, and the gains in municipal bonds can be particularly choice (but, as you'll recall, taxable). The closer to maturity a bond is, the less the discount as it nears the point at which the bonds will be paid off at par. The longer to maturity, the longer you'd have to hold the bond should the market turn against you. Municipal bonds, like corporate bonds, can be called before maturity—the issuer calling in a high-interest-rate bond and replacing it with something carrying a lower rate. Since a discount bond, by definition, carries a low interest rate, you don't have to worry that it will be called.

When you buy any bond, buy with the assumption that prices might not do what you expect them to do, and you might have to hold on for at least three years. That's all the more true for municipal bonds, in which price swings can be violent. Buy when your economic sixth sense tells you that interest rates are turning—or as close to the turn as you can get. But rallies in the bond market will tend to run no more smoothly than rallies in the stock market. Rates will fall, which will bring a flood of new issues to market, which will temporarily check the decline in rates. Then, the fall in rates will resume.

Buying In for Less

Granted that $5,000 per bond is a pretty steep price—but there are those cheaper ways of doing it.

You can put your money in a unit trust—a unit trust in municipal bonds being just like a unit trust in Ginnie Mae passthroughs. A bond dealer will take some millions of dollars of new bonds and put them into a trust, where they will stay, undisturbed, through the life of those bonds. You buy one or more units within that trust, with each unit usually going for $1,000, plus a sales charge of about $35 or $40 per unit. There's no management fee since the sponsor does no managing. The bonds that were there when the trust was created, will stay there through the years. One by one the bonds will be called, or they'll mature, until there's nothing left in the trust.

Because it's a fixed array of bonds, you know when you buy in what the trust will yield through its life. You get periodic payments of income from the bonds—distributed monthly by some trusts, and quarterly by others. When a bond is called, or when it matures, the proceeds are distributed to the owners of the trust, so bit by bit you get your principal back over the years.

New trusts appear all the time, and when you buy a brand-new trust, you're buying income, since the trust will offer a competitive yield when it's sold. After that, the price fluctuates according to what's happening in the market. If rates go down, your trust will yield more than newer issues are yielding. If rates go up, the price of your unit will fall and you're stuck, just as you would be with a bond.

The trust will buy back your units, if you want to sell, on the basis of the current price of the trust. If the price is up, you make a capital gain; if prices are down, you'll take a loss. You can buy into an older trust, at a discount, and gamble on a rising market to boost the price of your unit.

If you want to invest in a unit trust and you live in a high-tax state, shop around for a "single-state" trust, made up totally of issues from your state, that will be exempt from both federal and local taxes. As long as you're going tax free, you might as well go tax free all the way. The high-tax states (hence the ones most likely to have single-state funds) are New York, California, Pennsylvania, Massachusetts, Michigan, and Minnesota.

There is a condition under which a bond in a unit trust can be sold: if the sponsor thinks an issue is about to default. Then the proceeds are split among the investors. In theory, of course, the firm that sponsored the trust should have been smart enough to steer clear of any bond that might go into default. Even professionals get fooled though. In fact, sponsors of unit trusts have been known to cram a trust with bonds they brought to market and couldn't sell. By this point, you have a broker you can trust. Make sure he puts you into a unit trust that you can trust.

Having said that the yield on a unit trust never changes from Day One, there appeared in the spring of 1982 a floating-rate unit trust, sponsored by a clutch of big Wall Street names, including Merrill Lynch. The yield on the units changes as the prime rate of the banks changes (meaning that the yield fell through the summer and autumn of 1982). The entry fee is $1,000, and Merrill Lynch says it is selling well.

There are municipal bond mutual funds, and the money market funds that invest in very short tax-exempt issues.

A municipal bond fund is just like any other mutual fund, except that it invests only in tax-exempt securities. As a common stock mutual fund is always buying and selling in hopes of finding winning stocks, so a municipal bond fund is always buying and selling in hopes of finding bonds that yield the most, or that show the most impressive price gains. You may or may not pay a sales charge, depending on whether it's a "load" fund (in which case the commission can run to 8½ percent of your investment) or a "no load" fund (in which case there's no commission). There's no evidence that you can do better in a fund that charges a sales commission—and there's no good reason for doing so. You will pay a management fee to the fund managers. (You don't hand over cash: the fee is deducted from fund income before your dividend is paid.)

The yield on a bond fund will change from day to day, because the price of fund shares, based on the price of the bonds in the fund's portfolio, will fluctuate from day to day. Typically, you put up an initial $1,000 and then you can add as little at a time as you want to, to buy more shares. The funds will redeem your shares when you want to get out, at whatever the going price for shares is that day. Depending on the price of the shares when you buy in and when you get out, you can make a gain on your investment or take a loss. As with any other investment in a mutual fund, buy into a family of funds that lets you make unlimited shifts from one fund to another by making a telephone call. As circumstances dictate, you can go from a money fund to a bond fund to a stock fund and back to a money fund.

If you're in municipal bonds for the income, keep the concept of cash flow in mind. Any municipal bond salesman will have close at hand charts showing how much after-tax income you'll get, with a given yield, and at a given income tax bracket. The bond may yield 8 percent—but that's 8 percent tax free. It might take a 12 percent or (if your bracket is high enough) a 16 percent taxable yield to equal the 8 percent yield on a municipal bond.

But when it comes to cold, hard cash, what you get is 8 percent—$400 in income each year, if you paid $5,000 for the bond. The rest of the return is based on the taxes you don't pay—imputed income, not spendable cash. Try paying the mortgage with imputed income.

Seeking Shelter

It's really the idle rich that stick with municipal bonds. The active rich go into tax shelters. As noted in chapter 5, you can sometimes shelter more income than you have invested.

Tax shelters mostly are for the well-to-do, and by cutting the maximum tax rate from 70 percent to 50 percent, the 1981 tax law should have knocked some of the pins out from under tax shelters. But the 1981 law added some special features to shelters in real estate, oil and gas, and equipment leasing, and the business rolls on as briskly as ever.

Once again, the function of a tax shelter is to do just that—shelter from taxation, not merely the income thrown off by whatever the shelter invests in, but also some of your income from other sources. A shelter always operates with borrowed money, and the interest on borrowed money is a tax deduction. Each type of shelter further offers some special feature that provides fat tax deductions.

In real estate, as you'll recall from chapter 5, it's depreciation. The 1981 tax law helped out by reducing from as long as 40 years to 15 years the time in which you write off the property. It further provided for even bigger write-offs in the first few years you own residential property. In equipment leasing it's depreciation on whatever equipment the shelter is leasing —and depreciation on equipment was also speeded up considerably by the 1981 tax law. On equipment leasing there is also the investment tax credit that you get when you buy new capital equipment (which is what an equipment leasing shelter leases). In oil and gas, it's the deduction for the expense of drilling and exploring. In cattle it's the expense of fattening the cattle for market.

All these deductions should more than offset the income from the shelter—leaving you with deductions that you can take against other income. When you sell, the profit is taxed at the capital gains rate.

As you'll recall from chapter 5, nothing shelters like real estate shelters, thanks to the way the "at-risk" rules applies to real estate.

In all other shelters your deductions can't exceed what you actually have at risk: the cash you put up, plus whatever you'd be liable for should the deal fail and the lender come after you for his money. You have no further liability to the lender in a real estate deal: If the deal fails, the lender takes the property rather than dunning you for more money. Even so, in real estate (and only in real estate) you can take deductions up to the amount of the cash you put up—plus your share of the loan.

Your enemy in all tax shelters is the Internal Revenue Service, which tends to be very suspicious of tax shelters. That's hardly surprising, since the avowed purpose of tax shelters is to beat the government out of tax money. Nothing delights the IRS more than being able to flush out a phony tax shelter. The chilling word is "recapture," and what the IRS recaptures —at ordinary income rates, plus interest and penalties—are all the tax deductions you thought you had built up. You can further assume that anyone who invests in tax shelters will be marked as a moral leper by the IRS, that your every year's tax return will be scrutinized, and that you'll be audited as often as the IRS can get around to it.

Private shelters are definitely for the rich. Each investor

puts up a large sum, and the deal is put together by a lawyer or accountant who gets a fat fee for knowing every nook and cranny of the tax code. You can assume, in such a deal, that the deductions will be as promised, that the shelter will make economic sense, in addition to offering tax deductions, and that the IRS will be kept at bay.

The point about shelters making economic sense is crucial. There's no point in buying tax deductions, if the deal turns bad and takes your capital with it. You want the deductions, but you also want to keep—and enlarge—your capital.

Unfortunately, your chances of making it into one of those private deals is nil. You'd have to put up many thousands of dollars, and you'd have to convince those who organize the shelter that you had considerable wealth beyond what you put into the shelter.

Tax Shelters for You

That leaves public shelters—organized by a brokerage house or a real estate developer, for example—which are available to the general public. You can get in for as little as $5,000 or $10,000. For that, you become a limited partner—meaning that your liability is limited to the amount you've invested. Those who put the shelter together are the general partners. They make the arrangements, and you go along for the ride.

No matter what the shelter involves—real estate, cattle, oil and gas, or something else—you're at the mercy of whoever put it together. Your deductions may stand up against the IRS, but they may not. The economics of the deal may make sense, but they may not. Oil and gas shelters that looked like the greatest thing since sliced bread, looked awful when an oil glut developed in 1981 and 1982, and people pretty much stopped exploring for oil and gas. *The Wall Street Journal* estimates that investors put about $6 billion into oil drilling funds in 1981 alone. When the bottom fell out of the market, the *Journal* found that some partnerships were "being liquidated at less than 20 cents on the dollar."

The *Journal* also cited a private study stating that "less than half of the drilling partnerships registered with the Securities and Exchange Commission pay back their investors' money plus annual earnings of at least 10 percent, even in good times."

And that is only the oil and gas shelters. Bad times can hit any kind of shelter. You might have had the most marvelous equipment in the whole world available for lease—magnificent computers and spanking new freight cars—but when the economy crashed in 1982, what you had to lease would have gone begging.

It's a business made for fast-buck operators, and what's promised is not necessarily what's delivered. The business really heats up late in the year—the idea being that you're getting in near year end, but you'll grab the full year's worth of tax breaks. The IRS pays particular attention to shelters sold in the year-end rush, knowing that a fair percentage of them will be flawed in some fatal way.

I've mentioned only the most common shelters. After that, they get pretty exotic: fruit orchards, coal, films, and on and on. If someone invests in it, someone else will turn it into a shelter and dare the IRS to do something about it. The IRS usually takes the dare.

A shelter makes sense as you get above the 30 percent tax bracket, and it makes more sense the higher up the income ladder you go. But you must know whom you're buying from, and you must have a grasp of the economics of the industry your money will be invested in. No matter how much or how little you have in a shelter, a lawyer or accountant skilled in tax law must check everything out for you. Are the deductions likely to stand up? Does the deal make economic sense? Are the organizers of the shelter sound? Is their fee for putting the shelter together reasonable? What does your economic sixth sense say about it? Is it too good to be true? Is there anything about the deal that makes your nerve endings quiver?

If a shelter doesn't sound, feel, or smell right, walk away. There will always be more shelters than you could possibly invest in. You don't have to worry about letting one get away.

In tax shelters—and in every other investment under the sun—regard this as an absolute rule: IF SOMEONE YOU

DON'T KNOW PITCHES A DEAL TO YOU OVER THE TELEPHONE, HANG UP AT ONCE. A broker from a legitimate firm may have legitimately gotten your name, but he'll just invite you in to talk; he won't try to sell you something over the phone. Telephone sellers are trained to make every deal sound as though you've been given first crack at investing in the Mother Lode.

Don't buy a tax shelter—or anything else, for that matter—until you've read the prospectus, had a couple of days to think it over, and a lawyer or accountant has studied it.

The Taxing Plight of the Rich

When it comes to the tax laws, it's not as easy being rich as it used to be. Most of the foreign tax havens, in which you could bank your money away from the reach of the IRS, have been shut down. If you keep a foreign bank account, you must tell the IRS about it. If you move large sums of cash outside the country, you must notify the government of that. If you don't, and you're caught,. you're in very big trouble. If you're an American, no matter where your money goes, you still owe U.S. taxes on it. The only way around that is to renounce your American citizenship and live elsewhere.

The government, by the way, thinks most people who have foreign bank accounts, do report them—even if they understate the amount they have in the account. Remember that there's a fat bounty paid to anyone who informs on a tax cheat. More tax fraud is uncovered through phone calls from jilted spouses and lovers than by all IRS agents put together. If anyone knows what you're doing, you're their hostage forever.

Even the tax-exempt foundation, as a means of sheltering wealth, isn't what it used to be.

You can still donate your wealth to a foundation you've created. The income from that wealth would then be exempt from taxation, and you could bestow your name on the foundation—putting it alongside those of Ford, Carnegie, and Rockefeller. Unfortunately, in 1969 Congress passed a pretty stringent law about foundations. You can't, as you once could, pay yourself a handsome salary from the tax-free income of the foundation. No longer can you just give any old asset to a foundation—and, unlike some of the foundations of yore, you must spend a fair share of the foundation's assets each year.

When it comes to tax dodges now, foundations are far down the list.

It's Better to Give . . .

Even if you don't have the wealth for a big-time tax shelter, or a tax-exempt foundation, the 1981 tax law offers other ways of minimizing your tax bill. You can give your money away. If it doesn't belong to you any more, you don't pay taxes on it. There are even ways of giving your money away so you get it back someday.

Say you've got kids who'll be going to college in time. The money will go to them anyway. But each year you keep it, you pay the taxes. So you give the money to your kids, by setting up a custodial account, with you or your spouse as custodian.

Until 1981 each parent could give up to $3,000 a year, tax free, to each child. The 1981 law raised that to $10,000 a year, per donor and per recipient.

Once you give the money away, it's the recipient who pays the taxes, not you.

If you give it to a child, he or she will pay little or no taxes on the money, so there's more of it building up to pay those college bills. As custodian, you still decide where the money should be invested for maximum yield. Since there's no tax burden to worry about, you can go into a money fund or a savings certificate, without having to worry about the tax collector. You can buy a high-grade corporate bond, or a Treasury issue, maturing when you'll need the money to start paying college bills.

Harken back to lions and tigers and other zero-coupon government issues that we talked about when we were talking about IRA's. Recall that the drawback to most investors is that a zero-coupon issue pays no interest, but the IRS collects taxes as though it did. That's no concern when your money is sheltered by an IRA or a Keogh Plan. It's no concern when your child is the owner of the "zero," because it's the child's tax burden. Unless your child has lots of income, there won't be any tax burden.

Every state has its uniform gifts to minors law, and you make the transfer of assets under the provisions of that law. You don't need a lawyer to handle the transfer. Any bank or thrift institution or stockbroker can handle it. The only rule for you is that you must be prudent in where you put the money. You can't take it to the racetrack and bet it on behalf of your children.

Nor can you use the money once you've given it away. You have control over the money until the recipient is an adult, but you can't spend it because it's no longer your money.

If you don't want to give the money away forever, you can create a short-term trust, called a Clifford trust. The trust must run for at least 10 years, and you can create it with cash, stocks or bonds, or any other asset. During the life of the trust, all income goes on the tax bill of whomever you created that trust for. You decide where the income from the trust should be invested—again, for maximum yield, since you don't have to worry about taxes. At the end of 10 years the assets in the trust come back to you. A lawyer or accountant should help you with the trust, to make sure you're doing it right. But there's nothing very complicated about it.

Anything you give away can mean a tax break for you: old clothes, the old living room furniture, the TV set that doesn't work so well, old books, the children's old toys. Instead of running a garage sale, donate it to some worthwhile charity—the Salvation Army, Goodwill Industries, your church or synagogue thrift shop. If it isn't too beat up, or if it can be repaired at a reasonable cost, the agency will fix it up and sell it. You value the donation for tax purposes. If the valuation seems reasonable, the IRS will probably buy it.

Once a year, do a clean sweep of the house, gathering all the odds and ends you don't use, donate them to a charity, and take yourself a nice tax deduction. (By definition, all tax deductions are nice.)

If it's something of real value—a work of art donated to the local art museum, or an antique donated to the local historical society—the IRS will insist that you get a professional appraisal of its worth before it will accept the deduction. And you may not always find museums or historical societies interested in what you have to give away. Still, if you dabble in art and antiques, and the markets are so depressed you can't sell, try to give them away for the tax deduction.

If tax deductions are nice, tax credits are even better. Credits, as you'll recall, cut your final tax bill dollar for dollar. And the rules on credits—on child care, energy, capital investments, etc.—keep changing. Make sure you know all the rules about credits early enough in the tax year to do you some good.

That holds true for everything about your taxes. The time to think about taxes isn't in April of next year but early enough this year to plan your investments and your charitable contributions so they do you the maximum good. The point of going to a tax professional is not so much to prepare your tax return but to help you prepare a tax strategy, to go along with your money strategy. There are always changes in the tax laws that can make it worthwhile to shift income and deductions from one year to the next. That's where a tax professional earns his fee: making those suggestions early enough so they produce savings on your tax bill.

Guidelines for Action

Sometimes—all warnings notwithstanding—you do need expert help, and that includes doctors, dentists, lawyers, and tax professionals.

Once your income tops $35,000 a year (35 percent tax bracket in 1983), you're cheating yourself if you don't get help from a tax pro.

Take full advantage of all the tax breaks offered by Individual Retirement Accounts and Keogh Plans—but don't put your money where there's a chance of losing it.

Even if other kinds of bonds turn you off, look at municipal bonds, where income is tax free. Your best bet could be a single-state unit trust (exempt from federal and local taxes).

If you don't own something, you don't pay taxes on it. The 1981 tax law made it more advantageous than ever to give some of your wealth away. Tax shelters also gained from the 1981 law. Even so, approach shelters with extreme caution—and some of that professional help.

CHAPTER 12

Earning More in the Job Market of the Eighties

You can scrimp and save until your fingers bleed and you'll have more money for saving and investing.

Or you can go the other way and have more because you earn more. That can include everything from doing something for a profit that you now do for fun, to moving up faster at your present job, to starting a new career with better prospects.

One thing you can't do, in these uncertain eighties, is just stand pat.

Without knowing a thing about you, I can, with certainty, tell you this:

1. Whatever your age, you'll find the job market more competitive in the 1980s than in any other decade of your working life.
2. No matter how our economy does, unemployment will stay high by historic standards clear into the 1990s.
3. No matter what industry you're in, still more of your industry's products will be made abroad before the end of the 1980s.
4. No matter what industry you're in, or what sort of work you do, a microcomputer or other smart machine, or a robot, will start to make a major difference in the way you work before the decade ends.

It's a difficult time in the economy, and raises and promotions don't come as they used to. You can't count on rapid economic growth to carry you along, while you can count on intense competition for choice spots as the baby-boom generation floods the job market.

It's a time of great change for our economy, with old industries dying and new industries and new technologies emerging. Your present job may be a one-way ticket to oblivion because what you do is being done for less in Mexico or Malaysia, or is being done for less here by some supersmart machine.

You have to work extra hard to find the right job in the 1980s and beyond and you have to work extra hard to be noticed and promoted when you do get the right job.

You need a job strategy if you really want to take charge of your own financial future. As usual, the only one who can do that for you, is you.

Maybe you're pretty comfortable where you are, and you just need a few extra bucks a week to flesh out what you earn, for saving and investing. That's when you try some moonlighting—not a full-time second job but something that will bring in that little extra.

I know a writer who does carpentry in his spare time, someone who bakes pastries to sell at flea markets, and a woman who caters parties for a fee. I know a doctor who's an auto mechanic at heart. He buys old heaps, has fun fixing them up, and sells them at a profit. I know someone who does magic shows for parties, someone who runs a travel business part time, and someone else who sells and installs heating systems in his spare time. All do nicely from their part-time work, and I've known people who did well enough at a hobby to turn it into a full-time job.

Thinking Ahead to More Income

The next step in earning more money, is to play a "what-if" game with yourself. Sit down one day, when you have the house to yourself, and think about what you'd do if you lost your job and couldn't find another. How would you get by?

What skills or talents or hobbies do you have that might earn some money? Do you do quality house painting? Can you build kitchen cabinets? Can you refinish furniture and woodwork? Are you a skilled gardener? Can you do cement work? Can you groom pets or clean swimming pools?

Is there another field you'd like to try? What additional skills and training would you need, and how long would it take to get them? Is there another part of the country where you'd like to live? Might job opportunities be better there? Is there a business you'd like to start? How much would it cost to get started, and could you lay hands on the money?

You're turning your back on the past, and all of its comfortable niches, and looking at the future in a new way. The years go by, and we learn to live with our jobs and our incomes. Inertia keeps us from stepping out into something new. It's not a bad thing to do on general principle—taking the blinders off and thinking about the future. Jobs do vanish in these hard times, and people do have to change and adapt to get by. Should it happen to you someday, you have some idea of what your options are. And it could point your life in a whole new direction.

Even if you're madly in love with your job, sort through all the ways in which you might supplement your income—turning your talents and possibly your hobbies into extra cash. Should you actually do it, you'd become part of the fastest-growing sector of our economy—the $400 billion "underground" economy. Part of it involves drugs and gambling and prostitution. But most of it involves people just like you—selling goods and services for cash to other people who are seeking bargains and would rather not pay a sales tax. You're dealing with the underground economy when you buy something at a garage sale or a flea market, or when you pay a handyman in cash for doing some work around the house.

What you earn from your sideline business is taxable income even if you're paid in cash. Probably $1 in $100 that changes hands in the underground economy is reported to the IRS.

Your sideline business can be anything from free-lance gardening to selling those hand-painted birdhouses you've been giving away. If you have a product or a service to sell, let your friends and neighbors know about it, and let them pass the word along. Put up notices on the bulletin boards around town. Put a small ad in the local newspaper. Once things get off the ground, try a listing in the Yellow Pages.

Whatever you do, remember that you're in it for the profit. You don't have much in the way of overhead, and you can sell your services for less than a full-time professional might charge. But you want to turn a profit, so price yourself accordingly.

Still, this is sideline stuff—a little extra that can add to your savings and might generate some extra capital. It could turn into a new business for you. Most likely though, the big bucks will come if you can push yourself ahead in your main job—or turn to another job that pays better.

Positioning Yourself for Personal Growth

When the economy was booming, it didn't take much to move up at work. Rapid economic growth pulled most people ahead—not because of superior ability but because growth generated opportunities for all. With employment and economic growth subnormal, that isn't so today. To get ahead now, you must position yourself for growth, and you must do what is necessary to achieve this growth. You must establish yourself as an achiever. This means not just doing your job well but letting your supervisors know that you're a candidate for advancement.

You have to work twice as hard to move ahead because you've got a lot going against you.

There is the sluggish economy, which is reducing opportunities. There is, further, the postwar baby boom, which has filled companies with people who are in their thirties and are clogging up the avenues of advancement. The number of jobs in our economy will increase by less than 20 percent in the eighties. Growth among people in their thirties and forties, competing for the choicest jobs, will be twice that much.

If it were just too many people competing for too few jobs, it would be bad enough. Beyond that, is a very fundamental change in our economy—a change more fundamental than anything we've experienced since the start of the industrial revolution early in the nineteenth century. The age of the machine is ending in America, and we're moving into the age of information, and that is transforming the American job market.

America's forte used to be producing things in vast quantities, better and cheaper than anyone else could produce them. Already, much of the actual production—the heavy, dirty, dangerous, polluting work—is being done in other countries, and still more of it will be done in other countries in the future.

Much of what is produced in America in the future will be produced by robots, working under the control of smart machines, and with a minimum of human control. We will plan, design, analyze, sell, and manage here, but the factories will be elsewhere.

Whole American industries are shrinking, and even a strong economy won't restore those industries to their former grandeur. The economy lost 4 million jobs to the recession—most of which will be recovered as the economy recovers. But we've already lost 4 million jobs as we shift from machine age to information age, and few, if any, of these jobs will be recovered. That's why our unemployment rate will stay high even in recovery. We used to consider 5 percent unemployment the maximum tolerable for our economy. Even the White House concedes that we'll be lucky to bring unemployment to as low as 7 percent by the late 1980s. And that assumes five years of uninterrupted economic growth.

The government reckons that a quarter-million auto industry jobs are lost forever, and the steel industry will probably employ only half as many people as it used to. Farming used to employ every other American. Now, it's one American in thirty, and it will be fewer than that in a decade.

Much of our production of chemicals, machinery, textiles, apparel, shoes, and home electronics equipment has already gone overseas, and more will follow. Each of these industries has support industries that are similarly in trouble.

We have a teacher glut because the national birth rate

dropped so sharply in the 1960s and 1970s. We've had something of a baby boom lately, but it will touch only kindergarten and elementary school teachers in the 1980s. The children of the 1980s won't reach high school until the 1990s, and they won't reach college until close to the year 2000.

There are fewer newspapers today and fewer commercial banks. The thrift industry—savings and loans and savings banks—is going through a bloodbath. We had 40,000 different financial institutions in 1980. It will be 20,000 by 1990.

America's Changing Work-Force

So, for reasons economic, technological, and demographic, our job market is going through a period of great change, all of which will loom very large in your career prospects.

Consider, for instance, that most of the jobs being lost in our economy are "men-only" jobs: production-line jobs in basic industry; hard-rock mining; and jobs in such industries as railroading, the merchant marine, etc. At the same time, most of the jobs in our postindustrial economy are jobs that can be done by both men and women. It is probably not so surprising that recent surveys show very little difference between the kinds of careers that young men and young women seek today.

There still are profound differences in what men and women are paid. Labor Department figures, published in 1982, show the average woman earning only 65 percent of what a man doing comparable work earns. Among younger women, however, that climbs to close to 70 percent of a man's salary, so the gap does seem to be narrowing. The recession did not, as many feared it would, drive women back out of the work force. The increase in the jobless rate among adult women was even less than it was among adult men.

Since it figures to be, more than ever, a unisex work-force in the 1980s and beyond, the salary gap should narrow more —and the competition between men and women in the work force figures to become more intense.

The Labor Department has done the most extensive work in estimating the labor market of the 1980s: the jobs and professions that will be most in demand, and those that will be least in demand.

To a degree, the list fits all the current stereotypes—but only to a degree. There are plenty of high-tech, computer-oriented jobs on the list. But there are plenty of jobs that have nothing to do with computers and high-tech.

The fact is that our world is changing in many ways, of which the shift from machine-age jobs to information-age jobs is just part.

Another part of it is that we're living longer. Another is that the two-income family, with neither parent at home, is now the typical American family. Another is that the high price of energy has led to a growing demand that products and services be brought to us so that we don't have to leave home for them. Another is the dramatic shakeout among financial institutions.

The Jobs of the Eighties

The Labor Department expects jobs to be harder to find in the eighties for workers in heavy industry, the building trades, and farming. Other slow-growth fields include aircraft mechanics, bakers, butchers, bus drivers, cabinetmakers, elevator operators, garage workers, hairdressers and barbers, printers (but not lithographers or photoengravers), and taxi drivers. Nearly all, you'll notice, are jobs typically held by men.

Among professions, growth will be slowest for school administrators and for teachers in high school and beyond; also for clergymen, funeral directors, librarians, pharmacists, restaurant and bar managers, and stock and bond salespeople.

Finally, the demand will be down for the unskilled and the semiskilled in every field: for stenographers, bookkeepers, file clerks, key-punch operators, sales clerks, bank tellers.

The growth areas of the 1980s (and beyond) will certainly include plenty of high-tech jobs. Anything related to computers and advanced electronic devices looks promising: designing them, making them, operating them, and repairing them.

In fact, the Labor Department sees data-processing repair as the Number One growth field of the eighties.

It isn't just computers, either: the field looks very bright for people able to repair anything, from heavy equipment to radios and TV sets.

Other fields will make use of smart machines, but swapping a typewriter for a word processor hardly makes it into a high-tech job. The jobs of the 1980s will require skill and training, but that doesn't make them high-tech jobs either.

There will be fewer jobs for stenographers but more for medical and legal secretaries. The keypunch operator will become a computer operator. So will the bookkeeper. So will the file clerk, in an age when all company files are stored in a computer.

One area of particular concern to women these days is that the video arcade is seen as the training ground for the sophisticated, computer-oriented workers of tomorrow, and girls simply don't visit video arcades (or play video games on home computers) to the extent that boys do. The concern is that unless video games are made more attractive to girls, these girls will be left behind in the race for jobs.

Still, not all the jobs of the future will be built around computers or other smart machines (and you see the unisex nature of most of these jobs).

Medical workers of all sorts will be heavily in demand—not only doctors but health administrators, dieticians, practical nurses, registered nurses, dental assistants, and veterinarians. Health care generally will be more readily available, but there will be a particular need to care for the elderly, as the over-65 portion of our population grows in size.

With both husband and wife in more families working, there will be more opportunities in child care, food preparation, and household service. Travel is expected to be a growth industry as the baby boom generation moves up in the world and begins to spend big. With so much turmoil in the job market, career counseling and personnel recruitment should boom. Years of change and economic turmoil will take their psychological toll, and those who can provide psychological and psychiatric care will be heavily in demand. To study

America in transition, the demand for social scientists—sociologists, economists, political scientists—will be strong.

The cutback in government jobs is showing up. There will be fewer jobs for policemen and firemen, and more jobs for private security guards.

Finally, the demand for people to manage will be enormous, all across the board. There will be fewer jobs for bank tellers but more for bank managers; fewer jobs for sales clerks but more for sales managers; fewer jobs for purchasing agents but more for purchasing managers.

If there's a moral in it all, it is this: Fewer people in the future will work with their hands and more will work with intelligent machines. Not all jobs in the future (not even a majority of jobs) will be high-tech, but the typical job in the future will require more specialized training than the typical job in the past. There will be fewer jobs for doers and more jobs for thinkers; fewer jobs for underlings and more jobs for managers.

It certainly will be a time of rapid changes in the workplace, and we can't be sure of what all these changes will be. Those who forecast too far ahead, you'll remember, are the wrongest nearly all of the time. Anyone who set about in 1978 to start looking ahead to 1980 and beyond, would have paid little attention to the video cassette recorder as a consumer product—and no attention at all to the home computer. Yet by 1982 we had sold 3 million home computers.

As far as your job future goes, skills and training are fine—but overspecialization could be lethal in the years ahead. You want an education, and you want sufficient training in a field that you can find work in. But you don't want to become so specialized that you become unemployable should your job disappear. The wider the range that your skills cover, the better off you are.

It doesn't automatically follow that all the best jobs of the 1980s will be in the Sunbelt and that the older cities of the urban North will wither and die.

The rush to the sun has left most of the Sunbelt cities with rising rates of unemployment—particularly as the oil glut hit the Southwest and Mountain States. On the other hand, some of the areas of the North have become inventive in finding new industries to replace decaying industries. New England has already turned itself into an area for high-technology industries. Remember that through most of the 1981–82 recession, the jobless rate in Massachusetts was lower than the jobless rate in Texas.

Building Your Job Strategy

Even if you're in an industry that shows the promise of future growth, you still face a problem because others will head for those growth areas. Computer programming is a big growth area—except that there currently are more programmers than programming jobs. Whatever field you're in, your problem today is to make yourself heard above the throng—letting management know that you're an achiever, ready to move up in terms of responsibilities and in terms of pay.

Let your economic sixth sense explore the world where you work. By what rules does your company play? Do the rewards go to the creative, innovative types, or to those who rock the boat least? Do the prize jobs mostly go to those from sales? From finance? From production? Do you need a hitch in an outlying sales office before you're taken seriously? Some companies are content to have you work from nine to five and then go home. Some think more of you if you put in overtime, and if you take part in some after-hours activity. Does your company want you involved in community activities? Would it help if you played an active part in the United Way drive, or in the Boy Scouts?

Every company has what has come to be called its "culture." You can't expect to move ahead until you figure out how your company sees itself, and what it really wants from those it makes its leaders. I've known companies that rewarded managers who offered fresh ideas, and companies that rewarded managers who said "no" to fresh ideas. Some companies are innovators and some are followers; some encourage initiative and some penalize it.

If you can't identify, identify with, and encourage your company's culture, move elsewhere, because you'll always be the square peg in the round hole—and no one ever gets ahead that way.

What help does your company offer people who want to move ahead? Are job opportunities posted so you always know what's available? Is there someone in the personnel department who tries to keep employee career goals in mind when jobs present themselves?

Does your company like to promote from within, or do most higher-level jobs go to outsiders? To what extent will your company let you plan your own career path—as opposed to having the company make all the decisions for you? Fewer companies play the old game of "you'd better say yes to whatever we offer you, because if you say 'no,' we'll never ask you again." Saying "no" to the Nome branch office no longer means that you've killed any future chance for promotion. Yet, if you say "yes" to Nome when everyone else is saying "no," you can score a lot of points with your employer. I've known plenty of people whose first big step up involved taking a job that no one else would take. You might like Nome, and your boss will surely like you.

Don't expect your company to know what you want from the future. Everyone has his or her own concerns, and the only person who can plan your career is you.

At least once a year, sit down and think about your career. Think as openly and honestly as you can about where you are, where you want to go, and how best to get there. Where can your present job lead? How good (being absolutely honest with yourself) are your chances of moving to the next level? Where do you want to be 10 years from now? Twenty years from now? How good are your chances of getting there (again, being absolutely honest with yourself). Think about your company and its future, and the industry you're in, and its future.

The Extra Things That Count

Think about additional skills you might acquire that would help you move ahead. Are there night-school courses you could take? What in-house training does your company offer?

Most companies are impressed with employees who are willing to work at improving their skills. It's one of those things that makes you stand out in the crowd.

What about a couple of courses in your field? A writing course so your reports get notice, a course in public speaking to help you stand out at meetings? What about a course in microcomputers—to teach you all about the machines that will play so important a role in the office of the future? What about going whole hog and getting a Masters in Business Administration? Most cities have colleges that offer an MBA at night, and some schools have programs in which you work four days a week, and spend the fifth day going to school. Most companies will let you work out such an arrangement, because an MBA—or any other sort of advanced or specialized education—makes you a more valuable employee. Certainly it marks you as an achiever.

If something nice happens to you, let people know about it. If a client sends you a complimentary letter, send a copy of it to your supervisor. If you publish something, or give a speech, or win an award, make sure your company's newspaper or newsletter makes note of it. When you've done anything out of the ordinary, let people know about it. You want people higher up to know that you're something out of the ordinary.

Don't ignore one of the most basic rules of all: Tie onto the people whom you see moving up in the company. Never play the toady; it won't get you very far. Do make sure the up-and-comers know you, and know your special talents and abilities. Let them see how you can help them achieve your goals.

Raw talent still counts, but economic distress limits opportunities to advance. The rewards these days go to those willing to do that extra little bit to move up—the writing courses that make your reports better organized and more readable, the computer course that gives you an edge as the smart machines move into the office.

When to Change Jobs

Maybe there isn't any way up. Maybe it's a dying company, or a dying industry. Maybe you'd be happier someplace else.

As our economy changes—old industries fading away and new, growth industries appearing—people will change jobs more often. As machines become smarter, we may return to school several times in a career to keep up with the changes. As machines get smarter, new businesses in new industries will open up—creating new job opportunities. The home video cassette recorder is less than a decade old, and the home microcomputer is barely five years old. Each is already a multibillion dollar business—and each is spawning new industries in its wake.

Take your immediate situation. Maybe you've done your best for old Imperial Butter and Egg and it isn't getting you anyplace. Your company isn't growing the way it once did, the ranks of middle management are choked with eager aspirants to higher office. Anyway, the job just doesn't grip you as it once did. You could be ripe for a change.

This quiz (with an assist from *Money* magazine) should help you decide if you're ready for a job change:

—When you first get up, do you on most days really feel like going to work?
—Do you feel your job is making use of most of your special skills and talents?
—When you daydream, do you often have ideas relating to your work?
—Do you feel good about telling people what you do and where you work?
—Do you talk so much about your job—about the people and events at the office—that you sometimes feel you're boring your friends and family?
—Do you sometimes work late, or drop in on a weekend—not because there's a specific project that must be done, but "just to catch up on things"?
—Do you like mixing with people from your company, or your profession, after hours?
—Are most of the people you're close to at work happy with their jobs?

If you can't answer "yes" to at least five of these eight questions, you may be ready for a change.

It might be a change from one company to another in the same industry. Or you may be ready to change careers completely. If it's a dying industry, you probably want to get out altogether, to someplace where the future looks brighter.

Again, do as totally honest a self-appraisal of yourself as you can. What are your strengths and weaknesses? What special talents and skills do you have that might be useful in another job?

Where to Search

If you're in sales, finance, marketing, merchandising, production, or any of the basic corporate functions, you have skills and experience that can work for more than just one company and in more than just one industry. If you're skilled with your hands, you'll find that most industries are crying out for people able to repair things.

If you aren't under pressure to make a jump, you can take classes in subjects that would make you more marketable to another company. Don't let go of one job before you have another, and don't job-hunt in a panicked way. The more calm and confident you feel about making a change, the more calm and confident you'll appear to a potential employer.

If you can, try part-time work in the industry you're thinking of moving to. Read up on the subject and talk to people in the industry. Learn what the best companies are—and the worst.

If you've worked for a big company all your life, don't limit your search to other big companies. There are likely to be more job opportunities in the future among smaller companies, that aren't burdened by some of the huge fixed costs that are crushing many of the corporate giants. There have been a near-record number of corporate failures the past few years, but there has also been a near-record number of new companies born—and not just in the new-technology areas. Specialized publishing is red hot. So is mail order. Nor do you have to be a high-technology whiz to land a job even with one of the high-tech companies. It's your job function that counts. If you can merchandise can openers, you can apply the same skills and experience to selling computer software or medical equipment.

A big company may offer a more lavish benefits package, but it may not be able to offer much growth potential. A smaller company will certainly offer fewer rivals at each step up the ladder. At each step, you'll be closer to where the decisions are made. Growth can create all sorts of new opportunities. If there are stock options and incentive bonuses, you can participate very profitably in that growth.

The future may see less hiring by companies and more subcontracting of jobs. Instead of going to work for one company, you might become an independent contractor, selling your expertise in sales or marketing or design or production to a company—or to several companies.

If you've worked in a big city all your life, you may have to move someplace smaller when you change jobs. Many of today's fastest-growing younger companies have set up in smaller towns, where the living is easier. Thanks to advanced communications and smart machines, a company can locate anywhere and keep in close and constant touch with all the people it must stay in touch with. The job of tomorrow could as easily be in rural New Hampshire as in midtown New York.

You Have to Do the Searching

When you job-hunt, you'll have to do most of it on your own, because the system doesn't do much to help people find jobs. Most middle- and upper-management jobs are filled with the help of executive recruiters—"headhunters" as they're known in the corporate world where executive heads are hunted. Unfortunately, they don't work for people looking for jobs but for companies seeking talent (and usually pretty high-priced talent).

You may come in contact with a headhunter who'll promise to keep your résumé on file, "just in case anything comes up." That's a nice way of brushing you off—of saying, "Don't call us, we'll call you." The headhunter goes to work only when he's hired by a company to fill a spot, which is what he's paid to do. Then he checks with his contacts in the world of business to find the most suitable people for the job. Only in the rarest of circumstances will he turn to his file of unsolicited résumés. More likely, your résumé went into the waste basket the instant you went out the door.

The more you've built a reputation as an achiever, and the more people at higher levels you impress with your abilities, the more likely a headhunter will seek you out. A former boss who's gone to another company might be a source of names to a headhunter. A speech you made at an industry gathering could bring your name to the attention of people who make the recommendations to those executive recruiters.

Employment agencies do find jobs for job seekers—though usually lower down the corporate ladder than where the headhunters work—and there are as many kinds of agencies as there are stars in the sky. Many specialize in a single industry, and some of them are standard industry sources for lower and middle management. Ask around your industry about the agencies that specialize in your field, and find out which among those agencies are the best.

Beware of the career counseling outfits that charge fat fees (in the thousands of dollars) to help you "define your career goals" and "market yourself." A tip-off is an ad that talks about the "thousands of jobs that are never advertised." The implication is that the counseling firm knows where those jobs are, and can help you land one.

You'll get a battery of tests, of dubious value, and you'll get help in writing what you'll be assured is a "résumé that gets results." There will always be, lurking in the background, but never stated explicitly and never put down on paper, the promise of a job. You can read the contract you signed until the cows come home and never find that promise put into writing. Seldom will what you get from one of these firms be worth what you paid. Before you sign anything, read the contract, word for word. If it isn't there, in black and white, you don't have a legal leg to stand on. No verbal promise is worth anything. Your chances of actually landing a job through one of these career counseling firms is about 1 in 10,000.

If you want to change jobs, do your homework. Read the want ads daily. The Tuesday edition of *The Wall Street Jour-*

nal and the Sunday edition of *The New York Times* are crammed with job listings. The *Journal* publishes its *National Business Employment Weekly*, which is nothing but job listings. Read the professional literature—the trade magazines and the newsletters—of the industry you want to move to. Talk to people in the industry and let them know you're looking. Find out the executives at each company in the industry who actually do the hiring, and write each a personal letter, letting them know you're available—and letting them know of your qualifications. Include a one-page résumé.

The obvious danger here is that word of your search will drift back to your company. Still, that could bring things to a head at your company. If they really want you to stay, they may pay more attention to you, now that they know you're unhappy. Contrariwise, you could find yourself relegated to corporate Siberia—a disgruntled worker looking to go elsewhere. You don't want to be fired from your old job before you've established yourself someplace else.

The more committed you are to making a change, the more aggressive your search should be. And, of course, if you are out of a job, you can be as aggressive as you like.

Doing a Résumé

I screened thousands of résumés in my days at *Business Week*, and I found most of them unreadable. An employer wants to know your educational background, what you do best, and how your career has gone. The résumé most likely to whet a prospective employer's appetite is one that shows steady growth in responsibility and salary. You started at one level, moved to a higher level, and then to a still-higher level. That shows that your previous employers have thought well of you.

When it comes to writing a résumé, simple is best.

First, identify yourself (name, address, telephone number, marital status, number of kids). Then list your work experience, starting with your most recent job. Give that job a nice fat paragraph: what you do, areas of responsibility, number of people who report to you, and some of your triumphs on the job (increased sales by 50 percent, designed a new production technique that saved the company a million dollars, or whatever). Then, in shorter paragraphs, list your previous jobs—marching back into history. Again, the idea is to show growth in your career—additional responsibilities, more people reporting to you, growing salary.

Near the bottom, list your educational background, any job-related organizations you belong to, any honors you've won, anything that you've published. Finally, at the very bottom, list anything else about yourself that's relevant. If you're a graduate of a public-speaking course, or if you took a writing course, or if you did anything at all that sets you apart from the herd, list it.

Keep it to a page, even if you have to edit and re-edit it to get it down to that page. Don't be clever or cute with your résumé. Don't print it in red ink on a blue background to make it stand out. Keep it neat and clean, and have it reproduced professionally, not copied on the office Xerox machine.

You want to put your best foot forward, but you also want to keep it honest. If you lie about your education, your work experience, or anything else, you can be found out, and then you're dead. Word of such things has a way of getting around.

The whole business of preparing a résumé (of searching for a job, for that matter) gets a lot trickier if you've been out of the job market for a time—if you've been home raising kids, for instance. You have an education, and presumably you did work. But that was years ago. If you prepared a standard résumé, it would be ancient history.

But you do have strengths to sell, starting with maturity. And you probably have done things through the years that would interest a prospective employer. Did you play an active role in the PTA, or the League of Women Voters? Did you run a charity drive in your town? Did you do part-time work or handle free-lance assignments in your field? Did you take courses that might make you more attractive to an employer? During the years my wife was at home raising our children, she took on all the free-lance assignments in her field she could get. She then went back to school and got an advanced degree, and then took a secretarial course, to round out her skills. That set her apart from the hordes of other women rejoining the job market.

One approach, if you're re-entering the job market, is to use a "functional" résumé. Instead of selling a job history, you're defining your areas of strength—the skills, talents, and experience you have to offer. Pick three or four such areas, and do a paragraph about each: what you can do, what background or training you have in each. Stress all you can do, and all you know that might interest a would-be employer.

Another approach is to put everything down in a letter. Keep it tight: no more than two pages. Explain who you are and your situation. Explain what you want to do and why. List all the qualities that might sell you to an employer.

You want all the preparation for work you can get. Assume that you'll go back to work once your youngest is in school full-time. Spend the last year or two before that taking all the courses you can handle and doing all the part-time work you can get your hands on. You're training yourself to re-enter the market, and you want to do everything you can to make yourself a marketable person.

The functional résumé—or the letter in place of a résumé—may also be best if you're caught in a work situation where promotions just come very slow. You may be a potential superstar, but there's just no way to move up through the throngs of babyboomers. You have something to sell, but it won't show up on a standard résumé. So you try what's likely to work best for you.

Once You're in the Door

The best résumé in the world won't get you hired. It will merely get you in the door. That's when you get into high gear—in the job interview, where the final decision is made about who gets hired and who doesn't.

As I read scads of résumés in my time, I conducted plenty of job interviews. I looked for three essential qualities in everyone I interviewed, and I never hired anyone who didn't measure up on all three counts.

1. Knowledge
2. Stability
3. Enthusiasm

The knowledge part is obvious. Unless it's an absolutely entry-level job, the interviewer will expect you to exhibit a certain degree of expertise in the trade or craft. You're in the interview, because your résumé promised certain things about yourself: your experience and your training. Now the interviewer wants to examine it close up.

Are you as you billed yourself? Can you do the job? How well can you do the job? Do you seem the sort who can be trained to advance to higher-level jobs?

If you were doing the hiring, what would you want to know about you and your background. Plan your answers in advance, based on the questions you'd be asking if you were conducting the interview. Have a practice interview—preferably with someone in the field—so you'll gain experience in fielding the sorts of questions you're likely to be asked. Try taping your answers, so you hear what you sound like. You don't want to sound cocky; neither do you want to sound shy and weak. Sound confident.

Let the interviewer ask the questions—no filibusters on your part. Neither do you want a lot of one-or-two-word snap answers. Answer as fully as necessary to let your strengths show through. Where possible, weave in examples that show your experience in handling situations ("I had an assignment along those very lines . . ."). Unless there's some very reason for doing otherwise, keep your answers to 30 seconds or less. In a two-person conversation, 30 seconds can sound like an eternity.

Above all, be yourself—the role you know best—and be honest. The person who is interviewing you will have a pretty good idea of what you should know at a given stage of your career. If you pretend to more than that, you'll be found out —and you can write off that job.

The stability part is more subjective. The interviewer will be looking for evidence that you bring maturity and professionalism to the job.

RULE: DO NOT COME LATE TO A JOB INTERVIEW.

I don't care what the reason is, if you're late for a job interview, you start out with two strikes against you. You certainly make me wonder if (1) you want the job, and (2) you'll be late coming to work and late meeting deadlines. Arrive early enough for a job interview to comb your hair, touch up your makeup, and use the toilet. (Job interviews are stressful, so don't forget that last point.)

Dress appropriately and in good taste—conservative clothes in keeping with the workplace. Avoid extremes in clothing, hair-style, makeup, or jewelry. Remove all pins and buttons pleading special causes. Let the interviewer crack jokes: You keep it serious. Sit up straight and don't fidget. Avoid excessive gesturing. However you feel inside, you want to convey poise, a coolness under fire. I expect you to be nervous, but if you're panicked at the job interview, I'm certainly going to wonder about how well you'll stand up under the strains of the job.

Enthusiasm is absolutely essential. You must not only convey your qualifications for the job; you must show the interviewer that you want it. You're not in a position to demand anything, but don't for an instant let the interviewer doubt that you are totally, completely, 100 percent interested in the job.

Have a half-dozen reasons in mind why you want the job (none of them having to do with salary or fringe benefits). Stress why your background is right for the job and why the job is a natural next step in your career. Stress what the job can do for you—and what you can do for the job. Convey your enthusiasm from the second you walk in the door until the second you leave. Don't be afraid to follow up in a couple of days with a telephone call just to reassure the person doing the hiring that you want the job.

I once had to decide between two very qualified people. One called up the day after the interview to stress his interest in the job and the other person did not. The person who made the telephone call got the job. I don't want to sell you the job: I want you to want the job. If you have to be sold, I don't want you.

A job interview is just another skill to be mastered. The more interviews you have, the more you'll get used to them. The more practiced you get at them, the better you'll do.

Practice those dry runs with friends, spouse, or anyone else you can get to play the other side. A course in public speaking, assertiveness, or confidence building can help you in the job interview—particularly if you're returning to the job market after some years away. Never turn down a chance for a job interview, even if you don't think you have a chance for the job, or even if you don't think the job is right for you. Time spent in a job interview that doesn't lead to anything, can give you the skills that nail down a job that you want.

You might invest in a copy of *How to Turn an Interview into a Job*, by lawyer and placement consultant Jeffrey Allen, which was published in 1983. It's barely 100 pages long, but it covers the waterfront on preparing for a job interview.

Even if you're dead sure you do want to change jobs, never burn your bridges behind you. There may be fewer jobs out there than you think, and it may take a long time to find one. And sometimes an odd thing can happen. You get so revved up as you seek to change careers that you stir up excitement at the old job, and you suddenly get moved ahead there.

Twice during my years at *Business Week* I decided I was ready to change jobs, and I went through the whole process of talking to people, doing up a new résumé, all of it. Each time, while my job hunt was in full fury, *Business Week* promoted me.

Guidelines for Action

You must increase your income to survive the economic future—and you must do that in a job market that is changing because the economy is changing.

Figure on more job changes in the future until you find something where the avenues to the top aren't so clogged.

A small company may offer more than a big company, and you may sell your services to a company on a contract basis, instead of being an employee.

All the advice of experts to the contrary, most jobs in the future won't be high-tech jobs. But most jobs tomorrow will require more skills and training than jobs today.

You must learn how to write a job-winning résumé. And you must learn how to apply that combination of knowledge, stability, and enthusiasm to clinch it for you in a job interview.

CHAPTER 13

The New Realities About Retirement

All is prelude.

You're youthful and vigorous now—at the peak of your form and at the peak of your earning power. But time flies, and in time you'll retire. Further, you'll retire into an uncertain world, with your income barely half what it is today. There may be Social Security to soothe your Sunset Years. But there may not. If there is Social Security, it may be because the government has printed so much money to keep it going, that inflation will be your lot.

You may have a company pension to sustain you. But you may not. ERISA—the Employee Retirement Income Security Act—is supposed to protect those whose company pension plans go under. But ERISA doesn't cover all pension plans, and when it does cover, its coverage is limited. You may change jobs so often in these uncertain years that you never stay at one place long enough to qualify for a pension.

If there is a pension in your future, it may be different from the pension that's common today. You'd pay most of the cost of your pension, and the payout at retirement could be less than you'd get under your company's present plan. Should you have one of these new plans—called a "defined-contribution" plan—you'll find it isn't covered by any of the rules of ERISA.

You've certainly contributed in full measure to an Individual Retirement Account (IRA) or, if you're self-employed, to a Keogh Plan. If your money was invested prudently, and the institution you invested it with is still around, you'll have a nice piece of change. But it won't be the fortune you were led to believe it would be.

Assume, as you reach your mid-sixties, that you were twenty-five back in 1982 and that you put $2,000 into an IRA each year for forty years. Assuming that the 12 percent interest rate of early 1982 stayed in effect for those full forty years, your pile at age sixty-five would have grown to more than $1.7 million. Add $2,000 a year for forty working years for your spouse, at the same rate of interest, and the pile climbs to nearly $3½ million. You are, just as they promised, a millionaire.

But if you assume a 12 percent interest rate over forty years, you must also assume forty years of torrid inflation. You put up $80,000 and your spouse another $80,000 over those forty years. After four decades of heavy inflation, that $3½ million —circa 2022—would have the purchasing power of just about the $160,000 the two of you put up. Your millions are paper millions.

A Look at the Future

When it comes to thinking about retirement, hope for the best—but prepare for the worst.

The best is that you'll live a longer, healthier life than any previous generation in history, thanks to all the breakthroughs science has already made and those it will make during the rest of your lifetime.

If you're a forty-year-old man, you'll live until close to eighty. If you're a forty-year-old woman, you'll live well into your eighties. If you're under thirty now, man or woman, you'll probably live until close to ninety. You'll feel better more of the time than most older people do today—able to partake of more activities, able to travel more, able to live life more fully.

That's the best. The worst is that, by living longer, and by being able to do more, you'll need more to retire on. Yet it's impossible to say that those twin bulwarks—Social Security and the company pension plan—will deliver as they're supposed to.

If you have a corporate pension fund, you must first worry about keeping a job long enough to qualify for a pension. You must next worry about whether your company will survive until you retire—and, if it fails, whether the government will pick up all the pieces of all the pension funds of all the companies that don't make it. You must further worry about whether your company is basing its ability to pay your pension on earning so great a return on its money that nothing but more years of high inflation would make it possible. You must finally worry about whether your pension, if and when you do receive it, will keep pace with the rate of inflation of the day.

Few pension plans are indexed to inflation, although some companies have unilaterally increased the payout to keep their retired employees from starving. Someone who retired in 1960 with a pension of $10,000 a year was considered to be pretty comfortable. By now, inflation has reduced the purchasing power of that $10,000 to such a pittance that the person receiving it is officially living in poverty.

Social Security labors under a double whammy.

Near-term, it was brought to the point of insolvency because of all the burdens placed upon it—of which the indexing of the payout to inflation is the most glaring example. Wages for the average worker rose 5 percent in 1982, but every recipient of Social Security got an automatic 7¼ percent increase in benefits, because the cost-of-living feature of Social Security mandated it. A study by Morgan Guaranty Trust Company in New York shows that the income of those over sixty-five grew more rapidly in the 1970s (an average of 9 percent a year) than did income for any other age group. For the average person over sixty-five, 38 percent of annual income comes from Social Security.

Short-run, the congressional rescue of Social Security may do the trick—though only by stealing from the future growth of our economy. Increases in the Social Security tax on workers have outrun the rate of inflation, year after year. Now, the plan is to be rescued from immediate bankruptcy through even heavier taxes on workers. This will further diminish what the 1981 tax cuts were supposed to do to the economy.

And that's just the here-and-now. It's the year 2010 that you really have to start worrying about. That's when the baby boom generation starts drawing fortunes out of a system that will then be supported by the smaller birth classes of the 1960s and 1970s. By then, every fifth American will be sixty-five or older. Now it's one in nine. In 1940 it was one in 15. The answer in Congress is to raise the retirement age to 66 by 2009 and to 67 by 2027. That is like to cover a gaping wound with a Band-Aid.

You must assume that Social Security will do less for its recipients in the future. At the least, cost-of-living increases in benefits will be the exception, not the rule. At the worst, Social Security will pay only the genuine hardship cases, and the rest of us will have to pay for more of our retirement.

That's just for the general population. Salaries for women trail salaries for men, and that's likely to be true in the future —even if the gap narrows. If you're a woman on your own, you probably have limited financial resources to fall back on, and your pension—if you have one—probably will be smaller than for a man doing comparable work. But because you are a woman, the odds are greater than for a man that you worked at a job that didn't provide a pension. As a woman, you can further count on living longer after retirement.

Finally, with people living longer, you could face retirement and still have parents living that need your help. In fact, if the economy turns bad, you could have both parents and children living with you when you retire—the empty nest of today becoming the full nest of tomorrow.

Your Retirement Burden

The long and short of it, is that you'll bear more of the financial burden of your retirement than you've been led to believe. And that will change the whole concept of retirement in America, in some important ways:

1. Fewer people will take early retirement.
2. More people will work beyond what's now considered

the normal retirement age (which is still sixty-five for most people).

3. Many people who do retire will take new full- or part-time jobs to carry them through retirement.

The implications of this are considerable. Fewer of us will move to retirement communities, and more of us will stay put, where the job opportunities are. Even after retirement, for instance, you may continue working parttime for your last employer—a practice that is already becoming widespread. An alternative is that more companies will regard the elderly as a vast pool of trained talent and move their businesses to where the retirees are. More skills in the information age now dawning will be such that they can be used by someone in his seventies as easily as by someone in his thirties and forties.

The office of the future may be a decentralized office—computers and other smart machines making it possible for people to work at home, and still remain in constant touch with a central office, and with coworkers. Without the wear and tear of commuting, people could continue working to any age.

An important piece of legislation to know about is the Age Discrimination in Employment Act, which extended the mandatory retirement age from 65 to 70. The law says that an employer can't force you to retire before age 70. You can't be pressured into retiring earlier. Nor can you, because of your age, be forced to:

—Take a less responsible job.
—Give up privileges made available to other workers.
—Accept a smaller salary than other workers doing comparable work.

You can be forced to retire at sixty-five only if you've held a high-level corporate executive job and will be getting retirement benefits (not counting Social Security) of at least $27,000 a year.

Your rights under the law are guaranteed by the Equal Employment Opportunity Commission, an agency of the federal government, with offices all over the country.

This idea of letting the elderly work longer makes great sense for the economy. There will be a surplus of workers in the 1980s and 1990s. But then, as the baby boom generation begins to retire, or die off, early in the twenty-first century, the smaller birth classes of the 1960s and seventies won't produce enough bodies to fill all those jobs. We'll need to keep the elderly in the work force to keep our economy going.

Nor are most people likely to balk at working past the normal retirement age. Johnson & Higgins, the big insurance brokers, did a study a couple of years ago on how people felt about working-versus-retiring. Among those fifty to sixty-four, one-third said they weren't looking forward to retirement. Among those not covered by a pension plan, it was 40 percent. Of those currently working, 51 percent said they wanted to continue working after they retired—either in the same job, or a less demanding job. Among retirees, 46 percent were either working or wanted to. Among those not covered by a pension plan, it was 52 percent. An interesting sidelight is that the percentage wanting to work was as high for the best off of the retirees (earning more than $15,000 a year) as for the worst off (earning less than $10,000 a year).

If you want to work after retirement, you benefit from changes in the Social Security law. If you're sixty-five or older, you can make $6,600 a year without losing any benefits (raised from $6,000 in 1983). If you're 70 or older, (dropped from 72 in 1983) you get all your Social Security benefits no matter how much you earn.

Looking Ahead

So, not only will you most likely work after age sixty-five, in some capacity or another, but the odds are that you'll want to. The time to start planning for that is right now—before you move a step closer to retirement. Every question you asked yourself, in Chapter 12, about your career future must now be asked again in light of your retirement. Your career is not from now to whenever you plan to retire, but from now until the end of your life.

The sideline business you're using to supplement current

income may become your full-time career when you retire. Changes in your career now may be shaped by the need to have something you can turn to upon retirement. If your passion now is to drive a bus, think about how many seventy-year-olds drive buses.

Your thoughts about where you want to live after retirement will be shaped by the availability of work. A resort-area condominium complex for senior citizens may offer thousands of candidates for a limited number of jobs. Your own town, where you live now, may not offer a warm sun in winter, but it may offer more jobs.

If the idea of planning for retirement seems obvious, it's also obvious that most people don't do enough of it.

In 1981 the American Council of Life Insurance commissioned a study on retirement planning, and some of the points it made are chilling. It found that 72 percent of working Americans felt they weren't saving enough toward retirement, and almost half said they couldn't afford to retire. Half were saving nothing toward retirement, and only 6 percent believed they were putting aside more toward retirement than was necessary. As the study noted, fewer than half the people working in the private sector are covered by a pension plan (and no one knows how many who are covered will ever get their money).

The moral is that like everything else having to do with your money, the job of planning for your retirement is up to you.

There isn't much you can do about Social Security. Its fate will be settled in Congress. But there are groups working to influence the debate. The American Association of Retired Persons, based in Washington, works for the interests of older Americans. It's open to anyone fifty-five or older, whether they're retired or not. Membership is $5 a year, and you become eligible for discounts on drugs, for various types of insurance, and for group travel.

Just don't count Social Security benefits into how much you expect to have when you retire. It might be there—in which case you're ahead of the game. But it might not—and it certainly will be less generous than what's now being promised.

The Future of Medicare

No less crucial to your retirement is what happens to Medicare, which provides health coverage for the elderly. It's part of the Social Security program, and it begins working for you when you reach sixty-five (earlier if you should become severely disabled). Part A Medicare covers hospitalization and some other health services, and that you get for free. Part B pays doctor bills and you pay a small premium to get it. There's a deductible—the first $180 on a hospital bill—and Medicare pays the rest.

The cost of Medicare has been staggering—in part because inflation in health care has been staggering. In 1982, when inflation in the rest of the economy dropped to near zero, it was still in double-digits for medical care. Of course, one reason for the superinflation in health care has been the billions of dollars of Medicare payments dumped into the system.

Something had to give. In 1983, as part of its plan for saving Social Security, Congress made some changes in Medicare. Past practice had been to pay whatever a hospital wanted to charge. Between now and 1986, the government must set fixed rates on 467 categories of hospital treatment. This could save the government money; it could also mean cutbacks in what hospitals provide. And there could be more trimming. What you get from Medicare in the future could be based on what you can afford to pay.

Even now, Medicare doesn't cover hospital stays past 90 days, except for a 60-day once-in-a-lifetime "reserve." Nor does it pay for dental work, eye examinations, private nursing care (in or out of a hospital), or for medical treatment outside the U.S. Many retirees already buy supplemental coverage from a private insurer, and more will have to do so in the future.

If you have a company health plan or belong to a health maintenance organization, check now on what will be available to you when you retire. To what extent does your company plan cover retirees? Will it pick up where Medicare doesn't? If you have a choice between a company plan or an HMO, which offers elderly people a better deal? If you have private health insurance, what supplemental coverage, at what cost, will be available to you upon retirement?

Looking at Your Pension

You probably don't have much say in the kind of pension plan your company has, but you certainly should know all the details of the plan—and whether it's being handled properly and prudently. The most lavish plan isn't worth a thing if the company can't afford to pay off.

You should know some of the jargon of pensions, because you want to keep track of whether your company is doing an adequate job of safeguarding the money that you're counting on for retirement. The handiest source of information these days is your company's annual report to shareholders.

There are "pension assets"—how much the company has set aside to pay employees who are entitled to pensions. Balanced against that are "vested benefits"—what the company is obliged to pay those employees, past and present, entitled to pensions. By calculating the difference between the two numbers, you get the company's "vested funding position."

If the vested funding position is a positive number, chances are the company has sufficient assets set aside to pay pension benefits. If it's a negative number, the company may not. The larger these unfunded pension liabilities, the greater the danger that you won't see a penny of your pension money.

And that's just the tip of the iceberg. In figuring their pension status for their annual reports, companies are allowed to calculate on the basis of what you're earning now—not what you're likely to be earning years from now, when you retire. Presumably your pension will reflect the higher income you can expect in future years. But in figuring its obligations, your company pretends that your income will never go higher than it is today.

Every company calculates a rate of interest it expects to earn on its pension fund. The more that it assumes its pension fund will earn, the less cash it must pay into the fund each year to keep pace with its obligations. A company can play it straight—assuming that its pension fund will earn a reasonable 5 to 6 percent a year, and putting up enough cash to keep the fund healthy. Or it can arbitrarily assume that its pension fund will earn an unrealistically high rate of interest—enabling it to keep its cash contributions to a minimum but endangering the plan.

To make matters more confusing, what the company tells you in its annual report may differ dramatically from the way it carries the pension on its books.

Most companies, for instance, use a relatively high current interest rate in the annual report, to make the pension plan look good. when it comes time to decide how much it really will pay into the plan, the more prudent companies will use a lower interest rate, and they'll take into consideration your final, rather than your current, pay level.

You should know all you can about your company's pension fund: How much does it have in assets; how much will it have to pay out; are its pension liabilities fully funded and, if not, by how much do they fall short; what interest rate assumptions does your company make about the money in the pension fund?

You must dig for that information because no one will hand it to you. Your company is supposed to make details of the pension plan available to you, and it must maintain records that you can look at. You can ask all the questions you want about your pension plan, and you have a right to answers. Still, you're apt to run into a lot of resistance and a lot of fine print and plenty of double-talk—if not outright threats.

The cold, hard truth is that many companies aren't setting aside enough to pay all the pension benefits that are likely to pile up. If that's the case at your company, there's not a lot you can do about it, but at least you'll know the truth early enough to start making your own plans. Ask all the questions you can and, within the bounds of reason, demand detailed answers. If you belong to a union, the specifics of the pension plan are probably part of the collective bargaining agreement, and your union should have the details.

Pensions and Prudence

You should know who invests your pension money and where it's being invested. The criterion for investing the money of others, through the years, was the "prudent man" rule. You had to do as a prudent man would do in managing the money of other people. In the late 1970s the government changed the rules considerably by allowing pension money to be invested just about anywhere—in real estate, precious metals, anywhere. A lot of pension money has since been invested in strange ways—from speculative real estate to fast food franchises. That's not necessarily bad, of course. There have been some years recently in which a lone hamburger stand earned more than the auto and steel industries combined. Still, you should know who manages your company's pension fund. Nor is name everything here. Some of the biggest banks have had the poorest track records in managing pension fund money.

Some Pension Pitfalls

Even if your pension plan is funded down to the last penny, and even if the pension money is managed brilliantly, many things can go wrong. There can be a break-in-service, in which you leave the company. Most companies pay off on the basis of so many years of continuous service. In the old days, even a short break-in-service could cost you your pension. Now, under ERISA, the break-in-service must last for more years than you worked for the company before you risk the loss of your pension.

Those continuous years of service get into the whole matter of "vesting"—how many years you must spend with a company before you're guaranteed a pension benefit when you retire. If you leave the company (and its pension plan) before you're vested, you merely get back the money you put in. Once you're vested, the company owes you something at retirement even if you left the place years before your retirement.

Under ERISA you must be vested after 10 years of service, and for some smaller businesses, vesting must come within two to six years. If you change jobs frequently—and we may all change frequently in the economy of the future—you may never stay on one job long enough to be eligible for a pension.

If your company is acquired by another company and you weren't vested in your company's plan, the clock may be set back to zero in counting the years until you're vested at the new company.

Defined-Benefit Vs. Defined-Contribution Plans

Vesting could become less critical in the future because more companies are nowadays opting for the hottest thing in pensions, which is the "defined-contribution" plan, as opposed to the traditional "defined-benefit" plan. One feature of the typical defined-contribution plan is very fast vesting. Often you become vested as soon as you become part of the retirement plan. And that can come within a year or two after you join the company.

A defined-benefit plan is just that, and it's what we think of when we think of pension plans. The company commits itself to a specific payout when you retire, and it contributes what it must through the years so it can pay you as promised when you retire. In a defined-contribution plan, employees make their own contributions—usually (but not always) bolstered by a contribution from the company.

Companies like the idea because the employees do the bulk of the contributing to the plan, and a company typically pays far less than it would under a defined-benefit plan. Some companies have shifted from a defined-benefit to a defined-contribution plan, and the Employee Benefit Research Institute in Washington says that 75 percent of all new pension plans started in recent years are defined-contribution plans. Given the horrendous state of so many pension plans, and given the uncertain future for so much of American business, you can see a lot more companies going to the defined-contribution route in the future: terminating a defined-benefit plan and offering employees a defined-contribution plan in its place, or, perhaps, giving employees a choice between the two kinds of plans.

You wouldn't expect employees to like the idea very much. A defined-contribution plan costs employees more, typically pays out less, and is not covered by ERISA.

One advantage is that the employee has more certainty of getting money back at retirement with a defined-contribution plan than with a defined-benefit plan. The real lure, though, is the tax treatment of money contributed to a defined-contribution plan. Assuming the plan meets IRS rules, employee contributions to the plan aren't taxable until the plan begins to pay off. When it does start to pay off, you get special, very favorable, tax treatment.

It really amounts to deferred compensation and the tag is 401(k), which is the 1978 amendment to the tax code that made it all possible. In fact, it amounts to a super Individual Retirement Account, since you can contribute up to 25 percent of your total pay—against the $2,000 per person limit on an IRA. A certain amount of your paycheck is simply held back and put into the plan. Since you never see the money, you don't pay taxes on it until you retire. Further, you can have both a defined-contribution plan and an IRA, which amounts to a lot of tax breaks.

A financial institution will usually administer the plan, and employees usually have considerable say over where they want their money invested. Most plans let you borrow against your stake in the plan—to pay a big bill, or to send a child to college. Just understand that whatever you borrow from the fund will reduce the amount you get when you retire.

Immediate vesting has an obvious appeal. If you change jobs, you have something to take with you: your contributions, plus whatever your money has earned. Or there is at least a small pension waiting for you when you retire. Assuming we all do shift jobs more often in the future, the defined-contribution plan will be the way to go.

You can make a tax-free transfer of your pension fund money to another pension fund or to an IRA. The transfer must be made within 60 days of leaving your old job, and you can't touch the money: It must go directly from the old plan to the new plan or directly into an IRA.

Looking Beyond Pensions

Even if you have the best pension plan in the whole world, and even if you believe right down to your toes that Social

Security will never fail you, still build the biggest retirement nest egg you can. That's what all the budgeting and scrimping, and all the earning more, and all the careful investing is all about—building up the biggest pile that you can, because someday it's going to be very welcome—even if you do work past retirement.

We'll run through the rules on IRA's and Keogh Plans once more, because they're an essential part of your retirement planning. And remember that you can have both an IRA and a 401(k) retirement plan.

To sum up, a Keogh Plan is for the self-employed. You can put aside up to $15,000 a year ($30,000 starting in 1984) toward your retirement and pay no taxes on that money, or on the money that money earns, for years. You can't touch the money until you're 59½, and you must start drawing money out of the plan when you're 70½. You start paying taxes when you draw the money, but presumably you're in a lower tax bracket then.

An IRA is for anyone who's employed whether or not they're covered by a company pension plan. The maximum contribution is $2,000 a year for one person, $2,250 for a worker with a nonworking spouse, and $4,000 for a working couple. The same rules apply to an IRA as to a Keogh Plan: no withdrawals until you're 59½ and you must start withdrawing by the time you're 70½.

Your money can be invested anywhere, except in precious metals, precious gems, or collectibles, and you can't go into investments involving borrowed money. Anything invested in those forbidden areas will be counted as a withdrawal from the plan, and you'll be taxed on it. You can go into a bank, thrift institution, insurance company (an annuity, not life insurance), brokerage house, mutual fund, or anyplace else that meets the government's rules. If you're thinking of straying beyond the usual—banks, thrifts, annuities—get competent advice on whether it qualifies as a legal investment. If it doesn't, there goes the tax break.

You can invest your money one place and shift to another, tax free, so long as you don't gain possession of the money.

Even if you plan to work past 70½—when you must start drawing money—still get into an IRA or a Keogh. Assume that whatever you work at won't pay what your preretirement work paid you. The odds are good (or bad, if you will) that your tax rate at 70½ will be considerably lower than it was at forty or fifty. If by some happy turn of events you're still in a top bracket at 70½, you got a lot of tax-free years out of the money—each gain compounded by more because it wasn't being diluted by tax payments.

You want the best combination of high return and safety you can manage. You don't want to risk your money, which argues against stocks and bonds. You want your money in the strongest financial institution around. Accounts at both banks and thrift institutions are insured by the government—but only up to $100,000. At the moment, though, most commercial banks are in better financial shape than most thrift institutions. It's probable—but not 100 percent—that the government would pay off on all insured accounts, should depository institutions fail by the carload. Still, you'll probably sleep a little better at night, if your money is in a bank.

As indicated earlier, I put my IRA money into an insurance company annuity. It's a company I've been doing business with for years. I regard it highly, believe it will survive come what may in the economy, and feel I'm taking an acceptable risk by entrusting my IRA money to this insurance company.

Using an Annuity

In fact, an annuity is still another weapon you can use in planning for your retirement. You can buy a single-payment annuity, or an installment payment annuity. A single-payment is just that. Should you come into a large sum of money all at one time, you make just the single payment and the money earns interest through the life of the annuity. If you make a tax-free rollover from a pension fund, you can make use of a single-payment annuity. An installment payment annuity is also just that. You pay in a certain amount each month, or each year, and the accumulated money is invested.

Avoid variable annuities in which you're really buying units in a fund that invests in stocks or bonds or whatever. They do offer a chance for appreciation, assuming that what the fund has invested in increases in value. The greater the appreciation, the more your annuity pays off. But the other side is that the more depreciation there is, the less your annuity pays. You're gambling with money you shouldn't be gambling with. You want a fixed annuity that guarantees a specific income, to be paid to you in installments, after you retire.

Just remember that money in an annuity is being put there to build up, tax free, until you retire. It's to be left there for the long haul. The 1982 tax law slapped a heavy penalty on withdrawals from annuities that haven't run for at least 10 years, unless you're at least 59½ or unless you die or are disabled. That was to dissuade people from using annuities as short-term tax shelters—which they aren't.

A Retirement Money Strategy

As far as your investments go, the older you get, the more safety becomes the primary consideration and yield a lesser consideration. Since your tax rate will presumably fall when you retire, there's less need to take even moderate risks to pile up capital gains. If you continue working, and your tax rate does remain high, you can emphasize tax-exempt yield, but it's always yield that you're emphasizing.

But long-term investing is even more chancy in retirement, because you'll probably be dipping into capital to get by. It's bad enough waiting around for years for a bond to recover enough in price for you to sell out at a profit or to get back what you put into it. If you need money and the markets are falling, you lose—and sometimes you lose big—if you have to sell in a hurry.

Unless you're just rolling in it, stay away from commodities, options, speculative real estate, or anyplace else where the risk is high. You're out to preserve capital, not to gamble it.

Avoid the hurly-burly of the stock market most of the time. To the extent you own stocks, you should own income stocks—stocks bought for their high return, rather than because they offer the potential for gains. Even income stocks can be chancy in the sort of erratic, supercyclical economy we can expect through the rest of this century. Hard times have cut into the income of some of our strongest companies, and some of yesterday's blue chips have become today's dogs. You want stocks that historically have shown relatively little fluctuation in price because you don't want to lose your money.

Utilities are the classic stocks for retirees. Utility rates are set to produce a substantial return for the utility—meaning there's a high probability the income stream will continue uninterrupted. And utilities are seldom of much interest to the high rollers, so they tend not to fluctuate very much in price. Still, utilities are gigantic borrowers of money, and that's not so good in today's markets. If we practice energy conservation long enough and hard enough, that could cut into utility earnings. It's not always so easy politically to grant a utility a big rate hike, to make up for income lost because its customers are practicing the socially and economically desirable art of energy conservation.

There's also preferred stock, in which the dividend is set when you buy the stock, and the company must pay its preferred shareholders before anything is paid to the common stockholders. Because the high-rollers don't have much interest in preferred stock, there will mostly be mild price swings.

Sound income-producing property—a small apartment house or a small office building—can be particularly useful in retirement. You don't want something so big that managing it will be a problem, and the emphasis has to be on "sound." It must be in a neighborhood that will remain desirable, and you want tenants that will pay their rent and not skip, so that it becomes an investment and not a gamble.

A small apartment house with families—not singles—living in it is probably your top choice. It won't be too hard to manage, and you can usually count on increasing rents in line with inflation. A small medical center building would be another possibility. You can assume that doctors and dentists aren't going to skip out on you in the night. A small office building, with long-standing tenants, could be a good investment. Business tenants will usually make fewer demands on you than people who dwell in an apartment house you own.

You'll mostly be better off keeping the bulk of your money invested short-term: savings certificates, Treasury bills, Treasury and agency notes. You want top quality and you want as much of your money as possible insured. The best combination of convenience and safety may very well be a money market account at a bank—assuming rates on these new deposits remain competitive over the years.

You move more of your money into cash if it is clear that rates are going up. If there's a clear sign that interest rates are coming down, you can reach out longer-term with a 42-month savings deposit, or a government note running three to five years. You'll get a nice yield, and your money will be safe. And there's always plenty to choose from among all the Treasury and agency issues out in the world. Price fluctuations will be a little less in the government market than the corporate market, and all issues are either explicitly or implicitly guaranteed by the government. All Treasury issues, and some federal agency issues, are exempt from state and local income taxes, which gives you a little more return on your money. Ginnie Mae passthroughs, with their high yield and their government backing, are often brought by retirees.

As you get older, you catch one final break from the 1981 tax law. Your chances of having an estate big enough to get hit by estate taxes are now smaller, and you're spared the complicated financial planning that used to be necessary to avoid estate taxes.

You can now leave an estate of any size to your spouse, without paying taxes. Further, in 1981, an estate left to your heirs became subject to taxation once it went beyond $175,625. That increased to $225,000 in 1982, to $275,000 in 1983, and it will be $600,000 by 1987. Unless you can assume you'll leave an estate of more than $600,000, you can forget about estate taxes. That leaves more time for the basic chore, which is to prepare for retirement in such fashion that your retirement years will truly be golden years.

Guidelines for Action

Count on working longer in the economy of the future—until you're seventy at least, and maybe longer. And count on getting less help from Social Security and Medicare.

That puts more of your retirement planning up to you—including how and where you'll live, and even your choice of careers today.

It's a given that you make maximum use of an IRA or a Keogh Plan. And an annuity could be important to your retirement.

The pension plan of the past (defined-benefit plan) is giving way to the pension plan of the future (defined-contribution plan).

Make sure you know all about the plan your company offers. If you're given a choice, a defined-contribution plan will cost you more—but with some very nice tax breaks, and a greater chance of getting a pension when you do retire.

CHAPTER 14

Using Smart Machines to Manage Your Money

Were you grandly rich, a full-time bookkeeper would budget your money. Your investments would be handled by a blue-chip bank, or by one of the select Wall Street firms that manage the wealth of the wealthy. Battalions of lawyers and accountants would handle your taxes, and for the latest on the economic outlook, you'd hire a consulting firm that charges dearly for its services.

Since you're not grandly rich (yet), you do it on your own: burning the midnight oil as you budget your money, manage your savings and investments, and do all that's necessary to take command of your own financial future. Your economic sixth sense has been honed to the nth degree, but it's hard, lonely work.

But you can enlist an ally in your struggles: brilliant, tireless, witty at times, faithful always—a boon companion through thick and thin. It's the smart machine—the advanced calculator, for under $50, and the personal computer, for under $300. Both will do most of the hard, dull work required to survive financially. And when your computer isn't working for you, it will amuse and entertain you.

Picture this: Just after supper on a Sunday night, you adjourn to the study, where pride of place has gone to your brand-new Whiz-Bang computer. It set you back about $300, plus that much again for the extras. It speaks through your TV set, and it does things with numbers you couldn't do in a million years.

You give the Whiz-Bang one set of instructions, and it compares your spending with your budget. To make sure you get the message, it displays everything in four-color bar charts: a red bar showing that you're slipping on the food budget, and a green bar showing you're holding the line on utility bills.

Give the Whiz-Bank more instructions, and it balances your checkbook. Stored in the computer's copious memory is a list of everything of value in your house, kept up to date for insurance purposes, should your house burn down or be robbed. This night, you add your new stereo tape deck to the list.

Perhaps you subscribe to one of the new banking services that lets you pay bills through your computer. Assuming you do, you assemble all your bills and, by touching keys on the computer's keyboard, you instruct the bank to pay each bill and to hit your account for the amount. The TV screen shows your current bank balance. It further tells you of your bank's new Saturday hours, and a chore that used to take hours, now takes minutes.

You feed the Whiz-Bang more instructions, and it searches through the pedigrees of thousands of stocks, looking for a few that might outrun the market and produce gains for you. International Tennis Shoe catches your eye—its earnings up for three straight quarters, and the stock still selling at only six times earnings. You instruct the computer to search through its memory for everything on file on International Tennis Shoe, and your screen is soon filled with all the relevant financial facts. You further ask the computer to review the stocks, bonds, and options you own. It does so, and you decide to tell your broker, next morning, to sell 20 shares of Amalgamated Cough Drop and buy 30 shares of International Tennis Shoe. You also decide to sell a couple of options, which are running out of the money.

Some items of special note appeared in a recent issue of *The Wall Street Journal*. Feeding the Whiz-Bang new instructions, those *Journal* stories are brought to your screen to be read at your leisure. There's a hot new investment book, just published, and you strum the computer's keyboard a few times and order the book. It will be mailed to your home and your credit card automatically billed for the proper amount.

It's late now, and you're satisfied your finances are as they should be. To relax, you invite the computer to join you in a game of chess—which it does, willingly. More than a little pleased when the Whiz-Bang falls prey to your prowess as a chess player, you flip a switch and you and the computer retire for the night.

Tomorrow Is Already Here

Not a word of this is fantasy—stuff for the day after tomorrow. It's all here now. In fact, I make use of nearly all of it right in my own home.

My calculator is a Texas Instruments Business Analyst II, which I bought in the summer of 1981 for $42. With the calculator, came a fat guidebook, jammed with every sort of program imaginable.

Using the calculator, I can figure out how fast my savings will build at various rates of interest, and do the same for the future value of an annuity. I can figure the annual appreciation on my house, and how big a loan I could afford if I wanted to buy a new house. Should I get into creative financing in real estate—on either side of a second mortgage—it will figure out the amount of the balloon payment. If I want to make improvements in my home, it will help me decide whether to take out a loan or a second mortgage.

The calculator fits easily into my shirt pocket and will run for years on a single battery. There's nothing complex about operating it. For every problem, there's a formula already written down. Add in your numbers and you're off and running. If you want to spend more money, there are more complex calculators, able to handle more complex calculations—and to print out the answers on paper tape, so you'll have them for your records.

And those advanced calculators, as sophisticated as they

are, are mere playthings compared with the personal computers from such companies as Apple, Radio Shack, IBM, Commodore, Texas Instruments, and Atari—with new names appearing almost daily. I own an Atari 800 computer, which I bought in the summer of 1981 for about $800. As I write this, the same computer is being sold for less than $400. Even the cheapest personal computer can do serious computing, and the most powerful will match, in sheer computing power, the biggest commercial computers of a generation ago. Yet even the grandest of the personal computers will fit comfortably on a desk top, sell for no more than $3,000, and be of inestimable use to anyone willing to devote a few hours to understanding how a computer works.

Finally, since you'll be using the computer to manage your money and your investments, you can depreciate at least part of it for tax purposes, and you can probably take the 10 percent investment tax credit.

This won't be an intensive course in the care and feeding of computers. You'll learn more in an hour at a computer store, or by reading one of the many personal computer magazines, than I could teach you. I just want to open your eyes to some of the possibilities a computer offers anyone who's preparing for financial survival.

Getting Along with a Computer

Don't be intimidated by computers. A computer, from the very biggest to the very smallest—is just another tool: useful in certain ways just as a hammer or a drill or a paintbrush is useful.

A computer has no mind of its own. It can't think and it certainly can't out-think you. It won't bend you to its will and it won't—shades of *2001*—run amok. All it can do is handle a lot of mathematical computations in a short time: number crunching, as the computer folks call it.

The heart of your computer is a very advanced electronic device called a microprocessor. Hundreds of thousands of electronic parts—which, in the days of the first computers, filled a good-sized room—have been compressed until the whole microprocessor is smaller than a Chiclet.

You probably won't ever understand how a computer works. But you don't have to, any more than you have to understand the principles of jet propulsion before you board a plane.

A fear of computers is cyberphobia, and if you suffer from it, head to the nearest video game arcade and try a few rounds of PacMan or whatever the game of the moment is. An arcade game is just another sort of computer. It's built to respond in certain ways when you push a button or maneuver a stick. But every computer is built to respond in certain ways when you press a button or maneuver a stick. A PacMan machine lives with PacMan instructions all its life, while you can change the instructions you give your computer any time you want. But that's the only real difference, and if PacMan doesn't give you cyberphobia, neither will a home computer.

Any computer—arcade game or the most advanced computer made—can come alive only in partnership with a human being. When you aren't around, it sits there and gathers dust. Until you tell it what to do, it can do nothing. But tell the computer what to do, in a language it can understand, and it will do its best to serve you: crunching numbers by the hour, and each crunch producing answers that are useful to you.

Ask it, in the right way, how close to balance your budget is running and it will tell you. Ask it, in the right way, which dozen of 1,000 stocks have shown the biggest gains over the past year, and it will tell you. Ask it, in the right way, to play chess or PacMan, and it will do that. Ask it, in the right way, for the wisdom of the ages, and if that wisdom is stored someplace the computer can reach, that wisdom will be yours in a twinkling. All you have to do is ask—in the right way.

But also understand this about a computer: It won't work magic. It won't automatically pick the winning stock out of 1,000. It will look at all the information about those 1,000 stocks that has been made available to it, and it will tell you which stocks look the most promising in terms of past performance, or price/earnings ratio, or yield, or whatever you ask it.

The same holds true for any question you ask the computer: What you get out is no better than what you put in. The credo, among computer people, is "garbage in, garbage out." Give your computer the right sort of numbers to crunch, and it will reward you richly. Give it garbage and it will give you garbage back.

Making a Computer Come Alive

You tell your computer what to do by speaking in a language that the two of you—man (or woman) and machine—can understand. The most common language for the personal computer is BASIC (Beginners All-purpose Symbolic Instruction Code). There are other languages: Pascal, Forth, Fortran, Cobal. Most are for chores more complex than anything you're going to try. It really isn't important that you learn any computer language, because most of the time you'll use a packaged set of instructions bought at a computer store.

You could give your computer its instructions by typing them out on the computer keyboard (which is exactly like a typewriter keyboard). BASIC is 99 percent familiar English words, with a few special phrases. These instructions are the computer's program, and depending on what you want the computer to do, a program can be very simple or very complex. There are books that will teach you how to write a program, and books filled with programs that someone else has written and that you copy.

When I changed jobs, I had to decide whether to let my pension money stay with my former employer or do a tax-free rollover and shift the money elsewhere. I came across a program, in a computer magazine, that would calculate how much money I'd have, if I invested it for so many years at a given rate of compounded interest. It took about three minutes to type this program into my computer. Once the computer was programmed, it asked me three questions:

1. How much money would I start with?
2. How long would I invest for?
3. What rate of interest would I earn?

I offered different periods of years, and different rates of interest, and the computer—quick as a wink—would tell me how much money I'd have, year after year, until the final year. All the different possibilities took about 15 minutes and my decision was made for me (which was to shift my money to a single-payment annuity).

Even three minutes of typing may be more than you want to do. You can buy a program written by someone else and enter that into your computer. Programs start at just a few dollars and run into the thousands depending on what you want the computer to do. In your league, you'll rarely pay as much as $100 for a program, and most of the time you'll pay a lot less.

The Atari and Texas Instruments computers allow you to enter certain programs (mostly games) by inserting a cartridge. Cartridges for the Atari are about the size of a pack of cigarettes and pop into a slot in the computer. The whole thing takes about five seconds.

More likely, you'll use either tape cassettes or a distant cousin of tape called a floppy disk.

Programs are recorded on tape just as you'd record a song. Pop the cassette into a tape player that's compatible with your computer, and all the details of the program—those instructions—flow into the computer. The flow of data—from tape to computer—is called the "bit stream" and there's a lot of chirping and buzzing. It sounds like gibberish to you, but it's the King's English to the computer.

The right sort of tape player will cost $60 or $70. Unfortunately, the only virtue of tape is that it's cheap. Its drawback is that the program is fed into the computer, one bit of information after another, for maybe 15 or 20 minutes. There's a lot of chirping and buzzing before the computer is ready to work for you. Finding any single item of information on that 15-minute tape—where you put your list of 50 favorite stocks—can be a real chore.

The next step up is the floppy disk. It's a square bit of thin plastic—made from the same material that tape is made from. It's called a floppy disk because it's flexible. There's a hole in the center, and it plays the way a 45 rpm phonograph record plays, spinning around at considerable speed. It spins around in a disk drive, which will run between $400 and $500. One big advantage is speed. A program that might take 20 minutes to load from a tape, will load from a disk in about 20 seconds. And you can find any single bit of information in seconds, no matter where it is on the disk.

Again, you'll understand it better when you've spent an hour at a computer store. And there are now computer stores in every corner of the land. (When I bought my computer, in 1981, the nearest computer store was 20 miles away. Six months later, the nearest store was about 10 miles away. Now there are four computer stores in my town, and a dozen within a 15-minute drive.)

Now you have the computer and a way to give it its instructions. You can display the answers your computer provides on your TV screen, with a small adaptor that costs a few bucks. You get a clearer, sharper picture on a monitor, which looks like a TV but won't bring in regular programs. (A black-and-white monitor will run about $100 and a color monitor between $300 and $400.) If you want a printed record of what your computer is telling you, you can buy a printer for under $500. It will print answers at the rate of hundreds of characters per minute, and you'll have records of everything to read in bed or on the bus.

So, a computer will run between $100 and $1,500 (the higher the price, the more complex chores the computer can handle). A cassette recorder will run about $70 (but a disk drive for $450 will be far superior). You can use your own TV set, and a printer, for written copies of everything, will run under $500. Anything else will depend on the uses you put your computer to, and those can wait until you've bought the thing and spent some time running it.

But also figure this: The prices I cite are for mid-1983. At the rate prices in the computer business have been falling, everything will cost less by the time you read this.

What to Feed Your Computer

When you visit a computer store, or when you start poking through the computer magazines, you'll see all the programs available for your computer: everything from sophisticated financial planning programs to more games than you could play in a dozen lifetimes. If there's a game at the arcades, it's probably also available for your use at home. The magazines most aimed at the amateur computer user are *Popular Computing*, *Creative Computing*, and *Compute*, plus various magazines written for owners of specific makes of computer. Any well-stocked magazine shop will carry them, and all computer stores have a wide range of these magazines on sale.

The last issue of *Creative Computing* I read carried ads for 51 different money programs of one sort or another; personal money management, taxes, investments, and even some financially oriented games. And that's toward the end of 1982. By the time you read this, there will be twice as many.

I've tried a couple of personal finance programs, and now I use one that I got directly from Atari for about $20. It's not as fancy or as comprehensive as some of the others, and it doesn't break down spending as many ways as I would like it to. I've seen ads for a couple of other programs that I might want to try. Still, the program is effective when it comes to monitoring my spending.

I also use an electronic "spreadsheet" program—copied from a computer magazine—for playing "what if" games with my money. That's a favorite business application of personal computers.

Say that I'm drawing up a budget, just to give me an idea of how my spending is likely to go, at quarterly intervals over the next few years. I would lay out a sample budget, assume a 5 percent rate of inflation over those years, and see what the computer has to say. It will show me how much my spending will increase, item by item, at 5 percent inflation over that period. But say I also want to know what will happen at 8 percent inflation. Using paper and pencil, I'd have to repeat every single calculation. With my electronic spreadsheet, I change the 5 percent inflation to 8 percent inflation, and the computer automatically changes every single calculation for me.

I can do the same for different mixes of saving and investing. Each time I change something basic, the computer will adjust every number I'm working with accordingly. With paper and pencil, it would take days. With the computer, it takes minutes.

There are other programs to help you keep track of your investments—stocks, bonds, options, commodities, real estate, or anything else. Without a computer to aid you, you may not even belong in options or commodities, because of the close attention you must pay to the markets.

Standard & Poor's Corporation, the big investment advisory service, has a program called Stockpak. It costs $200 a year, plus a one-time $50 charge for the operating system that makes it work. You get a disk each month listing 900 widely traded stocks, including the 500 stocks that make up the S&P 500-stock index. For each of the 900 companies, there's an enormous array of financial data, allowing you to study each company and compare one company with another. There's also a monthly newsletter suggesting various investing strategies developed by S&P market analysts.

You can play all sorts of analytical games with your 900-stock list—asking the computer to cull out stocks that look cheap, stocks that feature an extra-high yield, and so on. You can look for stocks that you own that are suddenly going bad, and you can sell out quickly. If you tried to do that all on your own, you wouldn't have time. And that's the beauty part of a computer—that ability to cull and sort and analyze and select in a twinkling: crunching millions of numbers in the time it would take you to crunch a dozen.

Your problems won't be finding helpful programs but knowing which are best. The store you bought the computer from should be able to help. More stockbrokers are using computers all the time, and maybe your broker has some advice. The computer magazines review programs each month. There are groups of owners of different makes of computers all over the country. See if there's one for your computer in the area and attend some meetings. Talk to other computer owners—a growing band these days. You'll find most are tolerant of fledgling computer owners.

Reaching Out with a Computer

So far, we've just talked about the computer as a computer. Every computer can be turned into a terminal that will let your computer talk to other computers. There's some very high-powered data stored in other computers, and you can tap it—for a fee.

The three most widely available computer data services are The Source, owned by the *Reader's Digest*; CompuServe, owned by H & R Block, the tax people; and the Dow-Jones News/Retrieval Service, owned by the publishers of *The Wall Street Journal*. Dow-Jones is primarily for business users and investors; the other two are for more general audiences, but each still has plenty of information you'll find useful. I subscribe to both The Source and the Dow-Jones service, and I make considerable use of both.

You reach each service via telephone. For that you need a gadget called a modem, which ties your computer into a telephone line. You also need a program that will convince your computer that it's now a terminal. The one from Atari is called Telelink. It costs about $25, and it's in the form of a cartridge that drops right into the computer.

To reach Source or Dow-Jones, I dial a local telephone number (different local phone numbers all over the country), and when the number answers (with a shrill tone), my computer screen asks me whom I want it to talk to. I use a code to tell it I want either Source or Dow-Jones. When the appropriate service comes on, I provide my secret password, so the service knows that it's me—a paid-up subscriber and not an interloper. The password also lets the computer know whom to send the bill to. Then, using the instructions provided by each service, I ask my questions.

Dow-Jones will give me current price quotes on every stock, bond, option, commodity, or mutual fund traded on any stock exchange or over-the-counter. And I can get historic trading information on all these securities.

It will provide me with all the financial news of that day, available by subject matter, and cross-referenced several different ways. It will similarly provide me with all the news stories that have run on each of these subjects over the last 90 days. It will do that for news on general business subjects and on specific companies. If I want to review an item on General Motors that ran a couple of months ago in *The Wall Street Journal*, the Dow service will check its memory and produce a story that ran, say, 67 days earlier. It will give me the headline, and if I ask it—in the right way—it will produce the full story. I can read if off my screen, or I could use a printer and get a copy of the story to study at my leisure.

The Dow Service will further provide me with tons of detailed financial information on some 6,000 companies: earnings records, annual reports, copies of reports that each company must file with the government.

Finally, they keep adding new things to the Dow service. I can get sports scores, movie reviews, even the weather in U.S. and foreign cities. Each morning, at six o'clock Eastern Time, I can get a rundown of the stories appearing in that morning's *Wall Street Journal*. That's about an hour before the *Journal* is delivered to my door. Finally, I can search through the entire contents of the *Academic American Encylopedia*, because Dow-Jones calls up from it all the available reference material it has on a subject.

There are programs out that tie together investment analysis with the information available from Dow-Jones. Tell the computer what investment information to search for, and it will keep searching through the constantly updated statistics available from Dow-Jones.

There's a $50 charge for joining Dow-Jones. Depending on the information you need, you pay 60 cents to $1.20 per minute, for each minute of use during the daytime and 15 cents to 90 cents a minute at night and on weekends.

The Source is an even more ambitious project. You can harvest tons of financial data (current stock, bond, and commodity quotes; the latest on the performance of more than 3,000 stocks; and even all the news that moves over the United Press International business news wire each day). But you can also get a lot more.

You can check out—and order reprints of—stories that ran in any number of leading business publications. You can shop via your computer. You can send "electronic mail" to other

Source subscribers. You can "chat" with other Source subscribers, via your computer, much as ham radio people talk back and forth. I was up late one night and I chatted, via computer, with a banker 3,000 miles away. You can check airline schedules around the world and make plane reservations through the computer. You can get tips on where to eat in various cities—and on what wine to order.

It costs $100 to hook up to Source. Then you pay $20.75 an hour of connect time during the day and $7.75 per hour of connect time at night and on weekends.

CompuServe has its own features—financial data of all sorts, games, and so on. It's even a little cheaper than Source and charges no hook-up fee. To stay solvent, I limited myself to just the two services. If I become rich, I'll try all three.

Just about everything you can do with a desk-top computer, you can do with the newer-still portable units—small enough to fit inside a briefcase. The keyboard is skimpier than on a full-size machine, and you typically have a screen that shows only a few lines at a time.

Still, anywhere you go, a computer can now go with you. Prices on the portables are $700 or so in mid-1983—and obviously going lower, as prices of all computers keep going down.

There's still more coming—more computers, more programs, more sources of information you can tap into as the world goes electronic. As the world goes electronic, think about going electronic, too—to give you that little edge as you manage your money in difficult times.

The Bottom Line—Electronically Speaking

The basic rules of economic survival haven't changed—and they won't. You don't have to be able to forecast the distant economic future: Just take it a few months at a time. The economy is cyclical and it will remain cyclical. Armed with your knowledge of how the economy works, and armed with that intuitive sense that I call your economic sixth sense, you can spot change coming in time to do you some good.

You must take command of your financial future: using every trick at your command to budget, save, and invest in ways that will keep you afloat no matter what happens to the economy.

The time seems very right to invest your money, in markets that are working better than they have in years. You could bring home very big gains if the economy continues to do as it has been doing—and if the markets continue to do as they have been doing. Yet the potential for trouble is great, and you must know how to spot trouble in the making and to respond to it on the double.

There are experts aplenty who will tell you what to do. Just to say it one more time: Most experts are mostly wrong most of the time. Cut loose from the experts and do it on your own.

You want every ally you can enlist at your side. The smart machines won't work magic, but they certainly can do a lot. It's a dangerous economy out there—the past tumultuous and the future uncertain. You, with your trusty computer at your side, can do it a whole lot better than you all alone.

Guidelines for Action

You're smart, but think how much smarter you'd be with a smart machine at your side: a home computer, starting at just a few hundred dollars, and able to do the dog work as you take command of your money.

A home computer will help you work out your budget, pick investments, and keep track of what you invest in. You can learn to use it in a few hours. You don't have to know how a computer works to make use of it, any more than you have to know how a jet plane works to fly in one.

Picking the right programs makes all the difference. And those data services (from Dow-Jones among others) can fill your computer's screen with enough data to satisfy anyone.

You can take command of your financial future on your own.

You can do it—easier, better, and so much faster—with a smart machine to help you.

Index